MY BROTHER PAUL

Richard L. Rubenstein

My
Brother Paul

HARPER & ROW, PUBLISHERS
1817

New York, Evanston, San Francisco, London

FIRST EDITION

LIBRARY OF CONGRESS CATALOG CARD NUMBER: 72-124704

To my mother,

Sara Fine Rubenstein

TABLE OF CONTENTS

PREFACE   ix

I   The Point of View of the Observer   1
II   Identification   23
III   Damascus   34
IV   The Womb of Immortality   54
V   Totemic Atonement   78
VI   The Lord's Meal   87
VII   The Apostle and the Seed of Abraham   114
        a. Apostle of the Messiah or Turncoat?   114
        b. Israel's Conversion and Mankind's Salvation   127
VIII The Last Adam   144

NOTES   175

BIBLIOGRAPHICAL NOTE   195

INDEX   203

PREFACE

This book is the fruit of my long-standing interest in one of the greatest theologians the Jewish world has ever produced. I have not attempted to offer an exhaustive account of Paul's theology or career. I have attempted to share with my readers those aspects of the Apostle's life and thought that I have found to be of the greatest relevance to my own theological development.

I am indebted to far more men and women than I can ever acknowledge. I should like especially to thank my colleagues in the Department of Religion at the Florida State University, Professors Robert Spivey, Charles Wellborn, John Priest, George Bedell, and Charles W. Swain, for both their encouragement and their helpful suggestions during the course of the writing and editing of this manuscript. Dean William Hamilton, Portland State University, Portland, Oregon, and Professor Thomas J. J. Altizer, The State University of New York at Stony Brook, read portions of the manuscript and gave me much encouragement. I am also grateful to Bishop John A. T. Robinson of Trinity College, Cambridge, for the gift of his book, *The Body*. It proved to be exceedingly helpful to me in formulating my ideas about Paul. Similarly, I want to express my gratitude to Dean Krister Stendahl of Harvard Divinity School for encouraging me to undertake this endeavor and for offering a number of suggestions that aided me in rethinking my original position on Paul. Nor can I permit this occasion to pass without acknowledging the instruction I received concerning Paul while a graduate student at Harvard almost twenty years ago from Professor Henry J. Cadbury and Professor Sidney Ahlstrom, now at Yale University. Finally, I should like to thank Professor Jacob Neusner of Brown University, one of the preeminent Jewish scholars and thinkers.

I am indebted to Clayton Carlson and his staff in the Religious Books Department at Harper & Row for their editorial and research suggestions. Natalie Drache of Deya, Majorca, Spain, and Janice Donahoe of Tallahasee assisted me with the typing of the manuscript.

I am especially indebted to my wife, Betty, who read and helped to edit the entire manuscript. If I have been able to communicate my understanding of Paul with any degree of clarity, it is largely because of her thoughtful work.

Richard L. Rubenstein

The Florida State University
Tallahassee, Florida
December 14, 1971

MY BROTHER PAUL

Chapter I

The Point of View
of the Observer

In his own time men called Paul of Tarsus a madman, a villain, and apostate as well as Apostle of the Risen Christ. According to Freud, the most influential Jew of the twentieth century, Paul, one of the most influential Jews of all time, "was a man with a gift for religion, in the truest sense. . . . Dark traces of the past lay in his soul ready to break through into the regions of consciousness."[1] To this day opinion is divided concerning Paul's message, his spiritual origins, and whether his extraordinary influence has been a blessing or a curse. Some say he perverted the teachings of the Master he claimed to serve to the point of creating an entirely novel faith that Jesus could neither have recognized nor accepted. His person and his doctrine divide Jews and Christians more than those of any other Christian figure including Jesus. While he was born a Jew and raised a Pharisee, his letters have become part of the sacred literature of Judaism's greatest and most successful rival. There is universal agreement on the importance of his influence within Christianity. There is unending debate concerning who he was and what he taught.

For almost two thousand years, men of great learning have devoted their careers to the study of his letters, yet scholarly debate concerning Paul continues. Twentieth-century authorities as thorough and competent as Rudolf Bultmann, Ernst Käsemann, Jean Héring, C. H. Dodd, Albert Schweitzer, W. D. Davies, Béda Rigaux,

1

Hans Joachim Schoeps, and Johannes Weiss (to cite but a few), have disagreed in their interpretations of Paul. Contemporary research on the first Christian century has given us a far more accurate picture of its culture and spiritual climate than our nineteenth-century predecessors possessed. Nevertheless, *one arrives at a point at which one recognizes that each scholar presents his own Paul.* It is no accident that one of Paul's greatest nineteenth-century interpreters, Ferdinand Christian Baur, presented a Hegelian interpretation of him, while one of the twentieth century's preeminent New Testament scholars, Rudolf Bultmann, has undertaken an existentialist interpretation. Beyond a certain point, the quest for the "historical" Paul may very well be a will-o'-the-wisp. This does not mean that there remains no point in studying the Apostle's life or his thought. If it is true that each scholar presents his own Paul, it is also true that Paul's writings have elicited an extraordinary range of informed responses concerning the human condition in practically every generation since his own time. The theologies of Augustine and Luther are but two examples of Paul's perennial influence, for the reading of Paul proved decisive for both these men.

The subjective character of so many "objective" interpretations of Paul ought not to disturb us. One of the distinguishing marks of scientific investigation in the twentieth century has been that the observer is understood to be an integral part of the events he seeks to describe. When Freud began his self-analysis, he recognized the importance of the psychiatrist's involvement in the lives he seeks to help. Until Freud pointed out that the inner life of the therapist is crucial to what takes place in the therapeutic transaction, psychiatrists had tended to take their own objectivity and mental health for granted. A major turning point in the psychoanalytic revolution came when Freud realized that countertransference could not be ignored, that the emotional problems of the therapist play a very real part in the course of therapy.[2]

This insight had been anticipated in the first half of the nineteenth century by the Danish theologian, Sören Kierkegaard. During Kierkegaard's most productive years, Hegelian philosophy reigned in both Denmark and Germany. It offered the veritable key to the mystery of existence. Hegel described the incredible variety of events with human history and the totality of the transformations within the natural world as the expression of a single, unitary, purposeful process that he called the World-Spirit. Kierkegaard protested that only God could have the kind of knowledge that Hegel claimed for himself. Kierkegaard did not reject the possibility of objective knowledge. He did insist, however, on the priority of the subjective knowledge possessed by the individual arising out of his own unique circumstances. He called this knowledge *existential*. He insisted on the priority of existence, or subjective reality, over essence, or the strict objectivity that denies the transactional presence of the observer.[3]

The insistence by Freud and Kierkegaard on the importance of the point of view of the observer is directly relevant to this study of Paul. It is probably impossible to describe objectively the thought of a religious personality such as Paul, who lived almost two thousand years ago in a very different political, religious, and cultural world, and whose literary remains (as well as the Book of Acts) present so many textual and interpretive problems. One has only to consult the Pauline bibliography to realize how unlikely it is that any consensus can be reached concerning Paul's religious thought or his contribution to the religious life of western man.

There is, however, another way to study Paul's career. The investigator can begin with a description of his own involvement and then proceed to describe how Paul *appears* to him. This is admittedly a subjective approach, but it may heighten the only kind of objectivity a study of Paul can achieve. If the researcher can describe those elements in his own life that led him to devote himself to his subject, he may at least reveal to his readers the Apostle's impact on his work. An investigator, who seeks to establish the "true" facts after all the scholarly controversy over Paul, may do more to obscure than to clarify. The approach I am suggesting is indebted to contemporary phenomenology for its stress on the observer's perspective. Given this approach, events in the history of religion can become encounters between past and present.

Admittedly, this invites the criticism that I am reading my own concerns as a twentieth-century man into the literary remnants of a first-century man whose life was very different than my own. I can only respond that there is a limit to the extent to which Paul's situation can be distinguished from ours. If Paul's life were totally different, we would be unable to find relevance in anything he wrote. Yet men have read the letters of Paul and found instruction in them for almost two thousand years. If men were unable to recognize something of themselves in Paul, it is not likely that they would continue to read and study his letters.

Before discussing why I have studied Paul, I would like to explain the book's title, *My Brother Paul*. The most obvious reason for my choice was a desire to express my fundamentally positive appreciation of Paul as well as my dissent from the tradition in Jewish scholarship that regards him as the ultimate enemy in early Christianity.

As a theologian of Jewish origin, I am painfully aware of the fact that in the history of Judaism Paul is regarded as the supreme apostate. When Jewish theologians contrast their insights about man's relation to God with those of Christianity, the Christian theologian they are most likely to oppose is Paul. Seldom, if ever, have Jewish scholars found it possible to express appreciation for Paul. The greatest single failing of Jewish attempts to understand Paul has been a persistent refusal to take Paul seriously as both a loyal Jew and a theologian of extraordinary competence. I do not suggest that Paul was correct in his rejection of the Judaism of his time. Empathy for Paul is not agreement with him. Some men have personality structures that make it impossible for them to find fulfillment in traditional Judaism. They are neither better nor worse than traditional Jews; they are simply different. Paul was such a man. We are more likely to account for the differences between Paul and the rabbis by considering the differences in their experience than by attempting to establish whether Paul's religious position or that of his adversaries was the "true" one.

I have also another, sadder reason for calling Paul my brother. I concur in Paul's intuition, expressed in Romans 9–11, that the conflict between Church and Synagogue is fundamentally an expression of fraternal strife. I would hasten to add that one of the problems perennially bedeviling the Judeo-Christian encounter has been the fact that there has been too much rather than too little brotherhood. After all, the first brothers were fated to become murderer and victim. As long as we regard each other as rival brothers, we may be under the terrible temptation to slaughter each other. There is sorrow in calling Paul my brother. He is my brother; his contemporary followers are also my brothers. Regrettably, because we are brothers, we may never be quit of Cain's temptation.

My decision to write about Paul of Tarsus, a first-century Jew who became one of the most influential Christian theologians of all time, delayed work on other problems that might have seemed more immediately relevant to contemporary theology. I made this commitment partly because I believe that, long after many of the theological issues that now appear urgent have been forgotten, men will still be grappling with Paul's theology. I was also moved to begin this labor because I was convinced that Paul's most significant concerns often paralleled my own.

I first became interested in Paul as an adolescent in the late 1930s. At the time I had little affirmative sense of my own Jewish identity: I had had no religious education. I could not read Hebrew until I was eighteen years old. Nevertheless, I was intensely aware of the fact that I was a Jew living in a predominantly Christian culture during the period of Nazi ascendancy. I first read the New Testament as an act of self-understanding. I wanted to know something about the religious culture that constituted my fundamental environment but to which I was an outsider. As I read the New Testament, Paul interested me more than Jesus, and Romans interested me more than any of Paul's other letters. I was especially fascinated by Paul's vision of Christ as the Last Adam (Rom. 5:12–20). That fascination is apparent throughout this book.

At a superficial level, one of the parallels between Paul's career and my own is that I have found myself in as much tension in my own way with the establishment Judaism of my time, both lay and religious, as was Paul in his. Although my religious affirmations are very different than were Paul's, we share at least one common reason for rejecting establishment Judaism. Paul never ceased to believe that he was loyal to the traditions of his fathers, but he insisted upon interpreting those traditions in the light of his overpowering experience of the Risen Christ at Damascus. *Paul resolved the conflict between experience and tradition in favor of the authority of his own experience.*

I did not behold the vision of the Risen Christ or any other redeemer. I did have an overpowering experience that compelled me to reinterpret my own history and my community's religious traditions in its light. Like Paul's, mine was a conversion experience; like Paul's, the theme of death and resurrection was very much involved in my experience. There the similarity ends. Paul's conversion took place when he became convinced that Christ had defeated death; mine began when I finally gave up all hope that God would in the end redeem me from death. Unlike Paul's conversion, mine was neither sudden nor catastrophic, although it began with what was for me a catastrophic moment—the totally unexpected death of my infant son. Nevertheless, it took perhaps seventeen years for my experience to mature.

As my experience deepened, I came reluctantly to understand that, like Paul, I too had to choose between trusting my own insights and experience and what had been handed down to me. I made the choice with the certain knowledge that it would entail estrangement from the personalities and institutions that had comprised my communal and religious world: I elected the authority of my own experience.

One of the reasons for my interest in Paul was that he was what William James has called a twice-born man.[4] Paul experienced a radical shaking of all his personal moorings at a crucial moment in his life. All of the cultural and religious influences that had stabilized his life seemed to dissolve. Fortunately for Paul, this momentary dissolution was the gateway to a new and abiding reintegration through his identification with Jesus Christ as the Risen Lord of Jew and Gentile alike. The experience on the road to Damascus initiated a kind of second birth for him.

One does not have to be a Christian to be twice born. The experience of disintegration of personal foundations followed by a reintegration in which one feels reborn can take secular as well as religious forms. Second birth is often an adolescent phenomenon. It can also occur in the course of psychoanalysis or psychotherapy. Few persons enter analysis out of curiosity. I entered out of dire need. I felt emotionally trapped. In desperation I turned to analysis as a last resort. During its course I came to understand how appropriate the categories of death and resurrection are to the total experience.

I began my voyage from death, or more accurately, death-in-life, to resurrection in childhood. I was a good student. I was frequently advanced to higher grades. I finished high school just as I turned sixteen. However, in spite of the absence of religion in my upbringing, *I was unknowingly a true believer—in the secularized myths of my time and class.* Perhaps the best way to describe my development is to suggest that the intellectual and competitive sides of my nature were better formed than the emotional and fraternal sides. On one occasion, my father told me that he hoped I would become a distinguished scientist or scholar. He assured me that, if necessary, he would support me as a student until I was thirty-five. His offer was less important in terms of the material support it entailed than in its emotional impact. (I did not receive my doctorate in religion until I was thirty-six years old.)

Like most members of the middle class in the late 1930s, both Jewish and Christian, I had been trained from earliest childhood to believe in and live in accordance with a secularized form of the Law. I was constantly confronted with the Law's basic bribe (it is the same in both its secular and religious forms): Perform well and you will be rewarded; perform badly and you will be damned.

It didn't happen that way. I played the game by the rules. I did what was expected of me, especially in those areas of study that interested me. I was confident that I would eventually prosper. Nevertheless, I found that my life became increasingly distressed and anguished. The anticipation of a prosperous career was of little consolation to me during the frequent occasions when I was suddenly overcome by an anxiety attack of shuddering intensity. I might be walking in New York's Central Park on a spring day in the very springtime of life when quite unexpectedly I was overcome by an intense fear of death. Nor was the knowledge that I was progressing in my studies helpful in overcoming my painful adolescent sexual timidity.

Performing well and playing the game according to the rules, what Paul called "the wisdom of this world," were of little help to me in facing two of the most important realities of life: love and death. However, as long as I believed that the principal aim of life was "getting ahead," I was able to avoid facing the meanings that love and death really had for me.

Perhaps no event in contemporary history had so searing an effect upon me both intellectually and emotionally as the Nazi extermination of the Jews. The Nazis frightened me far more by my realization of how like them most men, including myself, could be, than by any feeling of how different they were. At the time, my greatest fear was my own nameless rage. Beneath the surface, my predominant emotion was objectless anger. I did not know what I was angry about. I had little conscious reason for fury; I did not even regard myself as an angry man. Yet if a stranger accidently pushed against me in a crowded subway or said an unpleasant word to me, I was tempted to strike him on the spot. I had all I could do to control myself. My inordinate commitment to performance, which in my case meant academic or intellectual excellence, undoubtedly heightened my tendency toward rage. At the same time, it left me with the fear that I might lose whatever control I possessed and explode in some violent act. In the late 1940s, fearful of my own fury, I began to reason that were I to submit to the disciplines of traditional Jewish Law, my life would be so constantly regulated in both the personal and the public spheres that I would have neither the time nor the energy to lose control of myself.

As I began to observe the traditions, I also began to believe in the God who had commanded them in Scripture. I urgently required a cosmic Lawgiver and Judge who could give my life a semblance of discipline. It was important that he be able to see me at all times.

I wanted no escape from him. Were he to avert his gaze for even a moment my slender capacities for control might instantaneously dissolve. Nevertheless, I did not really believe in him. I believed in him because I needed him, but somewhere within I was undeceived. I knew I had invented him because all other resources of control had become too precarious. At the time, I was beginning to study for the rabbinate at the Jewish Theological Seminary of America in New York City.

Obedience to the ways of the Lord has its own peculiar ironies. Initially, I felt great relief that I was leading a disciplined, compliant life, and that the ever-present threat of the breakdown of control had apparently been warded off. Nevertheless, there was still a problem. My initial observance was at best partial. I began by observing the major contours of the dietary laws. I refrained from work on the Sabbath. I also attended religious services every morning. However I quickly learned that I had only begun to observe the Jewish tradition. There were questions as to whether the meat we used was kosher enough (by this time I was married). Some people insisted that only meat purchased from butchers supervised by a rabbi known for his special strictness was really kosher. There were other questions, such as whether turning electric switches on and off on the Sabbath was permitted. I am especially fond of classical music. I had to ask myself whether I could turn on the radio on Saturday afternoons so that I might listen to the Metropolitan Opera broadcast. My greatest sacrifice in that area came when I refrained from listening to Mozart's *Don Giovanni.*

The more I observed, the more I became aware of whole areas of the Law that I was neglecting. Such scrupulosity may seem obsessive, but it became inevitable once I had convinced myself that all of the commandments had been given by God. If the commandments truly expressed the will of the Almighty Lord of life and death, who was I to decide which ones could be ignored? Picking and choosing constituted the height of arrogance. To the extent that I regarded any commandment as insignificant, I had set myself up as God's judge, an act of unspeakable hubris.

When I later read Galatians, as well as Paul's reflections on the first and Last Adam, I became convinced that he had been confronted with the same problem. Paul maintained that Adam had brought death into the world by a single act of disobedience (Rom. 5:12–21) and that any man's failure to keep every commandment warranted a similar condemnation (Gal. 3:10). In a religion such as Judaism, in which man's fundamental duty is to obey God, one becomes a rebel against God with the very first act of disobedience. Since no man can weigh the relative merits of God's commandments, any act of disobedience involves an intolerable self-assertion.

Having committed myself to the path of obedience, I was compelled to become ever more scrupulous. This may also have been true of Paul (çf. Gal. 1:14; Phil. 3:6). There was, however, a difference. Paul's letters reveal no conscious dissatisfaction with his religious life before conversion. In my case, no degree of religious practice ever seemed enough. The more obedient I became, the more intensely I felt that I was falling short.

My scrupulosity did have at least one advantage. I now had a way of identifying and explaining my hitherto amorphous feelings of anxiety and guilt. I felt that my continuing distress was due to the fact that I was not observant enough. This in turn led to ever greater scrupulosity in the smallest details. The new strictness always proved of no avail. Neither my anxiety nor my sense of guilt would go away. I felt worthless because I didn't really "mean" what I was doing and because I never did enough.

I did not have much affection for the God I had invented as my never-failing Watchman, Lawgiver, and Judge. I could easily have murdered him. I began to experience a hatred of God so deep that it cried out for deicide. I did not understand that my hatred of God was an expression of the same anger that had brought me to the Law in the first place. Here again, my hatred only served to heighten my fear of the most awesome of all retaliations, the vengeance of God. This in turn strengthened my resolve to be ever more submissive to his Law. By this time I was a student rabbi with my own small congregation. I was attempting to convince my congregants of the futility of their middle-class lives and of their need to lead the same kind of life that I was leading.

Later, while in analysis, I often read Paul's observations about the man under the Law in Romans 7 and found them very meaningful. Many scholars caution against reading this chapter as a psychological reflection on Paul's life as an observant Jew.[5] Nevertheless, it is my opinion that the chapter contains a retrospective account of Paul's life as a Jew living under the Law. Perhaps I found Romans 7 especially significant because I, too, was casting a retrospective glance at my life under the Law. What Paul did in the light of Christ, I did in the light of my psychoanalytic experience. I came to feel that some of Paul's observations paralleled my own experience. When Paul wrote, "I should not have known what it means to covet if the Law had not said, 'You shall not covet,'" I recognized a psychological reality I had also encountered. Every attempt I made to comply with the Law, thereby subordinating myself to God, contained an incitement to rebel against him. In spite of this incitement, I felt that the Law was holy and the fault mine. This was apparently Paul's feeling. He wrote, "The Law is sacred, and what it commands is sacred, just and good." Like Paul, it never occurred to me to challenge the sanctity of tradition. Unfortunately, belief in its sanctity only intensified my feelings of guilt.

Jewish tradition stresses that the gates of repentance are never closed by a merciful God. This assurance is often cited by Jewish scholars to prove that Paul was fundamentally ignorant of authentic Jewish tradition when he insisted that failure to fulfill all of the commandments condemns a man before God. However, I find no evidence that these scholars have taken seriously the peculiar mixture of rebelliousness and submissiveness involved in the act of obedience, whether one obeys a parent, God, or one's own superego. I shall never forget a little drama I saw enacted almost thirty years ago, in the lounge of Hebrew Union College in Cincinnati, among a group of students preparing to become reform rabbis. About five or six students were quietly conversing in the lounge when N. entered and came up to us. N.'s background had been strictly orthodox before entering the reform seminary. He was a very recent convert to liberal Judaism. N. took a sandwich out of a paper bag and said to us: "Look, I'm eating a ham sandwich!" Unlike traditional Judaism, the reform branch maintains no mandatory dietary restrictions. N. experienced this as a tremendous liberation. He was far less delighted by the taste of the sandwich than by the opportunity eating it gave him to rebel against a religious system he regarded as having enslaved him.

Any system of social control based upon obedience to external authority is likely to elicit rebellion as a symbolic act of self-assertion and liberation. Nietzsche once remarked that Christianity had by its antisensual bias eroticized love to an extent unknown in the ancient world. The attractiveness of forbidden fruit is at least as old as the story of Adam and Eve. N. was, of course, unaware of the extent to which his symbolic revolt tied him to the very religious system he wanted to overthrow. His need to assert his rebelliousness openly was an acknowledgement of orthodox Judaism's continuing power over him.

By imposing limits on man's autonomy, the Law incites men to rebel against its Author. Adam's rebellion is paradigmatic. Long before Nietzsche described the resentment of the servile consciousness, Paul understood how difficult it is for men to achieve genuine obedience to the Divine Lawgiver. It is also likely that Paul understood that a man could be religiously compliant and yet feel anxious and guilty. If men only felt guilt when they were objectively guilty, the problem of guilt would be far less urgent. Men often feel as guilty for offenses committed in fantasy as those they actually commit. In the language of psychoanalysis, at the primary process level of mental functioning there is no difference between fantasy and objective reality. The superego is just as punitive for offenses committed in fantasy as for real transgressions. Jesus seems to have understood the cruelty of the punitive superego when he declared, "You have learned how it was said: *You must not commit adultery.* But I say this to you: if a man looks at a woman lustfully, he has already committed adultery with her in his heart" (Matt. 5:27–28).

At the primary process level, all distinction between thought and reality is obliterated. It is impossible to be obedient without being tempted to overthrow those to whom we submit. As long as the inclination to rebel continues, feelings of guilt and self-reproach are inevitable. Since the entire process is largely unconscious, there is almost no realistic way to deal with the problem. It may be possible to repent for real misdeeds; it is often impossible to rectify matters without therapeutic intervention when one feels guilty for merely being tempted. Such irrational anxiety and guilt encourage further attempts to obey wholeheartedly. Unfortunately, the new resolve is usually followed by a repetition of the cycle of temptation, anxiety, and guilt.

In a system of external authority, it is often as difficult to repent as it is to be obedient. The rabbis taught that God would never reject a truly contrite sinner. Anyone who has ever participated in an authentic celebration of Israel's great Day of Atonement is aware of the power of repentance to reconcile man and God in the way of the Torah. Nevertheless, there is irony in repentance. Contrition begins with the recognition and confession of the offense. Confession is followed by the resolve to be truly obedient henceforth. However, every confession reenacts verbally the original deed. No matter how reprehensible the deed, some part of the sinner wanted to commit it. To the extent that any remnant of satisfaction for having offended remains, repentance can never be complete. Because men are creatures of conflict, wholehearted repentance may be impossible. It is impossible to obey all of the Law; it is probably impossible fully to repent for one's inability to achieve perfect obedience. When this is understood, it is possible to appreciate the psychological truth of one of Paul's most important insights: the fact that men can never make themselves right before God. This insight led Paul to his doctrine that God is graciously able to make just the sinner who is incapable of justifying himself. It is, however, possible to accept Paul's assertion that the sinner cannot justify himself, without concurring in his belief that God justifies the sinner through Christ. The doctrine of *justification by faith* presupposes a God who both makes demands upon and punishes men. Paul never ceased to believe in such a God. For those of us who find this God no longer credible, self-acceptance must replace acceptance by God. We shall return to this issue.

Perhaps Paul's observation in Romans 7 that contains the deepest psychological insight is his description of the conflict between the good he wants to do and the fact that "every single time I want to do good it is something evil that comes to hand. In my inmost self I dearly love God's Law, but I can see that my body follows a different law that battles against the law which my reason dictates. This is what makes me a prisoner of the law of sin which lives in my body" (Rom. 7:21–23).

Here again, there is profound psychological truth in Paul's description. I often found myself divided between what I knew to be right and something almost foreign within me that compelled me to do things of which I disapproved. When I read Paul's description of this conflict, I saw him as a spiritual brother. As I cast a backward glance at my life under the Law, I felt a strong sense of kinship with him in his retrospective reflection.

The most crucial problem that beset Paul, as it must all men, was death. Paul knew as much about the physical consequences of mortality as we do. He was undeceived concerning the inexorable fatality that confronts all flesh. He wanted a way out of mortality as urgently as do men in any age. The existential posture of hopefulness was possible for Paul because he believed that God had bestowed upon mankind a way out of Adam's terminal affliction, mortality. It is not necessary to concur in Paul's conviction that Jesus Christ is the true remedy for mankind's ultimate infirmity in order to feel empathy with Paul's yearning for immortality.

I had entered the world of the Law because it seemed to offer me a way of disciplining myself. Many years were to pass before I realized that I had far more compelling reasons for electing the path I did. Without the slightest conscious awareness, I had never really given up the hope that somehow I could escape dying. As a child, I was convinced that science would invent a cure for death long before I had to worry about it. I lost faith in the power of science to save me long before I lost faith in God's power. If somebody had told me, "You have become an observant Jew because you hope God will reward you with immortal life," I would have rejected the idea derisively. Yet the yearning for immortality was the most compelling reason for my life of religious discipline. At the most primitive level of my being I simply refused to accept the fact that, like all men, I was inevitably fated to perish.

When my infant son Nathaniel died suddenly on the morning before Yom Kippur in 1950 I could deceive myself no longer. I had been engaged by a congregation in Baltimore to serve as the preacher for their overflow services on the High Holy Days. My wife had taken our two children, Aaron, age eighteen months, and Nathaniel, age three months, to visit her parents in Cincinnati. I remember reviewing the sermons I had prepared as I rode to Baltimore on the train. When I arrived, I was told to come immediately to the rabbi's office. When I entered, he looked at me with a sadness that puzzled me.

"Dick," he said, "I have bad news for you. Nathaniel was found dead in his crib this morning." My first impulse was to cry out, "My God, what have I done that you have punished me like this?"

I flew immediately to Cincinnati. On the way I kept repeating to myself the text of one of the most awesome of all High Holy Day prayers, the *U-N'sane-Tokef*, which contains the sentence, "On Rosh Ha-Shannah it is decreed and on Yom Kippur it is sealed, (in the Book of Life) who shall live and who shall die. . . ."

The terrible pain of Nathaniel's sudden and inexplicable death was intensified by the peculiar symbolism of the High Holy Day prayer. In the prayer it is God who decides and passes judgment on "who shall attain the measure of man's days and who shall not attain it." It is God who gives life—and God who slays. The prayer assures the believer that "repentance, prayer, and righteousness avert the evil decree." One of the themes that constantly surfaces in this study of Paul is the conception of God as the Divine Infanticide. If, as both Paul and the rabbis maintain, death is God's punishment of his disobedient children, then God, though he be righteous and just, is the Divine Infanticide. The existential roots of my preoccupation with this theme are to be found in the sudden death of my infant son the morning preceding Yom Kippur. To this day I cannot utter the *U-N'Sane-Tokef* without thinking of Nathaniel.

My fellow students and the professors at the Seminary tried to console me. Their success was limited. There was, however, one man whom I wanted to see, Rabbi Isaac Hutner, the *Rosh Yeshivah* (leader) of Mesivta Chaim Berlin. I had acquired a great deal of respect for him. His words of consolation meant more to me than any other rabbi's. I visited him on Sukkoth, the festival of Tabernacles, as he sat in his Sukkah with his students.

"I want you always to remember," he told me, "that *Ribbono shel Olam,* the Master of the Universe, never writes guarantees in this life." As I was about to leave, he added, "I hope this doesn't cause you to lose your *emunah,* your faith."

I protested in surprise. In retrospect, he knew me better than I knew myself. It wasn't that I said, "God has done this to me, to hell with him." For at least three years I continued to lead a religiously compliant life. Nevertheless, I had been shaken far more than I realized.

As a result of my son's death, I came slowly to understand that observance of the Law would never give me what I really wanted, an escape from mortality. The purpose of the Law is to foster the obedience of the children of Israel before their Heavenly Father. The psychological posture of the believer before his God within the Law is always that of sonship. Even my remaining in graduate school until I received a doctorate had been an expression of my need to be a good son. I wanted the commendation of an expanding network of fathers. In the meantime, life was passing me by as my world became a carrel in Widener Library and a sea of file cards. And, I knew it. There were always more adolescent ordeals to be endured. There was always an ever-receding tomorrow in which the rewards of good sonship might finally be won.

My need to be a good son arose out of my fear of dying. When I began to understand my inner life, I realized that I had sought in every conceivable way to deny to myself that I was ever getting older. Fear of death was the goad of a strange "love" of learning that kept me in school until I was thirty-six years old. In my unconscious fantasy only fathers died; if I could somehow remain a "good" son and please my "fathers," especially my omnipotent Father, by perfect obedience, I might be saved from dying. The fantasy lacked logic; it did not lack strength. My willing servitude was born out of my quest for omnipotence, for I was really searching for a condition in which no possible harm could ever reach me. Only God enjoys such omnipotent felicity. It was my secret hope that, were I to become the truly obedient son, he might make me like him.

I find a similar idea in Paul's letter to the Philippians that I will discuss more fully in the chapter on Paul's vision of Christ as the Last Adam. In Philippians Paul quoted what may have been a primitive Christian hymn, which proclaimed that Jesus had been perfectly obedient to the Father, that he did not grasp at "equality with God," and that as a result God had raised him up from the dead to give him "the name which is above all other names" (Phil. 2:6–11). Because Jesus had been the perfectly obedient Son, the Father rescued him from dying and made him Lord over all. Paul knew that he could not by his own efforts become as obedient as Jesus had been. After conversion, he believed that God had done for him through Christ what he could not do for himself. I had no such assurance. I felt compelled to become the perfect son myself. I fell short constantly. When my three-month-old son died, too young to have given offense to either his earthly or his heavenly father, I knew with a deeper certitude than I had ever before experienced that I was doomed to die no matter how well I performed. When I read Paul's assurance to his churches that in Christ God has annulled the death sentence of Adam's progeny, I feel an especial sense of kinship with him. We have known the same terrors.

Paul's terrors were mercifully overcome by faith in the Risen Christ. I had no such boon. Had I lived in his time, I might have followed him. Once I realized that I had no escape from dying, I had to learn to live as if I were newly born. My new life was devoid of hope or illusion that the limitations of mortality could be overcome. My analyst was midwife to my rebirth. My conversion experience began in 1950. It took me years before I could emerge from my second womb. My rebirth did not involve faith in a messianic redeemer as did Paul's; it did, however, involve something Paul understood perhaps better than any other man of his time, the wisdom of learning to trust what we have been given. Today I am amazed at how long it took me to learn that lesson and how easily I forget it under stress.

My experience with the Law was obviously atypical. Most religious Jews accept the Torah as their normal way of life. Traditional Judaism is simply their folk culture. They are not normally driven by the compulsions that afflicted me. Like Paul, I came to rabbinic Judaism as something of an outsider. My friends at the Jewish Theological Seminary watched me agonize over the sufficiency of my religious observance with great kindness. Nevertheless, they regarded me as overly scrupulous. And rightly so; they were at home with Judaism in a way I could not begin to understand. They were also at home with their God. I was not at home with mine.

Freud has observed that "even those who do not regret the disappearance of religious illusions from the civilized world of today will admit that so long as they were in force they offered those who were bound by them the most powerful protection against the danger of neurosis."[6] I came to the religious group as a solitary individual seeking a way out of personal distress. Freud's observations on the difference between the neurotic and the member of a religious group are very applicable to what happened to me: "If he is left to himself, a neurotic is obliged to replace by his own symptom formations the great group formations from which he is excluded. He creates his own world of imagination for himself, his own religion, his own system of delusions, and thus recapitulates the institutions of humanity in a distorted way. . . ."[7]

The other students at the Seminary were at home with Judaism even when they were lax in ritual observance. I was not, although my scrupulosity extended to the observance of the rules of "family purity," which made my wife sexually inaccessible to me during her menstrual cycle and until seven "clean" days had elapsed. When I became religiously compliant, I did not exchange my private neurosis for the great religious institutions of my community. I simply utilized these institutions in a very private way. My experience has been too singular to cast doubt on the viability of the Jewish religious system for those acculturated into it in a normal way.

By the same token, I believe that the attempt to see in Paul's religious career the inevitable result of the breakdown of a fossilized Pharisaism misrepresents the extent to which normative Judaism was a viable religious way of life in Paul's time and during the ensuing two millennia. The fundamental issue between Paul and the rabbis has nothing to do with such questions as whether Paul's theology was an "advance" over first-century Judaism. The issue is whether Jesus is the Messiah and Redeemer of Israel, and through Israel of mankind. Unfortunately, neither those who accept nor those who reject Jesus as Redeemer have found a way to arrive at a consensus on this issue.

It is doubtful if the question of whether Paul's background was Hellenistic or Jewish can ever be resolved, especially because first-century Judaism was strongly influenced by Hellenistic culture. Nevertheless, all authorities agree that Paul's early years were spent outside of Palestine. Some scholars even deny that he lived in Palestine until after his conversion, despite the testimony of the Book of Acts.[8] I have come to believe that Paul's thought and religious life were far more Jewish than Greek, but that there were influences at work in him that set him apart from those whose native religious framework was Judaean Pharisaism. In all likelihood, Gershom Scholem is correct in his highly informed judgment that Paul was "a revolutionary Jewish mystic."[9] Nevertheless, Paul was different from his Jewish contemporaries in some inexplicably radical way. This difference enabled him to see both problems and potentials within the ritual and mythic structures of normative Judaism that were not noticed by his more traditional contemporaries. Although Paul's career has much to teach us, the failure of Pharisaism is not one of its lessons.

There is little direct evidence that Paul was afflicted with the kind of obsessive scrupulosity against which I struggled. Krister Stendahl warned against reading too much of the spiritual and psychological biographies of Augustine and Luther into Paul, especially Luther's struggle with his conscience. He asserted that Paul was equipped with what he calls "a rather robust conscience,"[10] citing autobiographical passages in Philippians and Galatians concerning Paul's life under the Law: "I was born of the race of Israel. . . . As for the Law, I was a Pharisee; as for working for religion, I was a persecutor of the Church; *as far as the Law can make you perfect, I was faultless*" (Phil. 3:5–7).

A similar thought is expressed in Galatians: "You must have heard of my career as a practising Jew . . . *how enthusiastic I was for the traditions of my ancestors*" (Gal. 1:13–14). Stendahl claims with justice that in these passages Paul recollects little of the divided self in his pre-Christian career that is often ascribed to him. Paul's description of the man under the Law in Romans 7 must in any event be seen as the retrospective thoughts of a man who has found his solution in faith in Christ. Although my own problems with the Law led me to understand the psychological force of Paul's observations in Romans 7, I did not arrive at similar insights by traveling the same spiritual road.

Above all, I cannot share Paul's solution. Paul saw Christ as the ultimate solution to the problems of mankind: "What a wretched man I am! Who will rescue me from this body doomed to death? Thanks be to God through Jesus Christ our Lord!" (Rom. 7:24–25).

I do not reject Paul's solution because he was Christian and I am Jewish. *I find the normative Jewish and Christian solutions equally unacceptable*. When I understood that my compulsion to obey God's Law with ever greater scrupulosity was in reality a reflection of an intrapsychic conflict and that I had, in fact, created the very God I sought to appease, Paul's solution became as impossible for me as the Law had been. The God-who-acts-in-human-affairs never ceased to be an objective reality to Paul. Paul's religious symbols never became transparent to him. He was not without profound psychological insight, but he never saw his conflicts as fundamentally psychological.

Even without psychoanalysis my religious symbols were destined to become transparent to me in the process of being trained in the history of religion and in the social sciences. The conflict between faith and history cannot be dismissed lightly. The objective historian is compelled to place the affirmations of faith in the context of the social and cultural movements out of which they arose. In the light of objective history, no religious position can be privileged. The same relativizing tendency is also manifest in the sociology of religion.[11] The fact that I came to see my conflicts as psychological was not unrelated to the fact that I grew up in an urban, middle-class, Jewish environment. Had my parents been rural peasants, it is not likely that I would have ever seen my conflicts as psychological.

Given my background, as soon as I recognized the psychological character of my conflicts, I had become another example of what Philip Rieff has called "psychological man."[12] Psychological man represents a type of demystified consciousness that neither Paul nor the rabbis could have anticipated, although both unwittingly contributed greatly to its appearance. There was a time when, I saw my problem as one of acceptance by God. As psychological man, such acceptance ceased to be meaningful. Neither the Law nor Christ could have taught me the resignation nor given me the self-acceptance I now required. Without self-acceptance, I would not have had the strength to trust the integrity and the authority of my own experience, especially when it entailed so radical a departure from the inherited wisdom of my religious community. Psychological man can only be healed, if indeed such healing is any longer possible, to the extent that he heals himself.

Here I have tried to spell out some of the more significant personal factors that contributed to my very strong involvement with a Jew who lived so long ago. I have not attempted to offer a spiritual autobiography, but have limited my account to experiences relevant to my interest in Paul. My involvement with Paul has never been identification with him. His times, his faith, and his life were very different from mine. And the description of my own point of view does not necessarily yield hints concerning those aspects of Paul's life and thought that I intend to discuss subsequently. Yet, if any single idea dominates the way I have come to see Paul, it is this: *Under the impact of the Christian religious revolution, which was at least initially an internal Jewish revolution, Paul came to understand, as did later Jewish mystics, that reality as apprehended by common sense offers only hints of the deeper and truer meaning of the human world.* Paul thus prepares the way for and anticipates the work of the twentieth century's most important secularized Jewish mystic, Sigmund Freud.

Finally, if there is one sentence in all of Paul's letters that has meant more to me than any other it is his autobiographical testimony: "I am no longer trying for perfection by my own efforts, the perfection which comes from the Law. . . ." While I cannot share Paul's yearning for perfection in Christ—"but I want only the perfection that comes through faith, and is from God. . ." (Phil. 3:9)—I can strongly empathize with him, for Paul had come to understand the wisdom of trusting what had been given to him.

Chapter II

Identification

More than any other figure in early Christianity, Paul of Tarsus stood at the crossroads of rabbinic Judaism and Christianity. No other figure embodied in his own life and thought the religious and psychological connections that both unite and render Judaism and Christianity enormously antagonistic to each other. Paul was initially a loyal and thoughtful Jew; he became a profoundly imaginative and completely devoted Christian. Both as a Jew and as a Christian Paul had the same fundamental problem, which did not change when he became a Christian. What changed was the way in which Paul and his spiritual heirs believed the problem was to be resolved. Throughout his life Paul saw mankind's fundamental problem as: *How can men achieve the right relationship to their Creator?* Before conversion his response was the classical Jewish answer: Men achieve the right relationship by obedient submission to the will of the Father. This submission was why normative Judaism has always been the religion of the Law. When Paul became a Christian, he found another way to achieve an acceptable relationship to his God: identification with the older brother. Identification is therefore a crucial category in which both the religious and the psychological worlds intersect in the experience of Paul and his spiritual heirs.

Largely as a result of the scholarship of Albert Schweitzer, we are able to understand the role of identification in Paul's thought and religious experience.[1] Before Schweitzer, Protestant New Testament scholarship tended to stress the doctrine of justification by faith as central to Paul's message; there was an understandable tendency to read Paul through the eyes and experience of Luther. Schweitzer maintained that the doctrine of justification by faith, while undoubtedly of great importance, was less central to Paul's thought than his "Christ mysticism" and his eschatology. Instead of regarding Paul as an opponent of Judaism, as earlier Protestant scholars tended to do, Schweitzer interpreted him as a loyal Jew who was convinced that the Risen Christ had initiated the Messianic Age.[2] According to Schweitzer, Paul understood the kind of existence baptized Christians enjoyed in the Messianic Age to be literally that of *corporeal solidarity with the glorified, immortal body of the Risen Christ.* He asserted that the fundamental conception of Paul's Christ mysticism is that the elect and Christ partake of a common bodily identity.[3] Paul's identification with Christ is expressed most graphically in his exclamation that, having been crucified with Christ, it is no longer he who lives but Christ who lives in him (Gal. 2:20). Paul described Christians as having "clothed themselves" with Christ, by which he meant that Christ was their new, heavenly body rather than new apparel (Gal. 3:27; Rom. 13:14; cf. II Cor. 5:3, 4; Eph. 4:24; Col. 3:10).

Paul also used an image drawn from the marital relationship to describe the baptized Christian's corporeal unity with Christ: "My brethren, who through the body of Christ are now dead to the Law, can now give yourselves to another (husband), to him who rose from the dead to make us fruitful for God" (Rom. 7:4).[4] Paul saw this union of Christ and Christian as a true unity. The Church is more than a collection of individuals united by common belief and hope. The Church is literally the body of Christ, and Christians are "living" members of that body (Eph. 5:30).[5] To be a member of the Church is to share a common identity with Christ. Paul asked the Corinthians rhetorically, "You know surely that your bodies are members making up the body of Christ . . ." (I Cor. 6:15). This is no mere figure of speech. Later in I Corinthians Paul illustrates the meaning of the Christian's existence in Christ by analogy with the human body: "Just as a human body, though it is made up of many parts, is a single unit because all these parts, though many, make one body, so it is with Christ . . ." (I Cor. 12:12–13). "Now you together are Christ's body; but each of you is a different part of it" (I Cor. 12:27). Bishop John A. T. Robinson has observed that the body Paul has in mind here is not that of "a supra-personal collective" but of a single, concrete individual.[6]

The unity of the Christian in Christ's body is such that Christ is the "head" and Christians who constitute the church are members of his body: "we shall grow in all ways into Christ, who is the head by whom the whole body is fitted and joined together. . ." (Eph. 4:15f., cf. 1:22; 5:23; Col. 1:18; 2.9f.).

Robinson has stressed the necessity of reading Paul literally. He claimed that Paul deliberately resorted to a "very violent use of language" when he asserted that individual Christians are actually parts of a single person. Robinson warned against any attempt to lessen the impact of Paul's words or "the materialism and crudity" of Paul's doctrine of the Church as the body of Christ.[7]

Robinson concurred with Schweitzer's assertion that the heart of Paul's doctrine is that the Christian's existence is a bodily being-in-Christ. Robinson amplified Schweitzer's work by stressing the centrality of the concept of the body as "the keystone of Paul's theology." Robinson further pointed out that Paul was fundamentally concerned with the vicissitudes of bodily existence throughout his religious thought.[8] The changes experienced by the Christian as he journeys from his pre-Christian life to the Resurrection are primarily bodily transformations. At baptism, his old body dies and he gains a new body, the body of Christ; he enters the Church as a member of the body of Christ; at the Lord's Supper he consumes the body of Christ; and at the Resurrection he will be changed into an immortal, spiritual body.

One of the effects of the work of Schweitzer and Robinson has been to heighten our awareness of what Robinson has called the "crudity of Paul's doctrine." For those who claimed that Christianity was "higher," more "spiritual," or more "advanced" than its predecessors, the contributions of these scholars must have been exceedingly difficult to accept. There has been a persistent tendency in Protestant thought to denigrate what Karl Barth has called "the concrete world of religion." As long as scholarship stressed the doctrine of justification by faith at the expense of other elements in Paul's thought, it was possible to regard Paul as a protomodern figure grappling with the problems of a man of divided conscience. But how could any modern man find meaning in Paul's crude, unabashed materialism, which seemed to violate so thoroughly the canons of common sense? How could any man with a normal ego regard himself as in reality identified with the body of another? Archaic men might have experienced a coalescence of identity into a kind of collective psychic unity in tribal ritual and dance, but the Christianity of twentieth-century men, especially individualistic Protestants, could hardly be understood in such terms. At first glance, the interpretation of Paul that stressed the believer's identification with Christ and the Apostle's utilization of concrete, bodily images seemed to lessen the relevance of Paul for the twentieth century.

It is my conviction that the scholarship of men like Schweitzer and Robinson allows us to see Paul for the first time as a figure who makes sense in contemporary terms. Paul's insistence on comprehending the Christian experience in terms of the human body links him with the world of psychoanalysis. Perhaps the central insight of psychoanalysis is that all of the "higher" productions of the human psyche—such as art, myth, and religion—are ultimately objectified expressions of the organism's developmental vicissitudes and its strivings for bodily gratifications within the emotional matrix of the nuclear social unit, the human family. Psychoanalysis has sought to uncover the organic, developmental, and familial realities underlying the symbolism of religion. Paul's bodily "materialism" and his persistent tendency to utilize the metaphors of paternity, fraternity, and filiation in his religious thought expressed a similar insight intuitively. The very crudeness of Paul's images testifies to their emotional honesty and their overwhelming power. The crudeness also makes it possible for depth psychology to comprehend Paul's theology in terms of its own symbolism.

The "corporeal solidarity" that Schweitzer described as the essence of Paul's Christ mysticism is analogous to identification as understood in psychoanalysis. Freud described identification as "the earliest expression of an emotional tie with another person."[9] Identification "endeavors to mold another person's ego after the fashion of the one who has been taken as a model."[10] Identification was used by Paul and his heirs whenever Christ served as the ideal of a truly Christian life.

Identification often occurs when a beloved object has been lost or is absent, as was Jesus after the Crucifixion-Resurrection sequence of events. Identification is the ego's way of regaining or retaining within itself the lost or absent object. It is often coupled with a strong yearning to be with a person to whom one is strongly attached. The oldest of all Christian prayers declared simply *Maranatha*, "May the Master come." This prayer expressed poignantly the primitive Church's yearning to be reunited with its absent Lord. Paul shared that yearning:

> I want to be gone and be with Christ . . ." (Phil. 1:23).

> . . . to live in the body means to be exiled from the Lord, going as we do by faith. . . . we are full of confidence, I say, and actually want to be exiled from the body and make our home with the Lord". (II Cor. 5:6–8).

Freud also regarded identification as "a derivative of the first oral phase of the organization of the libido, in which the *object we long for and prize is incorporated through eating*."[11] In a certain sense all identifications have an element of psychic cannibalism about them. When we identify with a person for whom we long, that person is taken in and becomes a part of our ego. Identification was involved in the case of one of Freud's patients, a child who reacted to the loss of a favorite cat by insisting that he was the cat. The child walked on all fours and refused to eat at the table.[12] There have been innumerable examples of identification with lost parents or relatives during mourning. There have been mourners whose hair suddenly turned the same gray color as their recently deceased parents. Other mourners have developed the identical disease which had proved fatal to the deceased as their way of denying the loss and retaining the lost object.[13] A very potent form of identification is manifest among very religious persons whose bodies exhibit the wounds of the crucified Jesus. In both the psychic act of identification and the physical act of eating, the prized object is taken in and made a part of the person. The parallel between identification and consumption is evident in the Lord's Supper as that rite was understood by Paul (I Cor. 10:16).

By replacing obedience to the Father with identification with the crucified older brother, Christianity introduced a radically novel element into the religious life of mankind. The denial of all semblance between God and man in Judaism has been called the "ultimate repression" by one psychoanalyst.[14] In the earliest childhood of the individual (if not the race), the gods are human figures with whom men can identify. Judaism repressed these identifications. Christianity made them available once again in art, religion, and in the general culture. Nevertheless, the divine-human figure who became manifest in Christianity was not the Father but Christ, "the first born of many brothers." The difference is crucial. Christ as the elder brother may have been a surrogate father, but he elicited a radically different kind of involvement from his disciples than did the real Father. It was impossible for religious Jews to identify with the Father in spite of the rabbinic injunction to model oneself after his holiness.[15] In Judaism the closest relationship one could achieve with the Father was obedience and, if one were extremely fortunate, trust, but never identification.

But identification was possible with the elder brother. He shared with the younger brothers their defeats, their humiliations, and their complex relations with the mysterious and inaccessible Father. Christ as the elder brother was a preeminently believable model with whom even the lowliest of men could identify. The psychological triumph of the Cross was such that through it no man could be so fallen, degraded, or devoid of worldly accomplishment that he was unable to identify with divinity. Because the elder brother has known the most terrible pain and defeat, any of the other brothers can say, "You are one of us."

When the older brother experienced the depth of human suffering and then fulfilled the most potent of all human yearnings, the attainment of eternal life, it is not surprising that the other brothers wanted to be like him. Christ, crucified and resurrected, became the most potent religious model for identification the western world has ever known, for he experienced the worst that men fear and the most glorious condition for which they hope. We need not wonder that the brothers wanted so badly to be like him that they were even prepared to eat his substance in the Lord's Meal in order to partake of his immortal glory.

Paul's belief that Christians achieve the only truly saving relationship with the Father through identification with the elder brother and his preference for concrete bodily images is related to another tendency that some scholars, including Bishop Robinson, have noted. Rudolf Schnackenburg has observed that Paul often used "picture language" and that he had a "gift and a predilection for plastic imagery."[16] A very good example of this is Paul's exceptionally striking use of the image of the Christian as buried and reborn with Christ in the waters of baptism as well as the symbolic interpretation Paul shared with others in the early Church of the bread and wine of the Lord's Supper as the body and blood of Christ. Although neither Schnackenberg nor Robinson utilize psychoanalytic categories, they have in effect noted the extent to which Paul's thought was dominated by the imagery and logic of primary process thinking, the id's level of mental functioning. It was very largely this quality that made Paul an authentic religious genius. His use of the imagery of the primary process greatly contributed to what can best be called the Christian psychological revolution. *Paul was able to express some of the deepest and most archaic emotional strivings of mankind because he was able to give objectified expression to his own unconscious mental processes.*

Throughout his letters, Paul's thought is permeated with the rich imagery and symbolism of primary process thinking. Paul exhibited a vivid *symbolic consciousness* that saw associations and connections where others saw only distinctions and disjunctions.[17] This capacity led Paul to distrust the day-to-day world of common sense. In the language of depth psychology, Paul distrusted the ego and the reality principle. This comes through with especial force in I Corinthians where Paul contrasted the wisdom of this world, the ego's wisdom, with Christian foolishness, which is God's wisdom, the only wisdom that will ultimately prevail: "The language of the cross may be illogical to those who are not on the way to salvation, but those of us who are on the way see it as God's power to save" (I Cor. 1:18). "For God's foolishness is wiser than human wisdom . . ." (I Cor. 1:25). Paul's insistence on the ultimate superficiality of human wisdom contains an insight that religion shares with psychoanalysis: Each in its own way asserts the reality of the unmanifest.[18] When Paul rejected the wisdom of common sense he was neither a fool nor an obscurantist. He understood intuitively that there was more to reality, especially emotional reality, than had been available to him as a Pharisee living in the pre-messianic world.

One of the most influential examples of Paul's symbolic consciousness is in the text already cited that Christians are members of one body of which Christ is literally the head (Eph. 4:15f.). The normal ego distinguishes the self from the external world; the id knows no such boundaries. The id unites what the ego treats as discrete. According to Freud, the distinction-making adult ego is a vestige of a very different kind of ego: "Originally the ego includes everything, later it detaches from itself the external world. The ego-feeling we are aware of now is thus a shrunken vestige of a far more extensive feeling—a feeling which embraced the universe and expressed an inseparable connection of the ego with the external world."[19]

The archaic ego has yet to be differentiated from either the external world or the id. This state, in which the self knows no boundaries and in which it experiences itself as omnipotent, has been called *primary narcissism*. In primary narcissism all sense of discrete personal identity is absent. Nevertheless, this undifferentiated state of consciousness contains a very important element of truth. No organism can exist apart from its environment. The sun, the earth, and the atmosphere are as vital as the internal organs to our bodily functioning. The boundaries of the self cannot realistically be restricted to the boundaries of the body. There is a sense in which all human beings together comprise a single organic nature. We are indispensible to each other for reproduction, nurture, and mutual support. Our egos are fundamentally transindividual. We are decisively affected by the memories and the experience of the race, the process of acculturation, and, most especially, the interaction between parents and peers. We distort reality when we insist on too rigid a separation of self and world. When Paul insisted upon the unity of all Christians in the immortal body of Christ, he wisely rejected the ultimacy of the ego's apprehension of the "real" world.

Here again we return to Freud's comment about "dark traces of the past," which were ready to break through into consciousness in Paul. Paul insisted that the Christian's ego boundaries had been dissolved into the larger unity of the body of Christ. Paul could not have made such an assertion unless he was in touch with the imagery of the earliest levels of his own experience. His insistence on the unity of the elect in Christ was an expression of a return to that period in his mental development that preceded the separation of self and world, the division into subject and object. In and through Christ, Paul saw the archaic solidarity of things restored. That is why he insisted that the transformation initiated by Christ had altered not only the elect but all creation: "From the beginning till now the entire creation . . . has been groaning in one great act of giving birth; and not only creation, but all of us who possess the first fruits of the Spirit, we too groan inwardly as we wait for our bodies to be set free" (Rom. 8:22–23). Paul's thought here is readily translatable into the language of depth psychology: The creation that groans "to be set free" is the day-to-day world of the normal adult ego. Paul envisaged the recovery of an older reality through Christ—the oldest reality Paul had ever known—one in which there was neither subject nor object, and above all, no death.

Throughout this study I shall have occasion to refer to the text in Galatians that states: "there are no more distinctions between Jew and Greek, slave and free, male and female, but you are one in Christ Jesus" (Gal. 3:28). We must follow Robinson's counsel and take seriously the literal meaning of this text, in which Paul asserts the unity of the elect in the body of Christ. It can be given ethical meaning and interpreted as Christianity's rejection of all forms of human social distinction, but Paul's assertion is far more concrete. Paul had broken with all of the regnant distinctions of tribe, sex, and social class of his time and culture. He was actually asserting in his own images that Christians can no longer rely upon the discriminations of the ego, as had the teachers of Jewish Law. Instead, they were to trust once again those archaic experiences in which the boundaries of self and world had yet to solidify.

There is, of course, great danger in insisting on the underlying unity of all things. We may be differentiated aspects of a unitary reality, but we must ultimately protect ourselves as individuals. Even within the family, too great an insistence on unity at the expense of individuality can be exceedingly dangerous. The ego may distort reality when it renders discrete the domains of self and world, but it does so in order to thwart the very real dangers the external world constantly presents to the organism. Had Paul merely reasserted the Christian's original unity with the world, he would have been faithful to a very archaic intuition of the nature of things, but neither he nor his churches could have long survived. Regression to a state in which the distinctions of self and world are lost characterizes the schizophrenic.[20] Fortunately, Paul did not collapse into psychosis in asserting the fundamental unity of all things in Christ because he insisted that the task of realizing that unity had yet to be completed. By stressing the fact that the process of redemption had been initiated but not yet achieved, Paul was able to give both the primary process and the secondary process (the ego's level of mental functioning) their due. He intuitively understood the limitations of the common-sense world without losing contact with it or the problem-solving capacities of the ego. Paul was thus both a visionary and an organizer, a mystic and an administrator. He was able to stabilize the two sides of his nature because of the unusual balance he achieved between his own conscious and unconscious mental processes.

In the next chapter we shall see that Christ as the elder brother became Paul's double and that Paul's strategy for achieving immortality and omnipotence was not to assert his own omnipotence uncritically, as would a psychotic, but to transfer his own yearning to the image of the Risen Christ and then to try to share in Christ's glorious condition of identifying a right relation to the Father. Paul was convinced that perfect obedience to the Father was impossible for him and that anything less would be of no avail, (cf. Gal. 3:10). He was also convinced that by perfect obedience unto death Jesus alone had achieved a right relation with the Father. Only by identifying with Jesus could Christians share in the Savior's relation to the Father (Rom 5:20). Here too we see that identification with Christ was decisive for Paul.

It is interesting to note that Paul did not entirely reject obedience to the Father, Judaism's way of achieving a right relation with God. He took it very seriously, but came to two conclusions about it: (1) it was impossible for any ordinary man to achieve, and (2) the fruits of Christ's perfect obedience were freely available to all who identified with him. For Paul, faith in and identification with Christ had become the Christian's new and perfect obedience before the Father.

Chapter III

Damascus

Karl Barth, one of the preeminent Christian theologians of the twentieth century, has observed that "the beginning and the end of the Christian message is the proclamation that Christ is risen from the dead."[1] The central issue in Paul's conversion was whether Christ had in fact been victorious over death. That issue was dramatically resolved for Paul when Christ appeared to him on the road to Damascus.

There have been innumerable attempts to understand Paul's conversion. Some scholars have seen the key to the conversion in the conflict to which Paul alluded in Romans 7. They describe Paul as caught, either between the demands of the superego and the id, or between his desire to comply fully with God's Law and the interior compulsion that inhibited his obedience until the conflict was resolved by the aparition of the Risen Christ.[2] One Jewish scholar explained the conversion experience as an epileptic fit.[3] Others have regarded the event as an hysterical outbreak.[4] The conversion has also been interpreted as a way of resolving homosexual conflicts, masturbatory conflicts, and ambivalent feelings of rebelliousness and submissiveness toward the Father God.[5] Still others reject all possibility of a psychological explanation whatsoever.[6] They see in Paul's conversion the workings of the grace of God, who can turn even the worst enemy into a faithful servant. Of one thing we may be certain: No attempt

34

at explanation can do more than offer a very partial illumination of what took place. Paul's conversion will always remain at least partly inexplicable. When we ask why Saul became Paul, we enter a realm that is frankly conjectural. Nevertheless, even a conjectural description may help us to understand Paul to some extent.

I believe that identification with the Risen Christ as the "first born of many brothers," abrupt and catastrophic at its onset, was Paul's way of resolving the conflict between his commitment to the worldly realism of the Pharisees and his perhaps subliminal hope that the crucified Messiah had truly been victorious over death. In the language of psychoanalysis, Paul's conflict was between the ego's common-sense realism and the id's refusal to recognize any limitation of space, time, or mortality.

Paul was one of the most influential Jewish messianists of all times. We shall not understand his conversion or his career without some insight into that perennially disturbing phenomenon, Jewish messianism, which provided the religious and psychological matrix out of which Paul's life and thought could arise. Jewish messianism has taken both religious and political forms, but it has always been a reaction against a harsh and often iniquitous world. In modern times Jews have often been in the forefront of radical political movements which seek to end the observed injustices and inequalities of the world around them. This is a contemporary, secular version of Jewish messianism. In the seventeenth century the Jewish community was overwhelmed by the faith that both the indignities of the exile and the sexual renunciations demanded by Jewish Law had been brought to an end by the apostate messiah Sabbatai Zvi. The belief that the Messiah had come encouraged a number of influential Jewish communities to abandon Judaism's traditional sexual restraints.[7] The primitive Christian movement was the most influential of all messianic transformations of normative Judaism, but it was by no means the only one. Messianism has been a persistent component of Jewish life for over two thousand years.

Throughout Jewish history, this worldly realism and its renunciations have been in tension with the kind of radical messianism which

surfaced in the primitive Church. The religious life of the traditional Jew roots him in the chain of generations and in his sexual,
familial and social roles. The religious Jew has always been encouraged to sublimate his surplus sexual and aggressive energies in
compliance with the behavioral expectations of his community. To
the extent that the commanding Father-God of Judaism is a superego figure, he functions to reinforce behavioral compliance. Attention
in normative Judaism is focused primarily upon behavior rather
than feelings. Feelings are never permitted to become dominant unless they can enhance the individual's capacity to comply with
the community's behavioral expectations.

The life of the religious Jew involves constant instinctual discipline.
Gershom Scholem has written of "the divorce of the Law from its
emotional roots" as one of the greatest yet most problematic achieve-
ments of the Halachah or legal traditions of rabbinic Judaism.[8] This
"divorce" was inevitable in view of the Jewish preoccupation with
behavior and role rather than feelings.

Inevitably, feelings had their revenge. Freud has observed that
"in all renunciations and limitations imposed upon the ego a
periodical infringement of the prohibition is the rule."[9] The id must
have its due. Freud cited the Roman Saturnalia and modern carnivals
as examples of "periodical infringements." Judaism has had its light-
hearted festivities both in ancient and modern times, but it never
allowed any real opportunity for the kind of relaxation of instinctual
renunciations most other cultures have found indispensable. One of
the functions of Jewish messianism has been to keep alive, at least
in fantasy, the hope that the inhibitions and frustrations of the
day-to-day world would eventually be annulled. That is why Jewish
messianists from the time of Paul to Sabbatai Zvi and even some of
the early reform rabbis have seen the "end of the Law" as one of the
most important consequences of the Messianic Age.[10]

Perhaps if Judaism had allowed for periodic carnivals of the flesh,
it might not have developed its persistent tendency toward messianism.
Unfortunately, that kind of release was exceedingly difficult for a
landless, powerless community whose survival depended entirely

upon the sufferance of their hosts. Apparently, most men have only a limited tolerance for instinctual repression. All men remember, perhaps indistinctly but nevertheless compellingly, a time in earliest childhood before deprivation, inhibition, suffering and death administered their humiliating scars to the precariously developed ego. Freud called this stage primary narcissism. Paradoxically, although the narcissistic ego is in reality powerless in relation to both its own instincts and the outside world, it comes to feel itself omnipotent. The primitive ego has no experience of limitation by the external world. Consequently, it experiences itself as all-powerful. When we seek to ascribe a meaningful content to the hope for immortality in terms of the development of the human organism, we can interpret that hope as the yearning to restore the infant's original feeling of omnipotence. Immortality is in essence a condition in which no possible hazard can threaten the organism. Only in the most impotent moments of infancy do men truly exist in such a condition. The experience is, of course, totally mistaken. Nevertheless, it is that condition, if not the objectless condition of womb-existence, which men seek to restore in their yearning for immortality.

Whenever the conflict between reality and the irrepressible memory of childhood narcissism becomes too great, the ego has a tendency to turn back to an earlier stage of development, when before the world was not experienced in so wounding a light. That is why some people take drugs and others daydream constantly; it is also why Judaism—which, of necessity, was so niggardly in tolerating periodic release—had to place its fantasies of release at the end of days. There is, however, an important difference between messianism and most forms of regression. In regressive strategies the reality principle ceases to hold sway and normal ego functions contract. *In messianism the abolition of the reality principle is projected into the future.*

Eschatology is born out of the recognition of a harsh reality and the refusal to settle for things as they are. What is at stake in all such strategies is the conflict between the reality principle and the pleasure principle. This in turn is an expression of one of the oldest of all intrapsychic conflicts, that of the ego and the id. Jewish messianism can thus be seen as the cultural objectification of the refusal of those forces within the psyche that are in the service of the pleasure principle to surrender completely to the reality principle. The messianist acknowledges the present power of the reality principle while looking toward its ultimate abolition.

Even before becoming a Christian, Paul could hardly have been indifferent to the primitive Church's claim that the Messiah of Israel had appeared in the person of the Crucified One. At the time, Jesus and the primitive Church exercised a very strong, albeit initially negative, impact upon Paul. We have his own testimony concerning his involvement: "You must have heard of my career as a practicing Jew, how merciless I was in persecuting the Church of God, how much damage I did to it" (Gal. 1:13; cf. I Cor. 15:19; Phil 3:6). As a Pharisee, Paul was not compelled to become an energetic persecutor of the infant Church. Rabban Gamaliel, who is depicted in Acts as Paul's own teacher, is also presented as taking a far more tolerant attitude toward the Christians (Acts 5:34–39). Paul's choice of role is in itself testimony to the fact that he was unable to leave the new movement alone.

Paul may have become a persecutor because he intuitively understood the revolutionary consequences of the belief that Jesus' Crucifixion and Resurrection had initiated the Messianic Age. Paul's mature theology was in all likelihood preceded by a period of gestation that began before his conversion. This does not mean that the developed theology of Romans existed unconsciously in the mind of Paul as a Pharisee. Nevertheless, in some rudimentary, perhaps subliminal way, Paul may have thought to himself, "If the Crucified One has really risen and is in truth Israel's Redeemer, we are no longer bound by the Law, its institutions or Adam's mortal curse." If Paul had in fact entertained this possibility, his first reaction would have been strongly negative. Paul's commitment to the world of the Pharisees was too strong to permit him to welcome initially what he correctly perceived to be as radical a challenge as the Christian movement. There is no reason to believe that Paul's capacity to understand the consequences of the dawn of the Messianic Age developed only after his conversion. Conversion altered Paul's convictions and his commitments; it did not alter his ability as a religious thinker. On the contrary, only if we assume that Paul's initial opposition to the Christian movement was due to the fact that he intuitively understood what was really at stake does his persecutory activity make sense.

Can we reconstruct Paul's preconversion attitude toward the Church from his letters? We can to some extent if we assume that before Paul's conversion he already understood that the career of Jesus confronted him and every Jew with the choice of the day-to-day Jewish world or the Messiah.[13] Then Paul's later writings, especially about the Law, can be used as an excellent source for his pre-Christian attitudes. After conversion Paul rejected much that he previously accepted and accepted much that he had previously rejected, but the same disjunctive alternatives continued to confront him. If we take into account Paul's reversal of position, we will often find that what Paul affirmed as a Christian offers us insight into what was most problematic for him as a Pharisee.

Paul has been regarded as an antinomian. Such a designation is neither accurate nor fair. After Paul became a Christian one of his fundamental convictions, as with almost all Jewish messianists in every age, was that the Messiah had abolished the authority of the Law: "Christ is the end (*telos*) of the Law" (Rom. 10:4). The word *telos* means end in the double sense of goal and termination. Paul undoubtedly meant that Christ was the goal toward which the Law had been pointing (cf. Gal. 3:24) as well as the one who finally abolished its binding authority.

Paul offered a number of arguments to support this position.[14] One of the most interesting is related to his doctrine of baptism. Paul wrote that "the Law only rules over a person during his lifetime." He maintained that Christians had died to their pre-messianic selves at baptism. Addressing himself to those "who have studied the Law" among the Christians at Rome, Paul argued that "through the body of Christ" Christians are now "dead to the Law." He concluded,

"But now we are rid of the Law, having died in that in which we were held. . ." (Rom. 7:1–6). As Schoeps has shown, Paul argued at this point from within the spiritual universe of rabbinic Judaism to prove that the Law had been abolished by the Messiah.[15] His argument rested upon the conviction that Christians are really dead men as far as the pre-messianic world is concerned. As "resurrected" men living in the age of the Messiah, Christians live a new kind of life and are no longer bound by the pre-messianic Law.

As resurrected men Christians are recipients of the gift of eternal life. The prize is yet fully to be won, but Christians already possess it in faith (cf. Rom. 5:1–11). As we shall see, Paul's eschatological vision of Christ as the Last Adam was decisive for his understanding of the destiny that awaits the elect. Paul was convinced that *the supreme importance of the Risen Christ for mankind is that he has overcome the death sentence that God had inflicted upon Adam and his seed for their primal rebellion against the Creator* (cf. Gen. 4:17–19).

After Paul became a Christian, he was convinced that the fundamental shortcoming of observance of the Law was its inability to assure men that they would not die. Paul was convinced that no matter how diligently a man observed the Law, he was doomed to fall short and perish, as had Adam, Abraham, and Moses. What had changed for Paul after conversion was not the sacred character of the Law (Rom. 7:12) but his understanding of where he stood in the divine timetable. Paul now believed that Christ had done what observance of the Law could not do. He had overcome mankind's terminal affliction and had made his victory freely available to all.

At the heart of Paul's postconversion conception of Christ's victory over death, we can discern a radical rejection of the ultimacy of all pre-messianic institutions.[16] Paul now rejected more than the Law: He rejected worldly status, worldly power, and worldly wisdom, for he saw them as manifestations of the world of death and dying. He understood that no human strategy could withstand the divinely inflicted condemnation. Christ became for Paul the only wisdom and the only power, because he alone had brought death to an end.

Some authorities have maintained that as a Jew Paul found himself caught between the conviction that he was obliged to fulfill
every last commandment and his perception that such obedience was
practically impossible. According to these authorities, Paul's dramatic
conversion was his way of resolving this conflict (cf. Gal. 3:10).[17]
However, as Stendahl has observed, we possess no evidence that Paul
found fulfillment of the Law burdensome before becoming a Christian.[18] Paul never claimed that the Law was no longer binding
because it was burdensome. There is little doubt that Paul would
have continued to observe the Law with the utmost scrupulosity had
he remained convinced that his age was pre-messianic or that faithful
obedience was necessary to redeem men from Adam's curse.

Paul rejected the Law after Damascus because he became convinced that it could not free men from death whereas Christ and
Christ alone could. He was not concerned with whether God for-
gives this or that sin or whether a man can stand in some trustful
I–Thou relation to the Eternal Thou. *For Paul the fundamental*
issue was whether death could be defeated. He was also concerned
with sin, but only because "the wages of sin are death," whereas
"the free gift of God is eternal life in Christ Jesus. . ." (Rom. 6:23).
Unless a man could be "made righteous," he would be condemned to
annihilation. Paul stated the issue succinctly: "The reason, therefore, why those who are in Christ Jesus are not condemned (i.e. to
death) is that the law of the spirit of life in Christ Jesus has set
you free from the law of sin and death. God has done what the Law,
because of our fleshly nature (*dia tes sarkos*), was unable to do"
(Rom. 8:1–3). The transformation envisaged by Paul might change a
man's psychological or ethical state, but that was by no means of
primary importance to him. *Human mortality is what was at stake for*
Paul. Sin brings death. The Law, though it be holy, cannot overcome
death because of "our fleshly nature," which is too rebellious to
achieve perfect obedience. Observance of the Law is therefore a dead
end from which men have been rescued by Christ's sacrifice.

In the autobiographical passage in Philippians, Paul described the
great pride he felt as a scrupulously observant Jew. He then observed

that everything that pertained to his old status was of no account in the light of his new life in Christ: "But because of Christ, I have come to consider all those advantages I had as disadvantages. . . . For him I have accepted the loss of everything, and I can look on everything as so much rubbish if only I have Christ" (Phil. 3:7–8). If Paul the Phraisee understood that all of his advantages would become "so much rubbish" in Christ, could his initial reaction have been one of welcome for the new movement?

Those who had little to lose, like the Galilean followers of Jesus, did not have Paul's problem when they joined the Christian movement. Paul, in contrast, had made a major commitment to a way of life that he understood the primitive Church was threatening. His initial strategy was to reinforce his old commitment by attempting to root out those whom he correctly perceived to be challenging it. However, the real arena in which the Christian challenge was played out was within Paul himself. His persecutory activities can best be understood as his response to both the threat and the promise implicit in the Christian message. Fundamentally, the threat and the promise were identical. If the Christians were right, none of the institutions to which Paul had given his loyalty were any longer of the slightest consequence, for the Age of the Resurrection of the Dead was in the process of dawning.

In all probability, Paul began to persecute the Church in order to reduce the tension arising from the internal conflict between his hopes that the Messiah had come and his own worldly realism. Instead of reducing the tension, his persecutory activities only intensified it, for in fighting the Christian movement Paul was fighting himself. Jesus' followers had made the astonishing claim that the deepest hopes and yearnings of the Jewish people for salvation were in fact being fulfilled by the crucified Messiah. Like the rest of us, Paul did not want to die. Until Paul learned of the Resurrection, it is likely that he was convinced that death was inevitable for all men. There may have been a time when he harbored the secret hope that, were he to fulfill the Law perfectly, God might save him from death. Some rabbis maintained that were a person to lead a sinless life of complete obedience to God's will, he might not die.[19] Nevertheless, Paul knew that even the greatest of the Israelites had died, save perhaps for Elijah. Eventually he must have concluded that no matter how scrupulously he kept God's commandments, he too was going to die.

One can safely guess that Paul's first response to the reports of Jesus' Resurrection was intense skepticism if not derisive rejection. Still, some part of Paul must have wanted the report to be true, for *if Jesus had been victorious over death, there was also hope for Paul.* Hence the Christian claim that Jesus had risen must have elicited an awesome hope within him, the hope that his own annihilation might be overcome. After all, death was no less threatening to Paul the Pharisee than to Paul the Apostle.

Nevertheless, the *way* Jesus died must have constituted a formidable obstacle to Paul at first. In one of the best known passages in his letters Paul referred to the "scandal" of believing in a crucified Messiah: "Here we are preaching a crucified Christ (Messiah); to the Jews an obstacle (*skandalon*) that they cannot get over, to the Greeks madness. . ." (I Cor. 1:23).

On the surface, it would seem that nothing in Jewish eschatology could have prepared either Paul or his contemporaries for the assertion that Jesus' degraded death on the cross was the beginning of his messianic role. Insofar as Jewish messianism was political, a Messiah who perishes at the hands of the conqueror was little more than a cruel joke. There is evidence for the idea of a suffering Messiah in first-century Judaism, but not a crucified one.[20]

Nevertheless, the "obstacle" of a crucified Messiah was overcome and the emblem of Jesus' disgrace became the symbol of his incredible victory. There is immense power in paradox. It reminds us that in the emotional life of men things are seldom as they appear to be. Paul came from a people with a tragic history. They had been slaves in Egypt, captives in Babylon, subject in turn to Persian, Greek, and Roman rule. From the point of view of worldly good fortune, the Jewish situation in Paul's time was not impressive. Subject to Roman domination, the events leading up to the catastrophic defeat of the year 70 A.D. were already in the making. When one measures the realistic situation of the Jews against their religious pretensions the contrast is extraordinary. In spite of their impotence, Paul's contemporaries were not only convinced that they were the elect of God, but also that their religious system had been divinely revealed to them. No matter how prosperous other nations might seem, no matter how difficult the plight of the Jews might be, they were in truth God's peculiar treasure, the children in whom he delighted. The Christian doctrine that poverty, weakness, and suffering—as symbolized by the cross—are the gateway to eternal victory had its roots in Judaism.

There is a strong masochistic element in Jewish messianism and the doctrine of the chosen people. Theodore Reik has pointed to the connection between personal masochism and group eschatology.[21] On the surface, a masochist appears to delight in the pain he endures. On closer examination, he willingly suffers because of his hope for ultimate satisfaction. The masochist expects to reach his goal *because* of the pain he has endured. To the extent that he willingly accepts pain, it is because he expects his ultimate reward to be consistent with the magnitude of his present sufferings. When a group looks forward to the time when its defeats will be recompensed and its enemies avenged, it resorts to an illusion akin to that of a child who consoles himself with the thought that he will someday get what he wants and pay back those who have injured him. Such collective daydreams occur regularly among defeated nations and oppressed minorities,[22] and it is not surprising that they were prevalent in first-century Judaism.

It is apparent from Paul's letters that he shared the masochistic component of his people's make-up. One is tempted to suggest that only a powerless, occupied nation such as first-century Israel could have provided the cultural and emotional preparation for the doctrine that the crucified Messiah achieved the ultimate victory through the most terrible defeat. Paul's tendency to masochism is visible in his writings. He gloried in his weaknesses, his sufferings, and his humiliations. He accounted them as gain as long as they were for Christ's sake: "If I am to boast, then let me boast of my own feebleness" (II Cor. 11:30). "I shall be very happy to make my weakness my special boast so that the power of Christ may stay over me, and that is why I am quite content with my weaknesses, and with insults, hardships, persecutions and the agonies I go through for Christ's sake, For it is when I am weak that I am strong" (II Cor. 12:9, 10). "But that is not all we can boast about; we can boast about our sufferings" (Rom. 5:3). "And if my blood has to be shed as part of your own sacrifice . . . I shall be happy and rejoice with all of you. . ." (Phil. 2:17). What has been called the "suspense factor" in masochism is also evident in Paul.[23] He welcomed his suffering because it anticipated joining Christ in his victory: ". . . he was crucified through weakness, and he still lives now through the power of God. So then, we are weak, as he was, but we shall live with him, through the power of God for your benefit" (II Cor. 13:4).

Paul knew grievous weakness and pain. He also saw them as emblems of special dignity. It is possible that his conviction that weakness was the gateway to victory was the result of the impact of Christ's Crucifixion and Resurrection upon him. It is more likely that he could find meaning in the Christian message because of the psychological preparation for the Christian interpretation of Jesus' suffering already present in the national psychology of the Jews. As a believing Jew, strongly influenced by the experience and the hopes of his own people, Paul was prepared to see in affliction God's "chastisements of love" long before he had ever heard of Jesus. And long before he came to regard Jesus' death on the cross as the Messiah's superlatively obedient act, Paul the Pharisee had been trained to regard martyrdom as the Jew's supreme act of obedience.[24] There was also the famous Suffering Servant passage in Isaiah 53. Scholars disagree concerning whether messianic ideas were applied to the passage in pre-Christian times.[25] Nevertheless, there is no doubt that the passage stresses the vicarious suffering of the guiltless Servant for "the sin of many." In addition to Paul's yearning for immortality, he shared with his fellow Jews a certain tendency to rationalize suffering as an emblem of God's distinctive favor. This tendency undoubtedly

predisposed him to respond affirmatively to the Christian proclamation.

Nevertheless, there remained the day-to-day certainties of the
Jewish, Hellenistic, and Roman worlds. People were going about
their business as if nothing had changed. Who could take seriously
the incredible tales about a Messiah who had died the death of a
common criminal? It is very likely that Paul was to some extent
ambivalent about his commitments to the traditions and institutions
of the Pharisees, for such ambivalence was prevalent in rabbinic
circles.[26] Still, Paul's personal and emotional investment in his
old way of life was far too great to be cast aside lightly. It was
exceedingly difficult for him to regard the world of the Pharisees as
"so much rubbish."

Paul's conflict over the infant Church was probably intensified
by the feelings of guilt his activities engendered. We cannot be certain of the extent, if any, of Paul's involvement in the death of
Stephen, a Hellenistic Jew like himself,[27] but we do have his testimony concerning his activities against the Church (Gal. 1:13; I Cor.
15:9). Paul's method of dealing with what was essentially an internal
conflict only served to intensify it. It is one thing to harm those who
do harm; it is quite another to aggress against men who proclaim
that mankind's most profound yearnings are in the process of being
fulfilled. Paul's persecution of the young Church led to even greater
inner division, which in turn spurred him on to more persecution,
thereby further intensifying the conflict.

This conflict was resolved on the road to Damascus. We shall be
in a better position to understand what happened if we consider
three aspects of Paul's experience: (1) his loss of normal ego functions; (2) his vision of the Risen Christ; and (3) his recovery of his
capacities.

Paul's loss of normal ego functions. There are three accounts of
the conversion in Acts: Acts 9:3–19; 22:3–16; and 26:4–18. They are
sufficiently consistent with each other that we are justified in regarding them as ultimately stemming from a single tradition.[28] They are
also impressive in their honesty. There is no discernible attempt at

artificial embellishment. Where these accounts do not contradict Paul's account in Galatians, I believe they offer us a probable description of the conversion as *Paul believed he experienced it.*

Paul does not seem to have had any doubt that the Risen Christ actually appeared to him. When we interpret the experience psychologically, we observe that Acts 9 contains a straightforward description of the abrupt and dramatic contraction of Paul's normal ego functions during and immediately after the event:

> Suddenly there came a light from heaven all round him. He fell to the ground, and he heard a voice saying, "Saul, Saul, why are you persecuting me?" "Who are you, Lord?" he asked, and the voice answered, "I am Jesus, and you are persecuting me. . . ." The men travelling with Saul stood speechless, for though they heard the voice they could see no one. Saul got up from the ground, but even with his eyes open he could see nothing at all, and they had to lead him into Damascus by the hand. For three days he was without his sight, and took neither food nor drink (Acts 9:3–9).

We do not know anything about Paul's physical state, the time of the year, or the weather conditions immediately before the experience; fatigue, hot weather, and thirst could easily have aggravated Paul's inner distress. Even today travel in that part of the world is far from easy, especially in the summer. However, while external conditions may have hastened the onset of the crisis, they could not have been decisive. Sooner or later Paul's inner conflict had to be resolved.

His loss of normal ego functions can be seen as the result of his inability to resolve the conflict between ego and id that we have previously described. The ego functions to guide the organism so that internal and external pain are avoided wherever possible. When Paul's ego failed in this task because of the intensity of his conflict, he regressed to a more archaic and primitive level of mental functioning. During the experience as described in Acts, Paul exhibited the physical as well as the psychological manifestations of extreme regression. He "fell to the ground," collapsing into the posture of a reclining infant or a sleeping adult. He was "without his sight"; his faculty of perception, one of the most important ego functions, was rendered inoperative. He "took neither food nor drink"; his ego functions were so greatly diminished that he was incapable of meeting his most elementary needs "for three days."

Paul also temporarily lost the capacity to distinguish between internal image and external object. This was an expression of the sudden dominance of id over ego. The primary process, the id's level of mental functioning, supplanted his normal thinking processes (i.e. the secondary process). The vision of the Risen Christ can be understood as an expression of the dominance of the primary process. What had happened to Paul was akin to a fainting spell under conditions of great fatigue or stress. It also resembled falling asleep after a very fatiguing day and having an especially vivid dream, save that it occurred in daylight. There is nothing strange or necessarily pathological about such regressions, unless we are to consider sleep, dreams, or normal fantasy pathological. In Paul's case, the resolution of his conflict began with such a regression.

Paul's vision of the Risen Christ. Paul was by no means the first man from that part of the world to have a vision under stressful conditions. At its most commonplace, thirsty desert travelers have hallucinated images of water or an oasis from time immemorial. Nor is it any accident that this harsh and often inhospitable landscape has produced far more than its share of the world's great religious visionaries. Technically, we can call Paul's vision an instance of hallucinatory wish-fulfillment. Unfortunately, such a designation makes the vision seem pathological, whereas there is no reason to regard Paul's experience as more pathological than any other apparition of that time and place. As we have seen, it is very likely that a part of Paul wanted to believe that Jesus had defeated death. As his normal ego functions collapsed, it became possible for Jesus to appear alive and glorious to him. Ironically, Paul's previous conscious inclination to reject the idea that Jesus had risen probably contributed greatly to the power of the vision when it finally burst into consciousness. Paul's inability as a Pharisee to examine his conflicted feelings about Jesus frankly and openly compelled him to relegate them to the unconscious and the primary process. This self-defeating strategy was his expression of the "divorce of the Law from its emotional roots" that Gershom Scholem has noted.

As far as primary process thinking is concerned, wishing something to be true is sufficient to make it true. The unconscious is entirely in the service of wish-fulfillment. Since the unconscious is oblivious to the laws of logic or the limitations of time and place, the Resurrection story was entirely credible to it, especially in view of the extraordinary measure of pain-reduction involved in settling Paul's conflict in favor of his wish to identify with Christ's resurrection.

It is also interesting to note how Jesus is depicted as posing his question in the vision. He does not ask Paul "Why are you persecuting my Church?" which is undoubtedly what Paul thought of himself as doing. Jesus asks Paul, "Why are you persecuting me?" which is precisely what Paul must have regarded himself as doing at the primary process level. In all primary process thinking words and abstract ideas are translated into pictures and concrete images. A number of scholars have commented upon Paul's preference in the letters for "crude, material" images and "picture language."[29] In both dreams and hallucinations, abstract ideas are translated into concrete images of persons or things. Even the primitive Church as a corporate institution was of necessity somewhat abstract. There was nothing abstract about Paul's identification of the Church with the Risen Christ in his vision.

When the imagery of Paul's unconscious mental processes became available to him, he saw his hostility toward the Church as personal hostility toward the Risen Christ. Later, his identification of the Church with Christ was to express itself in the doctrine of the Church as the body of the Risen Christ. Indeed, Robinson regards the vision at Damascus as the source of that doctrine.[30] Apart from divine revelation, only when the primary process became dominant could

Paul have experienced the resurrected Jesus as objectively present, addressing him, and, in effect, resolving his conflict.

The same kind of vision could have occurred to Paul in a dream after an unpleasant day spent harassing the new sect. Very similar psychological processes would have been at work. However the intensity of Paul's conflict, the strategy he used to resolve it—aggression against the Church—and the profound yearning for immortality that the conflict presupposed all combined to elicit from him a far more abrupt, dramatic, and unforgettable response.

Although the three accounts in Acts differ about what Paul's companions perceived during the experience, in no account does the Risen Jesus appear fully to anyone but Paul. Without entering into the question of whether this vision was a revelation as historically understood within the Christian Church, which no description of psychological processes can settle, we note that all three accounts testify to the private character of Paul's experience. It is therefore my conviction that the Risen Christ Paul beheld in his vision originated within his own psyche and was the objectified embodiment of his hope for eternal life. Since immortality is a state in which no possible harm can any longer afflict the individual, Paul's vision of the immortal Christ can be seen as an expression of his own yearning for omnipotence. At first glance, the equation of the yearning for immortality with the yearning for omnipotence may seem strange. They are in reality identical. To be immortal is to be exempt from all possible harm from nature, other men, or God. Only an omnipotent Being could enjoy so fortunate a condition.

Paul's recovery of his capacities. Paul's yearning for omnipotence could not have been very different from any other man's then or now. In some corner of our psyches we all want to become the God we once were as "his majesty the baby," to use Freud's metaphor. Occasionally the yearning is gratified through a psychotic breakdown in which an individual convinces himself that he is God or another superhuman figure. Such delusions are common among schizophrenics. They react to narcissistic wounds during adult life by the same kind of regression with which as children they had attempted to counter their earliest narcissistic wound, the painful realization that they are not all-powerful. They deny the wound and regress to the lost narcissism. This is especially manifest in megalomania.

Paul's experience did not prelude a psychotic breakdown. It took time for him to integrate the experience so that he could pursue a productive career. Nevertheless, the culture of the Christian world is permeated with evidence of the successful integration of his experience. Had Paul resolved his own quest for omnipotence with megalomanic delusion, he would have been quickly forgotten as one of humanity's countless psychotics.

Megalomania would have been exceedingly difficult for Paul the Pharisee in any event. Few aspects of Judaism are as insistent as its denial of all resemblance between man and God. Judaism thus strongly defended against the delusionary identification of man and God found in megalomania. According to Jewish tradition, such identification was in fact the ultimate blasphemy. It would have been impossible for Paul the Pharisee to avoid Adam's curse by repeating Adam's sin.[31] If immortal life, which we take to be psychologically and ontologically equivalent to omnipotence, was to be gained, Paul would have had to find an alternative to both megalomanic and blasphemous identification with the Father. Part of Judaism's permanent legacy to Paul and Christianity has always been the Father's inaccessibility and his radical transcendence. Another way had to be found to gain the ultimate prize.

Paul found the alternative for himself and his spiritual heirs in the vision of the Risen Christ, for it gave him the assurance of eternal life without identification with the Father. After the Damascus vision, it became possible for Paul to gain assurance of immortality through *identification* with the "first born of many brothers," the "first fruit" of those who were to overcome the limitations of nature and mortality. As we shall see, Paul believed that he and all Christians shared Christ's Crucifixion in dying to their old selves at baptism; he also believed that those who are truly one with Christ will ultimately share in his Resurrection. If Paul could not achieve omnipotence through identification with the Father, he could achieve it through identification with the resurrected older brother. He was thus able to resolve his conflict in favor of his oldest and most profound longings without resort to either blasphemy or psychotic collapse.

Identification with Jesus was not a solipsistic act that could not be shared, as megalomanic identification with the Father would have been. Paul's newly acquired faith was subject to constant reinforcement within the Church. Where identification with the Father would have been thoroughly isolating, identification with the elder brother brought him into the fellowship of the young Church. Furthermore, the primitive Church had never lost contact with the day-to-day world. The early disciples claimed that the Messiah had risen, but they never claimed that his work had already been completed. This meant that, then as now, there was a certain tension in Christianity between the Christian's awareness of the extent to which the world remained unredeemed and the proclamation that the Messianic Age had already begun. It was precisely this tension that allowed Paul to assert that mankind's hope for eternal life had been realized without doing violence to the practical necessities of the "real" world.

In effect, Paul was able to transfer his own hopes for omnipotence to the image of the older brother. Jesus became Paul's double, suffering the pain and winning the victory for him. Paul was then able to share in Jesus' omnipotence by becoming one with him. That is why Paul's "Christ mysticism" is so decisive to his experience. Only by becoming one with the Risen Christ could Paul become one with the Messiah's glorious destiny. Having projected his archaic hopes onto Jesus, it was possible for Paul to achieve them through identification.

Paul's fundamental goal was to find a way back to his earliest felicity as "his majesty the baby." That goal could only be attained at the final consummation of God's plan for mankind's salvation. In the meantime, Paul had achieved contact with his own "dark layers of the past" without permanently impairing his normal ego functions. One could almost think of the vision as initiating an opening to Paul's unconscious mental processes that were thereafter far more available to him than was normally current in Jewish culture at the time. Once the contents of the id burst forth into his consciousness, Paul was transformed into a person with a radically different emotional structure than his fellow Pharisees.

As a sleeper awakens from an unforgettable dream, Paul found his world transformed by his overpowering experience. The Pharisee had become the Apostle.

Chapter IV

The Womb
of Immortality

According to Cyril of Jerusalem, a fourth-century bishop with a profound interest in liturgy, the waters of baptism become both a "grave" and "mother" for the newly baptized Christian.[1] This identification of the baptismal waters with mankind's origin as well as its final destiny expresses graphically and explicitly a fundamental insight about baptism as Paul understood it. The texts in Paul's letters that come closest to this identification are Romans 6:3, 4 and Colossians 2:12: "Are you ignorant that when we were baptized in Christ Jesus we were baptized in his death? In other words, when we were baptized we went into the tomb with him and joined him in death, so that as Christ was raised from the dead by the Father's glory, we too might live a new life" (Rom. 6:3, 4). "You have been buried with him, when you were baptized; and by baptism, too, you have been raised up with him through your faith in the power of God who raised him from the dead" (Col. 2:12).

Admittedly, Paul did not state in either passage that the baptismal waters are a womb in which the Christian is born a new creature. Nor did he ever use the metaphor of rebirth to describe the Christian's postbaptismal condition, save in Titus 3:5 where baptism is described as "the cleansing waters of rebirth." (However, the authenticity of Titus as a Pauline letter is a matter of scholarly dispute.) The Christian is described as a "new creation" (II Cor. 5:17, Gal.

54

6:15), but not as newly born. Schweitzer maintained that Paul avoided the metaphor of rebirth because of its prevalence in Hellenistic religious circles.[2] Schweitzer apparently ignored evidence that the proselyte was regarded as newly born in first-century Judaism.[3] Paul gave this notion a Christian interpretation in the light of Jesus' death and Resurrection. The notion that at baptism the Christian enters a new life, actually true life for the first time, was central to his thinking. He contrasted the convert's pre-Christian existence, at best a kind of living death, with his Christian life, which was in the process of becoming life as it was intended by God before the sin of Adam, life devoid of the related curses of sin and mortality (I Cor. 15:21–2; Rom. 5:12ff). Paul repeatedly described the baptized Christian as *en Christo,* "in Christ," and he insisted that *en Christo* the Christian became a new man. He wrote to the Corinthians, "for anyone who is in Christ, there is a new creation" (II Cor. 5:17). So radically is the Christian's identity transformed by his existence in Christ that Paul could assert of his own postbaptismal identity: "I have been crucified with Christ, and I live now not with my own life but with the life of Christ who lives in me" (Gal. 2:19).

Paul frequently used the metaphor of stripping off the old and putting on the new to describe the dying of the old self and rebirth in Christ (Eph. 4:22–24: Col. 3:9f.; cf. Rom. 13:12, Col. 2:12). The new self the Christian acquires annuls both the old self and the premessianic world. All of the crucial distinctions that have cursed mankind are ended at least in principle with baptism: "All baptized in Christ, you have clothed yourselves in Christ, and there are no more distinctions between Jew and Greek, slave and free, male and female, but all of you are one in Christ Jesus" (Gal. 3:27–28; cf. I Cor. 2:13). If the term "rebirth" is absent from the undisputed letters of Paul, the spiritual and psychological reality of the Christian's experience as newly and truly born pervades his thought.

The Christian's life "in Christ" partakes of the two decisive events that together made Christ's life absolutely unique for Paul: He was crucified *and* he was resurrected. Having overcome death, Christ leads a new kind of existence that will never again be subject to suffering and dying. To be "in Christ" means to partake of Christ's death and his Resurrection. This does not mean that the new existence of the Christian is identical with that of Christ in his glory. The Christian undergoes baptism only once. Through suffering, he may die daily with Christ (I Cor. 15:31; 2 Cor. 1:5; Rom. 8:17). Christian resurrection *begins* at baptism with the bestowal of the Holy Spirit, but this bestowal is merely the "earnest money" or "pledge" (2 Cor. 1:22; 5:5) of the final transformation of mankind at the day of Redemption when the elect will put off their corruptible bodies and "be raised incorruptible" (I Cor. 15:52). Baptism begins a process that is not fully consummated until the last day. Nevertheless, faith in God's promise and fellowship with Christ make the Christian no longer subject to the powers and the vicissitudes of this world. To the extent that the Christian is truly one with Christ, baptism is a new birth into an imperishable life (Gal. 2:20).

At first glance, Paul's association of the Christian initiatory experience of immersion in and emergence from the baptismal waters with the Crucifixion and Resurrection of Jesus seems far-fetched. Jesus did not suffer death by drowning; he suffered an excruciatingly painful death on the cross. From the perspective of depth psychology, however, Paul's intuitive identification is startling in its appropriateness.

The use of purificatory lustrations was common throughout the ancient Near East. There were introductory rites of cleansing and rebirth in the Hellenistic mystery cults.[4] In rabbinic Judaism both baptism and circumcision were required for male proselytes. Only ritual immersion was required of females, who constituted the majority of the converts to Judaism.[5] Ritual baths were an important part of the rites of the Qumran community to which John the Baptist may have been related.[6] However, only in Christianity is baptism the indispensable initiatory ritual. Furthermore, there is no evidence of the identification of baptism with both the death and Resurrection of Christ by any early Christian authority other than Paul.[7] While it is possible that Paul was utilizing primitive Christian tradition in his identification, there seems to have been a very strong element of originality in his understanding of baptism that was thoroughly consistent with the principal contours of his mature theology.

Before Paul, baptism was used as a purifying and a penitential rite in which the sins of the novice's past life were washed away.[8] John's baptism is presented in the Synoptic Gospels as a rite of purification and repentance. John himself is depicted as looking forward to one greater than he who will baptize with "the Holy Spirit and fire" (Luke 3:16; cf. Mark 1:8; Matt. 3:12; John 1:26, 27). In addition to ethical cleansing, ritual purification was often involved in pre-Christian immersion.[9] Baptism sometimes involved reception of the Spirit even in pre-Christian sects.[10] There is an anticipation of Paul's conception of baptism as a dying with Christ in Jesus' words to James and John, the sons of Zebedee, in which he speaks of his coming ordeal: "Can you drink the cup that I must drink, or be baptized with the baptism with which I must be baptized?" (Mark 10:39; cf. Luke 13:50). Here to be baptized means to die. Nevertheless, only with Paul does baptism become both a dying and a rising with Christ.

Paul was able to associate the death and Resurrection of Christ with the experience of the newly baptized Christian because he understood intuitively and gave theological expression to the identity of womb and tomb in the subliminal consciousness of mankind. By his association of baptism with Jesus' death and Resurrection, he was able to bring to consciousness some of mankind's oldest and most profound responses to water. WATER

Water is the fundamental element of life. What is alive is moist; what is dead is desiccated. Perhaps the greatest adaptation ever made by living organisms occurred when they left their original acquatic environment and sought to maintain themselves in the utterly novel habitat of dry land. The greatest danger confronting them was desiccation. To this day the dependence of all land animals on water remains absolute. Sandor Ferenczi, one of Freud's original and most important disciples, has pointed to the relation between the sexuality of terrestrial animals and the profound adaptation required when living organisms left or were forced out of the sea. Ferenczi observed that sexual reproduction, involving bodily contact and the insertion of the male organ into the female, was not necessary for truly acquatic organisms. The ocean itself was a perfect and ever-present maternal repository for the male seed to wait to fertilize the female egg. At first a compromise was worked out in which certain amphibious forms of life ventured forth on dry land but returned to the sea in order to reproduce themselves. With the evolution of greater structural complexity, it became unnecessary for living organisms to return to the sea. Direct contact between the sexes and the development of the womb—which fulfilled all of the functions of the ocean for the offspring during the intrauterine period—obviated the primary peril of terrestial reproduction, desiccation. Not only are womb and water symbolically equivalent, they are in a very special way functionally equivalent as well.[11]

Ferenczi took one of Freud's most important observations and gave in greater depth. Freud had accepted Haeckel's formula that "ontogeny follows phylogeny," by which he meant that the development of the individual recapitulates the development of the race.[12] The truth of the assertion is obvious in the development of the human embryo, which recapitulates the evolution of the race in an abbreviated way in its nine-month growth within the womb from a single-cellular creature to a human neonate. Ferenczi pointed out that the very structure of our body as well as the organization of mammalian sexuality recapitulates the history of the race from cellular structures through acquatic existence to the highly complex existence of mammals who carry their own oceans with them.

Ferenczi also enriched one of Freud's most controversial insights, his strange definition of instinct: *"an instinct is an urge inherent in organic life to restore an earlier state of things* which the living entity has been obliged to abandon under the pressure of external disturbing forces. . . ."[13] Freud went on to write of "the conservative nature of living substance" and to assert that "instincts are historically determined."[14] He gave the example of certain fish such as salmon, who go through incredible exertions to deposit their spawn in waters very distant from their normal habitat. According to Freud, the spawning grounds were once the habitat of these fish, but they had long ago been abandoned. Nevertheless, the compulsion to return never ceased to operate. Whether or not the spawning grounds were where the species originally dwelt, the fish are compelled to return to their own place of origin by forces of overwhelming primordial power.

Freud cautioned against misinterpreting the forward thrust of human action. Largely through the impact of technology upon the political ideologies of the nineteenth and twentieth centuries, we tend to interpret human action as having a progressive thrust. We speak of moving forward to "higher" levels of development or consciousness. We tend to regard the goal of human action as the creation of novel and unanticipated stages of life. Behind these views we can discern a secularized but superficial reading of the Judeo-Christian view of time as linear and moving forward to a goal that is qualitatively "higher" at the end than at the beginning. Freud's observations on change imply a strong protest against the popular doctrine of progress:

> . . . instincts are therefore bound to give a deceptive appearance of being forces tending towards change and progress, whilst in fact they are merely seeking to reach an ancient goal by paths alike old and new. Moreover it is possible to specify this final goal of all organic striving. It would be in contradiction to the conservative nature of the instincts if the goal of life were a state of things which had never yet been attained. On the contrary, it must be an *old* state of things, an initial state from which the living entity has at one time or other departed and to which it is striving to return by the circuitous paths along which its development leads.[15]

For Freud, all forward motion is ultimately a return, albeit circuitous, to the original situation from which life arose. There are no exceptions. All forms of life are bound by their inner structure to conform to this compulsion. *All progress is disguised regress*. Humanity is trying to get back to its origins. When we discuss Paul's myth of the Last Adam, it will become apparent that both the Apostle and the analyst were moved by a similar vision.

Ferenczi accepted Freud's conclusions and applied them to the understanding of human sexuality. As we have noted, Ferenczi called attention to the way in which female bodily structure provides a miniature ocean in which the hazards of terrestial reproduction can be circumvented and the fetus can recapitulate that part of the history of the race that took place in water. Ferenczi also accepted Freud's idea of the conservative and regressive character of all instincts. He maintained that the conservative character of the male sexual instinct expressed itself in a multidimensional regression to the place of human origins, the female womb. He called the sexual act a "thalassal regression," indicating that by entering the female sexual organs, the male organ was returning—on behalf of the entire organism—not only to the place of individual origin, the womb, but also to the place of species origin, the surrogate ocean.

I do not believe that Ferenczi ever discussed Paul's doctrine of baptism or the utilization of ritual immersion in other religious traditions. Nevertheless, his work reveals the psychological appropriateness of Paul's association of the baptismal waters as the place of death and new life. We come from the life-giving waters of the womb. Water is womb and womb is water. If we are to live again, we must be reborn in and of the life-giving waters. Similarly, the watery womb is tomb. Burial in the fetal position is quite common in archaic cultures. In seeking to return to water, we seek the place of origin of both the individual and the race. And, as Freud and Ferenczi remind us, our ultimate quest is for the objectless state of quiescence out of which we have come. We shall see that Paul had a very similar image of the ultimate goal of creation.

Rituals often dramatize insights of which their participants have no conscious knowledge. When asked why they perform a given ritual, participants will frequently repeat inherited explanatory myths that disguise the fundamental intent of the rite. Such myths reflect a censoring process not unlike that at work in dreams. In pre-Pauline interpretations of ritual, water was often stressed as a washing agent.

Water as a washing agent can wash away all manner of dirt—physical dirt, moral dirt, and sacerdotal dirt. A lively process of association is evident in such interpretations of baptism. The censoring process is also visible. When water is regarded as a human tool, such as a washing agent, it is seen as something under human mastery. Such associations reflect the experience of the confident adult ego. One is only likely to regard water as a grave and a maternal matrix after the censoring process has been overcome. Neither the womb nor the tomb are ultimately subject to human mastery; they represent fatalities that are beyond choice. Men are more fearful of what is beyond their mastery than of what they can control. Such realities elicit from them archaic responses originating at a time when they were indeed confronted by a threatening environment they were unable to master. And, men are most anxious when confronted with realities that remind them of a time when they did not exist or will no longer exist. When they are drawn by an unknown inner compulsion to the primordial element that will ultimately spell their dissolution, their anxiety is likely to be especially intense.

Paul's interpretation of the baptismal waters as tomb and womb can thus be seen as less censored and more archaic than the interpretations of his Jewish and Christian contemporaries. Since the practice of ritual immersion was widespread, it is very likely that it reflected a common need to return symbolically to one's origin, and to come forth a new and reborn creature. It would seem that this need was consciously expressed in primitive Christianity for the first time in Paul's letters.

Mircea Eliade has observed that all initiatory rites involve ordeals that more or less imply a ritual death followed by resurrection or new birth.[16] He noted that it is characteristic of archaic mentality that *a state cannot be altered without first being annihilated.* In initiatory rites, death is the indispensable prerequisite for the beginning of a new mode of existence. Eliade comments: "It is impossible to exaggerate the importance of this obsession with beginnings, which, in sum, is the obsession with the absolute beginning, the cosmogony. For a thing to be well done, it must be done as it was the first time."[17] Since the person did not exist "the first time," he must die and be reborn in order to achieve the new mode of spiritual existence. The child, for example, must die in order that the man be born. In Pauline Christianity the "old man" must die in order that the new man "in Christ" be born.

Eliade has also observed that such initiatory death is frequently symbolized by darkness, cosmic night, the telluric womb, the hut and the belly of a monster. These images express regression to a "preformal state" corresponding to the original chaos, which was the way archaic man conceived the original state. This is in contrast to annihilation, which is how moderns regard death.

As you can see, Paul reversed the normal order of birth and death. For Paul, death came before true life. In the order of nature, birth begins an inexorable path that leads to death. Without belief in Christ's Resurrection, Paul would have seen nothing more in the rite of immersion than did any rabbinic Jew or any member of the Community of the Scrolls. The more archaic associations only became possible for him in the light of his overpowering Christian experience.

Paul's reversal of the order of birth and death in baptism accords with one of the deepest yearnings of mankind, the yearning for a new beginning, a new start in life. In the light of Eliade's observation that in the mentality of archaic man a state cannot be altered without first being annihilated, we can understand Paul's belief that a vitally new relationship to God could only be achieved by the death of the old self. The waters of baptism must be a grave before they can be the womb of the new man in Christ.

This belief may also have been related to Paul's views on human sexuality and marriage. Paul believed that baptized Christians were soon to enter the Age of Resurrection of the Dead in which, like angels in heaven, "men and women do not marry" (Matt. 22:30). That belief was consistent with a certain antiparental and antifamilial bias that can be discerned in primitive Christianity. The Gospel accounts make it clear that Jesus regards God alone rather than Joseph as his real father (Matt. 23:8–9). Nor is Jesus entirely willing to accept his mother (cf. Matt. 12:46–50; Luke 11:27, 28; John 2:3). Perhaps the strongest example of Jesus' antifamilial bias is to be found in Luke. Jesus says: "If any man comes to me without hating his father, mother, wife, children, brothers, sisters, yes and his own life too, he cannot be my disciple" (Luke 14:26, cf. Luke 18:28–30, Matt. 10:34–39). The Roman Catholic Jerusalem Bible notes that the expression "hates" in this passage is really an "emphatic way of expressing detachment." Nevertheless, the careers of both Jesus and Paul represent breaks with the strongly patriarchal family structure of Judaism. Neither married.[18] Paul believed that the chain of generations was to terminate in his time. The fundamental emotional ties that moved him were radically different than those of a Jewish *paterfamilias* of the time. One of Paul's strongest statements that the old order had changed decisively is in Galatians, where he asserted that the distinctions between Greek and Jew and male and female had been annulled in Christ (Gal. 3:27–28). Commenting on this passage, Rudolf Bultmann has observed that for Paul "this world's distinctions have lost their meaning."[19]

Anyone familiar with rabbinic Judaism is aware of the profound shift in sensibility involved in Paul's statement, for in rabbinic Judaism the distinctions between male and female were all-important —within the community of worship, the division of family labor, and in the rituals of sexual purity. Above all, sexual and tribal distinctions were real to Paul's rabbinic contemporaries because the vicissitudes of time and history had not ceased to be real to them. Although the quality of Christian life was a matter of the utmost concern to Paul, the family and the institutions pertaining to the chain of generations had become secondary to him. Günther Bornkamm writes of the "eschatological foreshortening of time in Paul's view of marriage."[20]

Paul was by no means indifferent to the problems marriage posed for Christians or to the moral and spiritual perils that both indifference or surrender to the promptings of the body might entail. His fundamental counsel on the question of marriage was consistent with his response to the question of how Christians ought to comport themselves in the interim between Christ's Resurrection and the final

[handwritten marginal note: Note — Neither Jesus nor Paul was married]

culmination of the redemptive process. He counseled that, wherever possible, Christians ought to remain in the same state (*klēsis*) as that in which they were baptized (I Cor. 7:20). Those who were married when baptized were not to "look for freedom" (7:27), nor were those who were "free of a wife" to "look for one" (7:27). Similarly, marriage was to be preferred to fornication (6:12–18; 7:5, 9) or resort to a prostitute (6:15—16), which at that time was frequently a ritual act involving communion with a sacred prostitute.[21] For Paul, the interim period had its special perils for Christians. Nevertheless, even when Paul counseled those who were married to remain so, he stressed his own belief in "the approaching calamity" (*ten enestōsan anangkēn*) (7:26)[22] and his conviction that his own celibate state was preferable to marriage in the interim (7:8, 28; cf. 7:32ff.).

Paul's personal rejection of marriage was not because he was homosexually inclined, as at least one incautious psychoanalyst has suggested[23] (cf. I Cor. 6:9), nor was it due to any special hostility toward women, as feminists sometimes claim. Admittedly, Paul carried over into Christianity many of Judaism's ideas about the subordination of women to men (cf. Rom. 7:2; I Cor. 11:2–16; Eph. 5:23), but his writings do not indicate that he ever intensified that position. On the contrary, his statement in Galatians 3:27–28 represented a profound alteration in current sentiment. Rightly or wrongly, *Paul's overriding concern was with death and resurrection, not sexuality*. Convinced of God's gift of eternal life in Christ, Paul became, of necessity, disinterested in the sexual act, nature's way of assuring the generational continuity of her mortal offspring. Paul believed that the End would speedily overtake the world (cf. I Cor. 7:31; 15:24–28; I Thes. 4:13–17; 5:2–9; Phil. 3:20–21). He also believed that the structures of the premessianic eon that were "so much rubbish" had been dissolved in principle if not actuality. What, after all, was the relevance of the family or the reproductive act to a man like Paul who confidently believed the End was imminent and that the redeemed cosmos would no longer be subject to the hazards of mortality? For Paul, baptism was literally the tomb of the old world that was passing away (I Cor. 7:31) and the womb of the new and perfect world in which there would be neither male nor female.

In *The Future of an Illusion,* Freud interpreted the God-who-cares largely as a projection of the child's encounter with his parents at a time when they were regarded as extremely powerful. There is, however, an element in the construction of the image of the God-who-cares that Freud neglected but that is crucial to an understanding of Paul's interpretation of baptism. Sooner or later the child discovers that his natural parents do not have the power to save him from death. That can be a moment of intense disappointment. The disappointment may, in fact, be so strong as to compel the child to seek for an omnipotent parent who could perform the act of redemption. Such a child might easily turn to God.

Freud also alluded to the "family romance," in which a person has the fantasy that he is not really the child of his parents but the orphaned child of parents of higher estate.[24] Such fantasies reflect disappointment in the capacity of real parents to bring about the gratifications the child seeks. Thus, *to be born anew involves the acquisition of a new parent as much as the attainment of a new status in life.* God is not only the child's projection of the image of parents into the cosmic sphere; God is often the disappointed child's projection of his wish for a truly powerful parent who can gratify his deepest yearnings. If Christians are born to a new parent at baptism, that parent is God himself.

Rabbinic Judaism stressed the role of God as Father, as did Paul, but never in opposition to natural parents or parental surrogates such as teachers. The integrity of the chain of generations was so firmly rooted in Judaism that the idea of second birth to a perfect parent was absent or suppressed.

I believe that the idea of second birth involving a new parent was repressed rather than absent. In addition to the quest for a more powerful parent who could bestow immortality, there may have been yet another very potent motivation for the quest for new birth in first-century Christianity. David Bakan has pointed to the fact that there are strongly marked infanticidal characteristics attributed to the God of the Hebrew Bible.[25] Among the examples he gives are the Flood, the killing of the Sodomites, the Akedah, the Egyptians, and God's temptation to kill all of the Israelites until dissuaded by Moses (Exod. 32:9ff.). Another example of the infanticidal aspect of God is implicit in the conviction that the sacrificial death of the Son of God cancels the debt of death all men owe to God (Rom. 4:25). Bakan claimed that the God of the Bible is "deeply ambivalent" about his infanticidal tendencies, manifesting what could be called a "neurotic" tendency to kill and then promising not to kill again. He argued that if the characteristics of God in fact derive from man himself, we may conclude that the infanticidal temptation must have been a crucial problem at the time.

Bakan's work rounds out the picture presented by Freud. Freud stressed the parricidal temptation in the Oedipus complex, which forever imperils the family structure. Bakan argued that we have far more evidence of infanticidal than parricidal violence in biblical Judaism. Both Bakan and Freud deserve to be taken seriously on this issue. Nevertheless, the real problem is intergenerational hostility on the part of both parents and offspring. Not only does the child turn away from the parent whose powers have proven wanting, he also fears the parent as a potential infanticide. Paul argued that under the pre-Christian dispensation God condemned all men to die for their sins (Rom. 5:12, 6:20–22). Paul was convinced that God's mercy was real, but only for those who were "in Christ." A God who inflicts death on his children in retaliation for their "sins" can with justice be seen as the Divine Infanticide. Baptism promises escape from the hostility of the Divine Infanticide; baptismal rebirth thus involves the hope for a noninfanticidal Parent.

In a book soon to be published, Bakan specifically links baptism and the infanticidal parent by interpreting the emergence from baptism as a rescue from drowning. There is some evidence that Paul indirectly associated baptism with drowning in addition to "being buried with Christ." In I Corinthians Paul contrasted Christian baptism with the journey of the Israelites through the Red Sea. Paul wrote that "they were all baptized unto Moses" (I Cor. 10:2). He made no mention of the Egyptians in the passage, but he was certainly aware that what he designated as Israel's baptismal waters became the watery grave of the Egyptians.

Dreams involving drowning often express fear of being cannibalized by the mother.[26] In another book, I have tried to demonstrate that fear of incorporation by the cannibal mother was expressed far more pervasively in the legends of rabbinic Judaism than fear of castration by the father.[27] When I began to study anxiety in rabbinic myth and legend, I thought I would be able to demonstrate that fear of the castrating father was the dominant form of anxiety in rabbinic Judaism. I was led to this hypothesis by the fact that circumcision, the indispensable male initiatory rite, requires a symbolic wounding of the penis. After several years of collecting legendary traditions describing God's punishment of the wicked, I realized that my original hypothesis could not be supported by the evidence. There were far more fantasies involving punishment through drowning and other forms of incorporation than through castration.

When these conclusions were translated into terms of the stresses of structure, it became apparent that in rabbinic Judaism, as well as elsewhere, fear of the pre-Oedipal mother was far more dominant than Oedipal fear of the father. I also concluded that rabbinic Judaism stressed the masculine character of divine paternity largely out of a profound need to minimize or repress the overwhelming and unmanageable fear of the mother, who constituted the most archaic aspect of the projection of parental figures into the cosmic sphere as God. Thus, at the deepest level, fear of the infanticidal parent is fear of the mother. This conclusion should occasion no surprise. In the course of psychoanalysis, fear of the father is usually uncovered first. Fear of the mother is older and less subject to therapeutic amelioration. If baptism involves the hope for a noninfanticidal Parent, the rite carries with it the assurance that the believer, after his return to the watery womb, has been rescued and need no longer fear his original mother.

In this connection it is interesting to note that Christianity never developed an image of a destructive, cannibal mother goddess such as one finds so often in pre-Christian religion. Throughout the Middle Ages the adoration of the Virgin played a central role in

Christian piety. Mary was a figure who inspired warmth and trust, with no apparent overtones of terror. On the contrary, when men found the stern judgments of God the Father too difficult to bear, they turned to her for solace and merciful intercession. Christians never ascribed to Mary the terrifying characteristics that had so often been ascribed to the pagan goddesses. It is impossible to go beyond conjecture, but I feel compelled to ask whether there might be some connection between baptism's function in enabling the Christian to be reborn to a noninfanticidal Parent and the apparent absence of an infanticidal mother figure in Christian piety.

If the waters of baptism are the waters of rebirth, we can locate at least two motives for associating new birth with the quest for a new parent: disappointment with the original parent's failure to cancel mortality and the yearning for a noninfanticidal Parent. But these are two sides of the same coin. Insofar as the old parent was regarded as omnipotent and hence capable of bestowing immortality, his unwillingness to do so constituted the great refusal. The real act of infanticide as seen by the child was the refusal of the parent to bestow immortality. As long as death is regarded as punitive, either the earthly or the heavenly parent (or both) must be seen as an infanticide. This conclusion is consistent with the view of death shared by Paul and the rabbis, for both regarded human mortality as punishment. Admittedly, nowhere does Paul assert that the Christian acquires a new parent through baptism. Nevertheless, he does claim that God truly becomes *Abba* for the first time after baptism. The elements of intimacy and trust conveyed by this Aramaic expression are such that no translation is required in the two passages in which Paul uses it. Similarly, Paul maintains that Christians truly become sons and heirs of the Father for the first time after baptism:

> Now before we came of age (i.e., became Christians) we were as good as slaves to the elemental principles of the world, but when the appointed time came, God sent his Son . . . to redeem the subjects of the Law and to enable

us to be adopted as Sons. The proof that you are sons is
that God has sent the Spirit of his Son into our hearts:
The Spirit that cries, "Abba, Father," (Gal. 4:4–6; cf.
Rom. 8:14–17).

Paul's teaching on the Christian's new relationship to the Father
is well summarized in Galatians 3:26: "You are, all of you, sons of
God through faith in Christ Jesus." It is Paul's conviction that
through baptism Christians for the first time find an utterly trust-
worthy parent-child relationship. For Paul, baptism carries with it
the assurance that Christians need no longer fear the oldest object of
human anxiety, the cannibal mother.

When the primitive Christian community ceased to be a sect
within Judaism and became an independent faith, one of the most
profound transformations that occurred was the shift from circumcision to baptism as the initiatory rite. As we know, the issue had
not been settled in Paul's time. We have a record of Paul's exceedingly strong reaction to a group of Jewish Christians or Judaizing
Gentiles who tried to convince the Gentiles of the Church at Galatia
that they must submit to circumcision. As translated by the Jerusalem Bible, Paul exclaimed: "Tell those who are troubling you I would
like to see the knife slip" (Gal. 5:12). This passage is shocking in
its bluntness. Paul wished that the Judaizers would castrate themselves. He associated circumcision not only with castration, but perhaps with the self-mutilation of the cult of the *Dea Syria* as well.
Paul always insisted that it was not necessary for Gentiles to be
circumcised in order to share in the blessings of the messianic kingdom. His rejection of circumcision for Gentile proselytes was consistent with his rejection of the old distinctions of Jew and Greek in
the new Messianic Age. Paul's insistence that one could in any
sense be a male member of God's elect community without circumcision was a radical departure from Jewish practice.

Many reasons have been given for the shift from circumcision to
baptism in primitive Christianity. For those who believe in the
divinely revealed character of the Christian faith, baptism ultimately

rests on the life, teaching, and example of Jesus. Some Jewish scholars have regarded the shift as part of a Christian strategy to lessen the severity of Jewish religious practice in order to facilitate the success of the Christian mission.[28] All authorities agree that there was a class of men known as *sebamenoi,* or "God-fearers," attached to the synagogues of the Diaspora, who accepted Jewish monotheism and attempted to live in accordance with Jewish moral precepts, but who did not commit themselves to circumcision or full observance of Jewish law.

Most of the converts to Judaism in Paul's time were women. To this day, it is physically and psychologically easier for a woman to become a member of the Jewish community. Although ritual immersion may carry with it the symbolism of death, burial, and rebirth, the actual hazards and pain of momentary immersion are almost nonexistent. Even with local anesthetics to remove the pain, it is impossible for an adult male to be circumcized without facing intense anxiety lest, in Paul's words, "the knife slip." No man can become a Jew according to traditional practice without undergoing a profound psychological ordeal involving this fear of emasculation. Hence it would seem that the shift from circumcision to baptism greatly aided the success of the early Christians.

Nevertheless, it is difficult to believe that the change took place because it was advantageous to Christianity in an organizational way. There is simply no evidence for that kind of pragmatism in the documents of the early Church. If we rule out revelation and pragmatic manipulation, we can most likely achieve a satisfactory perspective on what happened by asking what was at stake psychologically.

The most obvious difference between baptism and circumcision is that only males are circumcised whereas both sexes are baptized. When Paul asserted in Galatians that in Christ there is no longer a distinction between male and female, he claimed this as a consequence of baptism. Christians are not baptized because there are no male-female distinctions; baptism obliterates the distinctions, especially as they are found in rabbinic Law.

Circumcision emphasizes the infant's masculine sexual structure.

It also dramatizes the child's identification with his father and his place in the chain of generations. Jewish tradition makes it incumbent on the father to circumcize his male child on the eighth day after birth. In contemporary Judaism the father seldom performs the actual operation. Nevertheless, according to Jewish law, the officiant (the Mohel) performs the rite on behalf of the father and as his agent. Rabbinic law contains the principle that an act performed by one's agent is equivalent to an act one performs oneself. In all probability, the delegation of circumcision to a professional is a late development, for originally circumcision was carried out by the father.

Bruno Bettelheim has noted the profound difference between Jewish circumcision and circumcision as it is carried out in most other communities, where it is usually an ordeal of puberty.[29] In Judaism it is practiced upon infants who are in no sense active or consenting participants. As a pubertal rite, circumcision shares with all such ordeals the character of a test in which the young man proves his manhood. The young man who successfully masters the ordeal comes forth with greater self-confidence and independence. No matter how terrified he may be initially, there is an element of consent in his participation. After the rite, the initiate joins the adult males of his community. He is permitted to engage in sexual intercourse and to marry. His masculine indentity has been confirmed. Pubertal circumcision frees the initiate from parental authority. Because of his new feeling of mastery, the novice is *less* likely to be subject to castration anxiety after the ordeal. Furthermore, Eliade's observation that initiation rituals involve death and rebirth applies with special force to pubertal circumcision. The circumcised novice dies as a child and is reborn as an adult male.

According to Bettelheim, infant circumcision heightens castration anxiety, the son's dependence on the father, and the power of the superego. Sooner or later, every Jewish boy learns that his father has caused him to be circumcised without consent while he was a totally helpless infant. If the family is religiously compliant, as were Jewish families in Paul's time, the child is eventually instructed that it is God who demanded symbolic mutilation of his penis. This fact cannot but influence the growing child's image of God in later life.

Anyone who attends a Jewish circumcision ceremony is aware of an atmosphere of anxiety among those present before the ritual, often expressed in nervous joking about what is to take place. And after the operation there is a tremendous feeling of relief. The anxiety can be easily identified as anxiety lest "the knife slip," castration anxiety. It is felt by all, although its impact is probably greatest on young boys who are becoming aware of the meaning of the ritual.

Once the child realizes that his father has caused the foreskin of his penis to be cut off, he is painfully aware of the fact that his father had the capacity to cut off the whole penis had he wanted to. In addition to all of the factors disposing any normal male child to castration anxiety, the Jewish child must come to terms with the fact that his penis has been altered by the most significant adult male in his life, his father. When the element of divine sanction is added, castration anxiety takes on distinctive cultural forms for Jews that tend to intensify its impact.

It is, however, important to remember that Jewish circumcision is in no sense castration. Circumcision can be understood as a compromise attempt to deflect divine and/or parental hostility whose aim is castration. Although the God of Israel has been described as the castrating Father, it was Yahweh's mother goddess neighbor, Cybele, the *Dea Syria,* who demanded that her priests castrate themselves before becoming eligible to serve her.[30] In Semitic religion we find a castrating Mother but no castrating Father. Circumcision involves acceptance of the foreskin as a *pars pro toto* surrogate for the entire organ. It was as if biblical Judaism, developing in close proximity to a mother goddess cult that demanded real castration, intuitively recognized that intergenerational hostility could easily take the form of castration. In order to ward off the temptation, it permitted a harmless "acting out" of the surrogate ritual. This permitted symbolic expression of the hostile parental emotions without endangering generational continuity, as real castration was certain to do. Furthermore, circumcision bound the sons to the fathers in an especially powerful manner. The sons were aware of what the fathers, and the omnipotent Father, could have done to them in infancy. This knowledge cemented their resolve to be "good" sons. Obedience to the Law was partly maintained by the underlying anxiety lest the father finish what he had started on the eighth day.

Jewish circumcision is not a ritual of rebirth. It is premessianic. It ties the sons to the fathers and to their world. That may be one of the reasons why Paul referred to it as a "circumcision of flesh." It is a circumcision that roots the young Jew in his place in the order of the generations. Before circumcising his son, a father utters the blessing, "Praised be Thou . . . who has commanded me to cause (my son) to enter the covenant of Abraham our Father." It is the young Jew's entrance into his biological family rather than his rebirth into a new world, a new family, and a new temporal era. Insistence that the rite be carried out on the eighth day emphasizes the fact that it was an initiatory ritual into the very world from which Paul sought release.

Normally, Christians who were baptized in Paul's time received the rite as adults. There is some scholarly debate on the status of infant baptism in primitive Christianity, but Paul's experience, as well as that of the vast majority of newly baptized Christians, was that of adults entering a new way of life. Whether they came from Jewish or Gentile backgrounds, primitive Christians could readily feel that they had died to their old way of life, had been born to a radically new life, and had received a new Parent. A pagan converted to Judaism and circumcised according to Jewish tradition might feel that he had been reborn as a new creature, but the community he entered made no claims to the status of a messianic community in which sin, suffering, and death were in the process of being abolished. The newly circumcised proselyte might feel that he had been morally reborn; under no circumstance could he feel that he had been ontologically reconstituted as could the newly converted Christian.

We have noted several times Freud's observation about Paul that "dark traces of the past lay in his soul ready to break through to the regions of consciousness." Paul's distinctive association of baptism with both Christ's death and resurrection can be seen as demonstrating his ability to bring to the light of consciousness archaic intuitions that his contemporaries could at best express in the dramatics of ritual. This same capacity is also evident in Paul's discussion of baptism and circumcision. As bitterly as Paul fought attempts to impose circumcision on Gentile Christians, Paul never rejected circumcision entirely. Jeremiah had taught that while the nations were uncircumcised "all the house of Israel are uncircumcised of heart" (Jer. 9:26; cf. 4:4, Ezek. 44:7). Paul used the distinction between the circumcision of the flesh and circumcision of the heart to formulate his own doctrine of baptism as "the circumcision of Christ." The *locus classicus* of Paul's formulation of this doctrine is Colossians 2:11–13.

According to Rudolf Schnackenburg, the baptismal teaching of Paul in Colossians 2:11–13 is similar to that of Romans 6:4ff., although in a condensed form.[31] In Colossians Paul said:

> In him you have been circumcised, with a circumcision not performed by human hand, but by *the complete stripping of your body of flesh*. This is circumcision according to Christ. You have been buried with him, when you were baptised; and by baptism, too, you have been raised up with him through your faith in the power of God who raised him from the dead. You were dead, because you were sinners and had not been circumcized: He (God the Father) has brought you to life with him for he has forgiven us all our sins (Col. 2:11–13; italics added).

This passage contains the same association of baptism with the death, burial, and Resurrection of Christ we find in Romans 6. However, in Colossians baptism is identified with circumcision. It is "circumcision according to Christ," the true circumcision "not performed by human hand." Furthermore, the true circumcision is equated with being buried with Christ in baptism. It is "the complete stripping of your body of flesh." Paul's intent was to contrast Jewish circumcision, in which a small part of the flesh is "stripped off," with Christian baptism-circumcision–burial-with-Christ, which involves the total stripping of the flesh so that the old man may die and be reborn in Christ. Paul thus implied that only Christian baptism is true circumcision because it alone is real dying and rebirth. Implicitly Paul introduced a criticism of pre-Christian Judaism that we encounter frequently in this study: What is suppressed or distorted in pre-messianic Judaism becomes fully conscious in Christianity. Freud arrived at a very similar judgment when he characterized the central Christian affirmation that the Son died for the sins of mankind against the Father as an example of "the return of the repressed."[32]

By identifying true circumcision with the *complete stripping away of the flesh,* Paul intuited that the intergenerational hostility manifest in circumcision is much deeper than the father's desire to unman his male offspring. This becomes clear when we ask ourselves why any father would want to mutilate his son's penis and why any culture would find it necessary to institute compromise activities by which such hostility could be deflected. The reasons could only be sexual envy, rivalry, or jealousy. Nor is it surprising that the father feels such envy. After all, the father was once a child himself. At some level, he remembers his own desire to displace his father.[33] If, as Freud suggested, the unconscious is timeless, the father's memories of his early feelings toward his own progenitor never disappear. Although unconscious, the feelings have lost none of their potency. Every disguised expression of hostility and competitiveness on the part of the child is clearly understood by the father in some degree. No father ever really forgets what it means to be a son.

If one wishes to be rid of a rival one does not injure him, one murders him. The father's real temptation is not castration but, as Bakan pointed out, infanticide. This is reinforced by the father's memory of his own death wishes toward his father and his perception of the son's death wishes toward him. A ritual such as circumcision, which seeks to redirect harmlessly the parental temptation to castrate, is only viable as long as the infanticidal impulse is so completely repressed that there is little need to acknowledge it.

The infanticidal impulse was never completely suppressed in rabbinic Judaism. There was a time when ritual infanticide was practiced upon the first-born in Judea. Traces of such infanticide can be seen both in the Bible and in a custom practiced to this day by traditional Jews, the *pidyon ha-ben* or *redemption of the first-born* ritual. The ceremony essentially consists of the father presenting his first-born son to a *cohen* or hereditary priest on the thirtieth day after the son's birth; the priest must ask the father, "Which do you prefer, your son or your money?" The father then declares that he prefers his son and presents the *cohen* with five silver dollars, the symbolic equivalent of five biblical shekels, in order to "redeem" his son. The priest accepts the coins with the ritual formula, "This (the coins) in place of that (the child). This in exchange for that."

The ceremony has its roots in an attempt to deflect infanticidal hostility by an institutionalized exchange procedure that permits the child's life to be spared. Its original wisdom lay in the fact that men, who might find it difficult to alter their habits on the basis of verbal remonstrance, were able to change when given a surrogate activity. Today the ceremony is a happy family ritual, and few participants are ever aware of its origin or its ancient meaning.

A very potent reminder of the persistent strength of the infanticidal impulse can also be found in the reading from Scripture for Rosh Hashannah, Genesis 22, which tells the story of Abraham's aborted sacrifice of Isaac. On the holiest of days, Jews are reminded that God did not require the death of the tribal patriarch's son, for at the last moment a substitute was provided. The need to reiterate, under conditions of utmost solemnity, the fact that God demanded and Abraham was willing to accede to the death of the son, but that God "changed his mind" at the last moment, is testimony to the persistence of the very impulse the ritual seeks to ward off. Were the impulse without power, the reading would cease to be meaningful.

When Paul referred to the "stripping of your body of flesh" as the true circumcision, his words were psychologically appropriate in a sense. Paul's defense of baptism as true circumcision can be interpreted to mean that sons cannot overcome the hostility of the Father (in the double sense of heavenly and earthly) by a token removal of the flesh. The hostility is deeper; it can only be overcome by a consuming ordeal. Nothing short of death and rebirth will suffice. This argument was possible for Paul because of the Damascus experience, which overwhelmed him with the unshakable conviction that Jesus had in fact faced the Father's hostility in its most terrible form without perishing forever. Jesus' skin had been completely stripped away at his Father's command, and instead of this "stripping away" being his final destruction, Paul was convinced that it was the gateway to a deathless and glorified existence. Jesus had overcome parental hostility so completely that no further harm could ever come to him.

Paul did not say that any stripping of the body of flesh would rescue men. Their circumcision must be that of Christ and their death that of Christ. Ordinary water will not suffice. The waters must be filled with the Spirit of Christ to effect redemption. Only in that way will men partake of the Resurrection that has already happened to Christ and that will ultimately take place in all those who are "in Christ."

Under the impact of the Christian religious revolution, it was Paul's achievement to deepen immeasurably the meaning of one of mankind's oldest rituals of renewal, the rite of immersion in and emergence from the watery substance out of which the race began. In his religious imagination, Paul was able to associate baptism with mankind's most profound and archaic responses to earthly and heavenly progenitors as well as to water as the primordial matrix of all life. As we shall see in discussing Paul's doctrine of Christ as the Last Adam, the restoration of God, the cosmos, and the race to their common original condition was the culminating motif of Paul's eschatological vision. The Christian's return to the waters of rebirth and the womb of immortality anticipates that fulfillment. According to Paul, the initial act in the drama of cosmic restoration, which is destined to reach its climax in the reunion of all things in God, begins with the Christian's emergence as a "new creation" from the waters of baptism.

Chapter V

Totemic Atonement

At first glance, the idea of eating the body of the Son of God in the fundamental rite of sacred worship seems to violate common sense completely. Nevertheless, this form of worship is maintained by the majority of religious men and women throughout the Christian world. If Paul did not originate this conception of Christian worship, he was among the first to proclaim its truth. In the twentieth century, a far less believing Jew, Sigmund Freud, argued that there was a profound psychological truth embedded in this conception and that the Lord's Supper as interpreted by Paul was in fact a dramatic reenactment of the moral catastrophe with which human civilization, religion, and morality commenced.[1] Freud's attempt to reconstruct the origins of religion through a causal myth of original parricide is enormously enlightening without necessarily being literally true.[2] Freud's theory can help to illuminate our understanding of Paul, especially his interpretation of the Lord's Supper.

Briefly stated, Freud argued that before human religious and social institutions developed as we know them, men dwelt in small hordes dominated by a tyrannical father. The horde consisted of the father, his harem, and some of the younger male offspring. The older male had exclusive sexual possession of the harem, which consisted indifferently of all the females in the group. His sexual rights were maintained by aggression against his own male offspring, who were his potential rivals. By infanticide, castration, and explusion, the father prevented the sons from displacing him. The expelled sons were driven by sexual need to find a way to gain access to the females. Finally the brothers banded together and murdered the father. However, parricide proved to be an ironic and complicated act. Although the young men sought to be rid of the father, they also wanted to be like him, enjoying especially his sexual privileges. In spite of their envious hatred, there was much about the father they admired and wished to emulate. Thus hatred and love were intermixed in the first parricide.

We have already noted that there is a cannibalistic aspect to all acts of identification insofar as the object we prize is taken into and becomes a part of the psyche.[3] The crudest form of becoming one with an object is to eat it. According to Freud, the exiled brothers solved the problem of displacing the father while becoming like him by eating him. The primal crime of humanity was the cannibalistic devouring of the father by the sons so that they might become like him and take sexual possession of his females.

Since love and hate were intertwined in the original act, the sons were incapable of feeling satisfied with their victory. On the contrary, Freud maintained that their feelings of guilt were so great that they were driven to deny to themselves that the father was dead or that they had committed the crime. This only made matters worse, for by denying the parricide, the sons could not cancel their unconscious memory of the deed or their fear of the victim's retaliatory aggression. Denial led the sons to ascribe such extraordinary powers to their father that he became for them the Father in heaven. As a result, the sons were condemned to unending obedience to the dead father's will as their way of assuaging their fear of his retaliation. Freud's implicit definition of God is both paradoxical and compelling: *The heavenly Father is the first object of human criminality.* Men willingly obey his "law" because of their fear that he will retaliate against them as deicides.

Though the crime was never forgotten, the sons were unable to admit consciously what they had done and were inwardly compelled to repeat the act in dramatic form. The repetition took the form of the archaic totem sacrifice, which Freud regarded as "perhaps mankind's oldest festival." He maintained that the totem animal was normally sacrosanct, but on certain festival occasions the entire tribe was compelled to slaughter, consume, and mourn the very animal that was regarded as the tribal ancestor. According to Freud, the totem animal was in reality a surrogate for the murdered father. He pointed to many examples of animals that were identified with heroes, ancestors, and gods.

In dreams, poetry, religious symbolism, myth, and individual neurosis, a similar process of identification continues to this day. One of the most beautiful examples of this kind of identification in the history of art can be seen in the great van Eyck altarpiece in Ghent, "The Adoration of the Mystic Lamb," in which all of the figures are turned reverently toward the central figure, the mystic lamb, who is of course Christ, "the lamb of God."

The totem sacrifice was both a confession and a reenactment of the unconsciously remembered deed. Remorse and self-assertion were comingled in the reenactment, as love and hate had been in the original deed. The totem sacrifice also offered the possibility of "deferred obedience" to the murdered father.[4] The sons quickly learned that they could not indulge in unrestricted sexual license with the slain father's women without grave conflict among themselves. Having killed to acquire the women, the sons voluntarily imposed the father's sexual restrictions upon themselves in order to maintain fraternal solidarity. No man could partake of the totem sacrifice, thereby repeating symbolically the original deed, if he were guilty of violating the newly instituted tribal taboo against incest.

The totem sacrifice became the focal point of tribal memory, solidarity, and morality. Freud did not dismiss lightly the oft-proclaimed confession that we are all miserable sinners. The original basis of social solidarity was criminal complicity in the unconsciously remembered parricide. All who partook of the sacrificial animal were regarded as of one substance with both the victim and the other members of the tribe.

Freud's interpretation of the substantial solidarity of those who eat together was in part dependent upon the work of the Scottish scholar, W. Robertson Smith.[5] Freud cited an example Smith had given of the Bedouin custom that renders a stranger inviolable for a certain time after he has eaten with them. As long as the food remains within his body, the Bedouins regard the stranger as having shared a common substance with them and hence not to be harmed.

The idea that people who share a meal partake of a common bond persists to this day even in secularized forms. Few acts are as hostile as the refusal to break bread. Paul's vigorous opposition to Peter when he withdrew from table fellowship with Gentile Christians at Antioch indicates that he understood the extent to which the act of sharing a common meal is a profound expression of human solidarity (Gal. 2:11–16). This intuition is explicit in Paul's statement that "though there are many of us, we form a single body because we have a share in this one loaf" (I Cor. 10:17). The loaf to which Paul referred was, of course, the bread of the Lord's Supper.

The act of ingesting is one of the oldest ways in which we confront our environment. Long before living organisms develop the faculty of visual perception, they must consume a portion of their environment. Eating also partakes of the oldest expression of love: The mother gives of her own substance when she feeds the child. Originally, the beloved object, food and the feeder are one to the child. In totemic sacrifice they become one again. When a god is consumed, he is both food and feeder. Those who partake of his substance become one with him as do Christians with Christ in Holy Communion.

Freud rejected the theory that the sacrificial victim is a gift of the worshiping community to its god. He regarded the sacrificial gift as a later development that arose after the institution of private property. He stressed the perennial centrality of the Communion sacrifice as the decisive religious act. His view is in conflict with certain rationalizing and moralizing tendencies within both Judaism and Protestantism that regarded sacrifice as a "primitive" anticipation of more "advanced" expressions of religious worship such as personal prayer. Freud's emphasis was, however, by no means foreign to Roman Catholicism, which has always stressed the real presence of the body and blood of the Christ in the sacrificial elements of the Mass, Catholicism's sacrament of worship.

Freud also applied the myth of the primal crime to his interpretation of Christianity. As we have noted, Freud saw the distinction between Judaism and Christianity in terms of the "return of the repressed." One of the areas in which what Judaism had repressed became manifest in Christianity was the Lord's Supper. From the perspective of psychoanalysis, the sacrificial reenactment of the primal crime had been transformed in Judaism into a system of animal sacrifices. Admittedly, the Hebrew sacrificial system contained few overt traces of the surrogate character of animal sacrifices, but extensive knowledge of Canaanite and other Near Eastern sacrificial systems tends to corroborate the hypothesis that many of the biblically ordained sacrifices had their roots in human sacrifice.[6]

Freud argued that the archaic sacrifice of a divine-human victim was finally revived in Holy Communion. He maintained that Christ had redeemed man psychologically from the "burden of original sin" by laying down his own life. According to Freud, mankind's "original sin" was not Adam's eating of the apple. The biblical tradition censored a far graver offense: parricide. Had men been guilty of the lesser crime, Freud contended, God would have required a far less severe punishment in accordance with the measure-for-measure principle. Christ's atoning death pointed back to an archaic blood guilt.[7]

Freud also maintained that by offering himself on the Cross, the slain "son" took the place of the originally murdered "father" as the object of human adoration. As a result, son-religion (Christianity) took the place of father-religion (Judaism). As a sign of the displacement of the father by the son, the totem feast was revived, but now the community of brothers (i.e., the Church) ate the body and blood of the son rather than that of the father. The ritual permitted the brothers to identify with the son in the most concrete way, by eating his substance. It also repeated the primal crime in a novel form: By his prefect atonement, the Son had done in his way what the oldest group of brothers had done in theirs—he had displaced the Father. Freud therefore concluded that the Eucharist was "essentially a fresh elimination of the father, a repetition of the guilty deed."[8]

It is my opinion that Freud was in error when he interpreted Christianity as a religion in which the Father is once again displaced. Certainly in Pauline Christianity no such displacement takes place. As we have noted, the Jewish strategy of obedience to the Father has been altered to identification with the obedient older brother as Christianity's way of achieving a right relationship to the Father.[9] Nevertheless, the fundamental issue remains the same in both religions: How does man achieve the right relationship with the Father? We are therefore compelled to seek for a somewhat different psychoanalytic understanding of Holy Communion than that suggested by Freud, although our explanation will be along Freudian lines. It seems that, insofar as Holy Communion is a symbolic repetition and confession of the original parricide, Christ, by offering his body to the brothers in the Communion meal, pays once again the price of the original crime on their behalf. However, while Christ's sacrifice allows a dramatic repetition of the crime, he makes it possible for the Christian to avoid having to confess, "It is God we have murdered; it is God whom we seek to murder again, because it is God whom we wish to become." We have already noted that identification with God was impossible in Judaism and that this Jewish taboo was a permanent legacy to Christianity. We have also noted that identification with Christ allowed the Christian to identify with the elder brother's omnipotence without falling into megalomania or blasphemy against the Father.

We have, however, only told half the story. There cannot be two omnipotent beings. Every being limits or impedes any other being that is over against it. An omnipotent being could tolerate no such impediment; yet, if its opposing Other were also omnipotent, the first would be powerless to rid itself of the other's intrusive presence. In reality, *the omnipotence men seek is their oldest experience of undifferentiated unity with the world.* Here we recall Hegel's awesome dictum that initially each consciousness "must aim at the death of the other."[10] Hegel's observation parallels the psychoanalytic observation that when the neonate first encounters the environment, his initial goal is to obliterate it as a painful intrusion upon his original bliss. The quest for omnipotence must therefore contain a deicidal component insofar as God is experienced as the opposing Other. Freud stressed the brothers' desire to gain the father's sexual priviliges in his myth. When the earthly father became the Heavenly Father, the brothers had an additional motive for displacing him: They now wanted to take God's omnipotence unto themselves. That is one of the reasons why Judaism is so uncompromising in its denial of all resemblance between God and man and its insistence that the greatest sin is the quest to displace God in order to become omnipotent. In Christianity a way was found to express the quest for omnipotence through identification with Christ. A way was also found to express the deicidal hostility that, of necessity, attends the quest for omnipotence. In Holy Communion one partakes of Christ's omnipotence by the oldest of all forms of identification, the act of ingestion. *The very same act is the oldest form of aggression,* the act of consuming the desired person or thing.[11] This allows for both crude identification with and aggressive displacement of the omnipotent one. Loving union and deicidal aggression comingle in the ritual. Freud's comments about the cannibalistic character of identification are very much to the point.

Nor can we forget Judaism's legacy to Christianity in this matter. Omnipotence is gained from and deicidal hostility is expressed against the elder brother without the direct involvement of the Father. This may indeed be the deepest meaning of Christ's self-sacrificing in Christianity. Usually, the theory that Christ atones for the sins of mankind stresses the willingness of Christ, though innocent, to accept the punitive violence of God against mankind, thereby rendering it unnecessary for men to become the objects of the punishment they richly deserve. I believe that there is another side to Christ's self-sacrificing obedience: Christ becomes the stand-in for mankind's ambivalent yearning to become and, at the same time, be rid of God. When Christ offers himself he is, in effect, saying to men, "You want to become one with God's power and be rid of his punitive threat against you. You cannot be rid of God or identify with him directly. Take me in his place. I freely offer myself to you." Christ's gift is such that he offers himself in place of sinful men to a punitive God and offers himself in place of God to deicidal men.

Christ is thus truly a mediating figure. He mediates between the brothers and the Father by offering the Father an obedience even unto death of which the brothers are incapable, and by taking upon himself God's punishment for the brothers' disobedience. He mediates between the Father and the brothers by allowing the brothers to cannibalize freely and become one with him rather than the Father, thereby freeing them from the temptation to commit the worst of all crimes, deicide against the Father.

Freud's primal crime myth has been dismissed by some scholars as unfounded speculation by a man who overstepped the limits of his own competence.[12] Even Freud admitted that the myth was a "just so" story.[13] Nevertheless, although his attempted reconstruction can hardly be taken as factual, Freud deepens our understanding of the Christian religious revolution, of which Paul was perhaps the most decisive exponent after the Crucifixion of Jesus, and helps us to understand its extraordinary emotional power.

Freud's myth of a primal crime is important in understanding Paul. Both Freud and Paul accepted the doctrine of "the fall of man." Both agreed that human history began with an act of primal rebellion against the Father. Both saw Christ's fundamental role as that of undoing the consequences of the primal rebellion. As we shall see, Paul's myth of Christ as the Last Adam stresses his role in undoing the sin of the first Adam. Both Paul and Freud regard the Lord's Meal as the way the believer becomes one with the elder brother. We shall also see that both take very seriously Christ's "real presence" within the elements of the Lord's Meal. Above all, both Paul and Freud, for very different reasons, regarded the Jewish strategy of obedience to the Father as futile, and both saw Christ as uncovering a deeper level of the meaning of God's controversy with man, which Judaism had suppressed.

There were, of course, major areas of disagreement between Freud and Paul, the most important being Freud's conviction that the Christian solution to mankind's religious problem was ultimately as illusory as was the Jewish solution. Nevertheless, by permitting the hidden memory of mankind's oldest and most intolerable offense to resurface, Christianity brought the possibility of the self-understanding of man a step closer to realization. Like other forms of revolutionary Jewish mysticism and messianism, the Christian "return of the repressed" was a further stage on the road to psychological man, which culminated in the psychoanalytic revolution.

Chapter VI

The Lord's Meal

Freud regarded Holy Communion as a resurfacing of the archaic totem sacrifice within Christianity. Nevertheless, it is not at all certain that Freud's insights into the nature of the Eucharist apply to the ritual as it was understood by Paul. The question of what the Eucharist meant to Paul has aroused lively debate among scholars. Paul left no record of any systematic exposition of the meaning of the Eucharist. In the letters the Lord's Supper is discussed at some length in I Corinthians (10:1–18; 11:17–34), but these passages reflect Paul's attempts to deal with problems of moral and religious behavior that had arisen in the Church at Corinth; they are not systematic expositions of the Eucharist. In addition, here as else where in Paul's writings, there are textual and interpretive difficulties that frequently obscure his meaning.

To understand what the rite of the Lord's Supper meant to Paul, it is helpful to see the ritual against the background of primitive Christian tradition. Paul's description of the Lord's Supper in I Corinthians is the earliest written tradition we possess. In its written form Mark 14 is a few years later, but it probably reflects the same oral tradition utilized by Paul.[1] Although Paul's account differs somewhat from the Markan account in detail, there is a fundamental agreement that suggests that the primitive Church preserved a well-defined memory of Jesus' last meal with his disciples: During this meal Jesus broke bread with the disciples and said of the bread, "This is my body." He then took wine and after all had partaken of it said, "This is my blood." By identifying the bread and wine with his own body and blood Jesus opened the possibility of the development of a sacrificial ritual centering in his own person. Nevertheless, Jesus' *Last* Supper (in contrast to the *Lord's* Supper) is not yet a meal in which Jesus himself is the sacrificial victim. During the Last Supper Jesus declared to his disciples, "I tell you solemnly, I shall not drink any more wine until the day I drink new wine in the kingdom of God" (Mark 14:25). These words indicate that the Last Supper was primarily a feast of leave-taking and hopeful anticipation. Jesus looked forward to the time when he would once again eat in fellowship with his disciples "in the kingdom of God." It is the consensus of scholarly opinion that Jesus' promise refers to the future messianic feast that the Messiah will enjoy with the faithful when all is accomplished.[2]

It is very likely that Jesus' promise to return corresponded with his disciples' deepest need. They were aware of the terminal threat that hung over their Master's life. It was questionable whether their group could maintain itself without Jesus. The original disciples were bound to each other by the powerful emotional ties that united them with their leader. Their situation at the time of the Last Supper calls to mind Freud's description of the relation of a primary group to its leader: Such a group is constituted by the profound ties that unite its members with their leader. Loss of the leader, especially where there is no possible successor, can result in group disintegration and panic among the members.[3] By virtue of the absolutely unique impact Jesus had upon his followers, he simply could not be replaced. His words of confident assurance that he would return in all probability reflected his intuitive understanding of what he meant to his followers and what his loss would mean to them.

Oscar Cullmann has observed that the meals shared by the disciples immediately after the death of Jesus were initially meals of joy and thanksgiving rather than sorrowful commemorations of the Crucifixion.[4] According to Acts, the disciples "continued to meet every day in the Temple and, breaking bread at home, they ate their meals with joy and simplicity" (Acts 2:46). If the meals they shared had a distinctly sacrificial character, emphasizing the consumption of the body and blood of the Risen Christ, it is unlikely that they would have continued to meet "every day in the Temple" where the traditional Jewish sacrifices were offered. According to Hans Leitzmann, the earliest Christian sacred meals were communal meals of fellowship not unlike those the disciples had enjoyed with Jesus before his death.[5] Leitzmann maintained that the Risen Christ was in some sense present at these meals of fellowship. Luke recounts two occasions immediately after the Resurrection when Jesus appeared to his followers and ate with them. In both instances there was an initial lack of recognition by the disciples. At Emmaus two of Jesus' followers recognized the Resurrected Christ only after he had taken bread, blessed it, and distributed it (Luke 24:30–32). The Risen Christ then appeared at Jerusalem to the disciples, who initially thought they were seeing a ghost. He demanded that they touch him to verify that he was no ghost, and only then did he ask for something to eat, partaking of grilled fish with them (Luke 24:39–43).

There is no reason to doubt the psychological reality of the apparition of the Risen Christ. Although Paul, in the instance of his Damascus vision, was receptive to such a vision for somewhat different reasons, the disciples were faced with a conflict between their own worldly realism and the extraordinary meaning and promise Jesus had given to their lives. Both the continued viability of their fundamental community and everything that had given redemptive hope to their lives was at stake. If Jesus had definitively terminated his career with execution as a common criminal, all would have been in vain. The disciples were incapable of denying what Jesus had meant to them despite his apparently catastrophic end. As with the narrative of Paul's vision, the tradition of Jesus's Resurrection appearances at Emmaus and Jerusalem has a ring of psychological truth about it. The disciples' intense yearning for their lost leader may also have been reinforced by feelings of guilt at their inability to maintain an undivided loyalty toward him. Thomas doubted him; Peter denied him; Judas betrayed him. If the other disciples had emotions akin to most men, their own feelings about Jesus could not have been entirely uncomplicated. Both their yearning and their feelings of guilt were probably greatest in those early days when the shock of his departure was most deeply felt. Under such conditions, it is not at all surprising that Jesus was once again manifest to them as they sat together at their meals.

Since the publication of Leitzmann's great work on the Lord's Meal, scholars have debated whether there were one or two types of sacred meals in the primitive Church. Leitzmann believed that there were two distinct kinds of Eucharist: One was the "Jerusalem type," the other the "Pauline type."[6] The Jerusalem Eucharist ultimately derived from the ordinary fellowship meals the disciples shared with Jesus before his death. It was marked by a sense of the Risen Christ's spiritual, if not actual, presence and the hopeful anticipation of his return. Leitzmann regarded Paul as the creator of the other type of Eucharist. He maintained that Paul transformed the fellowship meal of anticipation into a memorial feast emphasizing Christ's death. Leitzmann elected an interpretive strategy in his research that has been quite common in German circles. He regarded the Pauline Eucharist as essentially Greek and modeled after Hellenistic memorial feats in honor of the dead; the earlier Jerusalem type was of Jewish origin. Leitzmann thus saw Paul as responsible for the Hellenizing of one of the most important rituals of the primitive Church.

This distinction between a primitive Palestinian ritual of breaking bread and a Hellenistic sacred memorial meal initiated by Paul has been challenged by later scholars.[7] Here I simply want to point out the the whole question of whether a particular mode of religious thought or action was originally Hellenistic rather than Jewish is subordinate to a far more important issue: *What was psychologically at stake in the shift from one type of belief or practice to another?* Even if it is granted that the form of the Eucharist that ultimately became dominant in the Christian Church derived from the Pauline type, and that Paul was indebted to Hellenistic sacred meals for his understanding of the Eucharist, we are still faced with the question of why the shift took place. Undoubtedly Gentile Christians were more familiar with Hellenistic cultic meals than with Jewish ritual. However, Paul himself was not only at home in Jewish custom, but, as T. W. Manson has shown, I Corinthians is permeated with the symbolism and mood of Passover, even to the extent of calling Christ "our Passover," and using the Jewish custom of cleansing the home of all leaven before the Passover festival as a metaphor for the moral self-cleansing of the Corinthian Church (I Cor. 5:6–8).[8]

Once attention is focused on the question of what was psychologically at stake, there is no need to go beyond the stresses inherent in Judaism and the primitive Church to understand the development of the Eucharist. Furthermore, contemporary scholarship has become exceedingly wary of rigid separations of early Christian belief and practice into mutually exclusive categories of Greek and Jewish elements.

A much more helpful way of understanding the evolution of the Eucharist is to be found in Oscar Cullmann's distinction between the earliest sacred meals, at which the disciples ate *with* Christ, and the later Lord's Meal, at which *Christ was eaten*.[9] The joyful meals of fellowship that followed the Resurrection were meals in which the disciples either ate with Christ or anticipated eating with him at the messianic feast. However, there came a time when hopeful anticipation of Christ's return predominated over the feeling of his presence. The sources depict Christ as present immediately after the Resurrection, but, within a short time, the disciples are left to carry on their work without him. It is at this point that their longing for his return must have intensified. That longing is powerfully expressed in the Eucharistic liturgy preserved in the *Didache*, which most scholars date no later than 150 and many date much earlier. As the sacred meal concludes the leader prays: "Let his Grace (i.e., Christ) draw near, and let the present world pass away." The congregation replies: *"Hosanna to the God of David."* Leader: "Whoever is holy, let him approach. Whoso is not, let him repent." The congregation concludes with the *Maranatha: "O Lord, come quickly. Amen."*[10]

The *Didache's* version of the Eucharist rests upon Jesus' assurance to his disciples that he would not drink wine again until he did so in God's kingdom. This Eucharist expresses the note of anticipation and expectation we have already noted in the earliest forms of the Christian sacred meal. Nevertheless, *there is a limit to the human capacity for unrequited yearning.* Ultimately, men must choose either to abandon the object of yearning and reinvest their emotional energy elsewhere or to find a way to rejoin the lost object.

The forces that made for the Christian's identification with Christ were overwhelming once his physical departure had finally become a reality. Christ had become the heart and center of the disciples' lives both in this world and for the world to come. As we have noted, identification with Christ gave Christians the means of achieving the most crucial of all relationships, the right relationship with the God who held the destiny of their souls in the balance. Identification with Christ provided Christians with their most awesome hope, hope for a way out of mortality; it also provided them with a primary community, the Church, in which their fears, hopes, and aspirations could be shared. Christ was simply too important to lose or even to remain a distant object of yearning. A way had to be found to assure the primitive Church that Christ was a present reality, as he had been in those first days after the Resurrection.

It is neither surprising that a way was found nor that the memory of Jesus' own words pointed the direction to union with him. There was more than one way in which Jesus could be present at the sacred tables of the primitive Church. He could be, as he had been, with them in spirit; he could also be with them as *both the food and the feeder.* Jesus' action in offering bread and wine with the words, "This is my body; this is my blood," contain the implicit message, "I am the food as I am the feeder." If it was no longer possible for Christians to share food with Jesus, it was inevitable that they would find in these words a way to be with him in body.

By construing the bread and wine of their sacred meal as the body and blood of Christ, Christians resorted to the oldest, the most effective, and the most crudely physical way of becoming one with the beloved object, physical incorporation. The Eucharist was a literal acting out of the basic Christian strategy for achieving the right relationship with the Father in Heaven, identification with the elder brother. We can recall Freud's observations that oral incorporation is the oldest form of identification and that Christianity is a cultural expression of the "return of the repressed." However, we must caution against regarding the Christian attempt to identify physically with Christ as pathological. By finding a way to overcome the gap that separated them from Christ, which was rooted in the most archaic, nonverbal, sensuous strategies of the organism, the primitive Christians preserved both the integrity of their community and its redemptive message. They also were able to cope with the inevitable tension between the Christian proclamation of *hope fulfilled* and the Christian reality of *hope deferred*. By partaking of the true substance of the Risen Christ, they periodically became "one body" with his immortal glory and anticipated sharing it completely at the end of days. At the same time, they prepared themselves for the rhythm of life in which the assurance of redemption was constantly countered by the harsh realities of the Roman Empire.

It is precisely the crudely physical aspects of the Lord's Meal, in which Christ is both food and feeder, that constitute its overwhelming power. Wherever the rite of the Lord's Meal has been taken seriously, and wherever the real presence of Christ in the elements has been honestly asserted, Christendom has had an incomparable way of expressing through religious drama its deepest conscious and unconscious yearnings concerning human morality, kinship, and mortality. I know of no ritual in any other contemporary religion of comparable emotional power. In our times, when men are rediscovering the body and learning once more the real power of touching and tasting, the Christian Lord's Meal may serve as an example to other religious traditions of the fact that not prayer but sacrificial communion is the decisive mode of human fellowship and worship; and that, by consuming bread and wine in the sacred precinct, all men, both Christian and non-Christian, can become one with each other and with God's body for a fulfilling moment that can carry over into day-to-day life.

It is my conviction that the transformation of the Lord's Meal from one *eaten with Christ* to one in which *Christ is eaten* would have taken place with or without Paul. Nevertheless, most scholars agree that Paul played an important role in the transformation. Some scholars maintain with Leitzmann that the Pauline type of Eucharist, in which Christ is eaten, derived from Paul himself. Others maintain that Paul's discussion of the Eucharist in I Corinthians 10 and 11 was dependent upon primitive Christian tradition.[11]

The crux of the problem lies in how one interprets the verse with which Paul established his authority for his interpretation of the Eucharist: "For, on my own part, *I have received from the Lord* that which I also delivered unto you: It is this: The Lord Jesus on the night in which he was betrayed, took bread. . ." (I Cor. 11:23, 24). Some scholars believe that Paul meant that he received a tradition of the primitive Church that he then handed down to the Corinthians.[12] These scholars interpret I Corinthians 11:23 as Paul's assertion that he had faithfully transmitted to the Corinthians the Eucharistic tradition that he had received from others who in turn ultimately received it from Jesus at the Last Supper. These scholars reject the originality of Paul's interpretation of the Eucharist.

Other scholars, including Leitzmann, insist that to ascribe such fidelity to Paul in matters of primitive Christian tradition is inconsistent with both his known independence of the Jerusalem Church and his own insistence that his gospel and his authority derived ultimately not from men but from Christ (Gal. 1:1, 2).[13] They find it difficult to reconcile him as a faithful traditionary with his assertion that: "The Good News I preached is not a human message that I was given by men, it is something I learned only through a revelation of Jesus Christ."

If convincing evidence could be found that the Pauline type of Eucharist originated with Paul and that he received the tradition by what he regarded as a direct "revelation" from the Risen Christ, it would simplify the problem of a psychological understanding of Paul. We could then regard the interpretation of the Lord's Meal in which Christ is eaten as having been initiated by Paul. This fact would be of overwhelming importance in understanding him. However, one must be careful in utilizing a view of Paul that lends itself so readily to psychoanalytic interpretation but that has been challenged by some of the best New Testament researchers. Let us for the moment rest content with the fact that some of the most distinguished scholars in the field have maintained that Paul originated the type of Eucharist in which Christ is really present in the elements. I believe that Paul did in fact originate the "Pauline" type of Eucharist, but the available evidence is not such as to warrant more than the assertion that Paul may have originated it.

Those scholars who reject the view put forward by Leitzmann do not as a rule deny that Paul believed in the real presence of Christ in the Eucharist. Today their dispute centers on whether this type of Eucharist originated with Paul. However, even if this type of Eucharist did not originate with Paul, Paul was certainly one of its most influential expositors in early Christianity.

As we have noted, Paul's teaching about the Eucharist is found primarily in I Corinthians 10 and 11. In the tenth chapter Paul contrasted Christian with Jewish and pagan sacrifice. He began with a *midrash,* or homiletic interpretation, on the two fundamental Christian sacraments, baptism and the Lord's Supper. In Paul's *midrash* Moses and the children of Israel are treated as anticipatory prototypes of Christ and his Church. Israel's journey through the Rea Sea and the cloud that preceded them are assimilated to the theme of Christian baptism: "They were all baptized unto Moses in this cloud and in this sea" (I Cor. 10:2).

In addition, the Israelites are depicted as being fed with "spiritual food" (*broma pneumatikon*) and drinking "spiritual drink" (*poma pneumatikon*), which they drank from "the spiritual rock that followed them as they went" (10:3–4). Paul identified the "spiritual rock" with Christ, referring to the rock to which God directed Moses in Exodus 17:4 where God is depicted as saying: "Behold, I will stand before thee upon the rock in Horeb; and thou shalt smite the rock, and there shall come water out of it, that the people might drink." There is no suggestion in Exodus that the rock moved with the people on their wilderness journey, nor is there any identification of the rock with a future Messiah. However, apparently there was a rabbinic tradition that "the well which was with Israel in the desert" was "like a rock" and that it accompanied the Israelites throughout their desert wanderings.[14] This tradition may have been the source of Paul's Christian *midrash*. After his conversion Paul understood Scripture in the light of the Christ-event so that the identification of the moving, water-giving rock with Christ seemed entirely natural, especially because he regarded the life-giving capacities of the waters as an anticipation of the life-giving powers of Christ.

The Protestant scholar Jean Héring has observed that when Paul used the term "spiritual" (*pneumatikon*) he did not mean something immaterial.[15] When Paul contrasted the natural mortal body (*soma psuchikon*) with the immortal spiritual body (*soma pneumatikon*) into which Christians would be transformed at the resurrection (I Cor. 15:44), he regarded the spiritual body as the true body. Nevertheless, it remains a body for him. Héring thus agreed with John A. T. Robinson and Albert Schweitzer concerning the corporeal nature of the "spiritual" realities of Christian life as understood by Paul. Héring pointed out that the "spiritual food" of the Israelites in the desert to which Paul referred was the manna sent by God (Exod. 16:15). Because the manna was God's own nourishment, it was for Paul an anticipation of the Eucharist. Ernst Käsemann has expressed a similar opinion, asserting that Paul regarded the God-given food and drink of the Israelites as a partaking of the body of Christ.[16] Käsemann has interpreted Paul's phrase "in Christ" to mean that Christians are members of Christ's body because Christ enters into them as *pneuma* (spirit). Käsemann maintained that, for Paul, *pneuma* is "the substance of resurrection corporality and the dimension in which the Risen Christ exists."[17] And whenever Paul described *pneuma* as Christ's gift to the believer, he was referring to the most radical form of the Risen Christ's self-manifestation. Consequently, Paul discerned an identity between the Eucharist and the spiritual food and drink of the wilderness rock. For Paul, Christians consume the Risen Christ's bodily substance at the Lord's Supper as the Israelites did in the wilderness.

Paul had a purpose in likening the food and drink of the Israelites to the bread and wine of the Lord's Supper. He used the example of the Israelites to warn the Corinthian Christians that the Eucharist was not a magic rite that automatically assured salvation to the communicant. According to Paul, the Israelites had been incorporated into Christ's glorious body by partaking of "spiritual" food and drink. Nevertheless, "their corpses littered the desert" (I Cor. 10:5) because they had turned from the true God to false divinities. The Corinthian Christians were similarly endangered. In their enthusiasm for "the end of the Law," they apparently regarded it as a matter of indifference whether they participated in pagan cultic banquets in addition to partaking of the Lord's Supper. Using the example of the Israelites as a warning, Paul pleaded with the Corinthians to "flee from idolatry" (I Cor. 10:14). At this point Paul introduced his first description of the Eucharist: "The cup of blessing which we bless, is it not a fellowship (*koinonia*) in the blood of Christ? Is not the bread which we break fellowship in the body of Christ?" (I Cor. 10:16, trans. J. Héring). Käsemann has commented that the usual translations of *koinonia* as "fellowship" or "participation" are not strong enough, and offered instead the conception of "falling into a sphere of domination."[18] By partaking of the bread and wine of the Eucharist, Christians enter into and become a part of the domain of the Risen Christ's spiritual (but nonetheless bodily) substance. Like Schweitzer and Robinson, Käsemann understood Paul to maintain that the glorified *bodily* substance of the Risen Christ is present in the bread and wine, and that Christians literally partake of this substance in the Lord's Supper.

Paul's insistence that Corinthians who participated in the Eucharist were obliged to abstain from pagan cultic banquets is an example of the way sacrificial rituals can be utilized for the purpose of moral and religious control. Since no man may partake of the sacrifice if he is morally or ritually unfit in the eyes of God, the sacrifice itself acts as a barrier against improper behavior. In sacrificial religion, the worst offense is to partake of the sacrifice when one is morally or ritually unworthy. This is beautifully expressed in Psalm 24: "Who shall ascend unto the mountain of the Lord: or who shall stand in his holy place? He that hath clean hands and a pure heart; who hath not lifted up his soul in vanity nor sworn deceitfully" (Ps. 24:3–4). One ascends the mountain of the Lord to partake of the sacrifice. The psalmist defines with utmost simplicity the conditions under which such participation is appropriate. Another side to this definition is the implicit warning against standing "in his holy place" unless one has "clean hands and a pure heart."[19]

Paul offered a similar warning to the Corinthians, which can be paraphrased as: "Do nothing which would render you unfit to eat at the Lord's table; you cannot behave improperly and partake of the body and blood of the Lord. The Israelites tried and were smitten. Take heed from their example."

Paul's horror at improper consumption of the sacrificial victim was expressed with especial force in I Corinthians 11 when he warned the Church: "anyone who eats the bread or drinks from the cup of the Lord unworthily will make himself guilty in relation to the body and blood of the Lord" (I Cor. 11:27, trans. J. Héring). To consume the Risen Christ's true substance unworthily is far more dangerous than never to have partaken of it at all. Paul then detailed the punishments that had followed from improper participation in the Lord's Meal: "That is why there are among you so many sick and ailing, and a considerable number have died" (I Cor. 11:30, trans. J. Héring).

We have already noted that for Paul neither sickness nor death were natural occurrences. Here he regarded the sickness and death manifest among the Corinthians as God's punishment for improper consumption of the Lord's Supper. Paul's concern with proper preparation for the Eucharist reminds us of Martin Luther's scruples over the celebration of his first Mass. Paul's insistence that Christians be properly prepared for the Lord's Meal reveals again the extent to which he regarded *identification with the elder brother* as the means of achieving a right relation with the Father. Nevertheless, even where such identification is overtly corporeal as in the Eucharist, for Paul it functioned as a regulative norm of Christian morality; only those "with clean hands and a pure heart" could partake of the Lord's substance at his table and achieve the fruit of identification with the Risen Christ, immortal life.

We have noted that Paul felt that the believer literally consumed Christ's body. There has been some confusion on this point because of the "spiritual" nature of the Risen Christ's glorious body. If we bear in mind the observations of Héring and Käsemann that for Paul the spiritual is not immaterial but "the substance of resurrection corporeality," we will understand that in the Lord's Meal the Christian becomes united with the body of Christ, which is the only true body. Since Christ is no longer subject to decay or death, he alone truly exists as God intended existence before the sin of Adam. Within a few years after Paul's death, Ignatius declared that when the communicant partakes of the bread and wine of the Eucharist he partakes of the "medicine of immortality, an antidote against dying, to live in Jesus Christ forever more."[20] For Paul, when Christians participated in the Eucharist, their identification with the Risen Christ was just as tangible and concrete as were the older forms of consuming the sacrificial victim, whether human or animal. There was, however, an important difference: The older victims were consumed either in the process of being slaughtered or after having been slaughtered. Christ alone is consumed *after* he had passed through the slaughter and had been resurrected to enjoy the only truly incorruptible existence. *Christ alone was therefore the sacrificial victim to whom no harm can come.*

One of the problems involved in sacrificial communion is that there is an inextricable union of the loving and aggressive feelings of the communicant toward the offering. The act of eating the victim is aggressive insofar as the victim is destroyed in the process; it is loving insofar as the communicant becomes one with the victim. Because of his Resurrection, Christ cannot be destroyed in the act of being consumed. He is therefore the perfect sacrificial offering.

The aggressive aspects of sacrificial consumption, while undoubtedly subliminally present in the communicant, are of no avail against the indestructible Christ. The Risen Christ is the only food that nourishes without being destroyed in the process of being consumed. Unlike one's natural mother, our earliest source of nurture, the Risen Christ can neither perish nor run out of milk. For Paul as well as Ignatius, when properly consumed, Christ is truly the "medicine of immortality."

There is enormous emotional potency in these images. One of the infant's oldest sources of pain is the experience of hunger. Before he comprehends hunger's power through the moderating perspective of experience, it is awesome in its encompassing terror. The oldest expression of love received by the infant is the mother's gift of food. The child both delights in the mother's milk, the tangible substance of her love, and fears profoundly her retaliation for his part in the act of being fed. In that act, the infant cannot initially distinguish between food and feeder. This makes the mother's earliest act of love fraught with danger. The infant can only receive the feeder's gift by consuming the feeder. At some level, the infant fears that the price to be paid for the original gift of love is that the feeder will do to him what he has done to her: He fears being totally consumed. The persistence and potency of this anxiety can be seen in both the archaic images of the child-devouring mother-goddesses as well as the regressive fears that come to light in contemporary psychoanalytic patients during the course of therapy.[21]

Paul's insistence that the Christian consumes the Risen Christ when he partakes properly of the Lord's Meal contains the assurance that the oldest and most profound expression of human yearning, the yearning to be truly fed, is being met at least temporarily and without danger. The believer consumes the perfect food, which saves him from annihilation. Furthermore, the believer need fear no retaliation from the feeder since the one upon whom he feeds can never be destroyed. By consuming the body and blood of the Risen Christ at the Lord's Meal, the believer thus eats the only true food, the food that nourishes for immortal life.

Paul continued his brief exposition of the Lord's Supper with his own explicit identification of Christ's body with the Eucharistic bread. He observed that Christians together constitute a single body because they share in common the bread of the Eucharist: "The fact that there is only one loaf· means that, though there are many of us, we form a single body because we all have a share in this one loaf" (I Cor. 10:17). We have noted that Paul regarded all Christians as constituting a single organic body of which Christ is the head. This theme is repeated here, and is associated with the idea that Christians derive their corporeal unity from the act of consuming Christ's body, which is the "single loaf" of the Lord's Supper.

In all probability, Paul's identification of the loaf with the sacrificial victim had Jewish roots. In the liturgical rites of the Jerusalem Temple, the showbread was regarded as sacrificial in character.[22] In some sense, this was also true of the unleavened bread of Passover. In addition, on the Sabbath and holy days it is customary to place two loaves on the table to symbolize the fact that on these days a second sacrificial offering (*korban mishneh*) was offered in the Temple in addition to the ordinary daily offering (*korban tamid*). When the bread is broken and blessed at the table, it is customary to sprinkle a pinch of salt on it before eating as if it were a sacrificial victim, for it was customary to sprinkle salt on sacrificial victims within the Temple.[23] Thus the bread at the festive table traditionally took on the character of a surrogate offering, just as the family table has always been regarded in some sense as a private altar in Judaism. There is a direct connection between the earliest celebrations of times and seasons in ancient Israel, which were sacrificial in character, and the family table, which to this day has never lost its continuity with the archaic celebrations of Semitic sacrificial meals. Viewed from this perspective, Jesus' identification of the bread with his body and Paul's insistence that Christians are one body in Christ because they partake of a single loaf can be seen as an example of how the muted and latent expressions of archaic sacrificial ritual in Judaism became explicit in Christianity.

Paul's second discussion of the Eucharist in Corinthians has been called "the oldest Christian document about the Lord's Supper" by one very distinguished scholar.[24] Paul had heard that abuses had crept into the celebration of the Lord's Meal at the church in Corinth. Originally the sacramental meal took place in conjunction with an actual meal, but we learn from the letter that the rich ate well and often riotously while the poor were hard pressed to satisfy their hunger. There was no fixed time for the meal to commence. The rich had more leisure and came early; the poor arrived late after they had finished their work. Drunkenness was also a problem: "But in view of the way in which you meet as a congregation, you cannot possibly eat what should be the Lord's Supper. For each of you hastens to eat his own meals, and one suffers hunger while another is drunk. Have you no houses in which to eat and drink? Or do you consider the Church of God of so little account that you do shame to the poor?" (I Cor. 11:20–22, trans. J. Héring).

After rebuking the Church, Paul reminded them of the true nature of the Lord's Supper: "The Lord Jesus on the night in which he was betrayed, took bread, and having given thanks, he broke it and said: 'This is my body which is for you. Do this in remembrance of me.' Similarly, the cup after supper saying: 'This cup is the new covenant in my blood. Do this in remembrance of me each time you drink it'." (I Cor. 11:24–25, trans. J. Héring).

An enormous amount of scholarly research has been devoted to this passage. One of the perennial theological issues within the Christian Church has been the manner in which Christ is present in the elements of the Lord's Supper. And as we have noted, a consensus seems to be developing that *for Paul* Christ is really present in the bread and wine. It has also been observed that, as reported by Paul, Jesus does not simply say, "This is my blood." Instead, he is depicted as saying, "This cup (*touto to poterion*) is the *new covenant* (*diatheke*) in my blood."

According to Bultmann, the original formula that Paul probably embellished was: "This is my body; This is my blood."[25] Paul's formulation has led to speculation that he may have been more interested in stressing the identity of the bread with Christ's body than the wine with his blood. In the passage about the "single loaf" in I Corinthians 10, Paul argued that Christians are one body with Christ because they consume the loaf that is his body. There is no mention of wine. This has led W. D. Davies to suggest that Paul "refined" the simpler and more graphic original formula (i.e., "This is my body; this is my blood") because of his rabbinic background and his consequent discomfort with the sacrificial system.[26] While it is difficult to argue against a scholar of such standing, I believe that Paul was by no means embarrassed by the identification of the wine with Christ's blood. Davies asserted that Paul's "sober rabbinism" "led him . . . to recoil from an over-emphasis on the 'blood' element in the primitive Christian presentation of the Death of Jesus."[27] And Paul's reticence parallels what Davies calls "the more 'rationalistic' sections of the Christian Church," which have often been "antagonized by certain 'Evangelical' presentations of the Cross of Christ."[28]

As an outsider, it is my conviction that the "Evangelicals" may very well be closer to Paul's meaning than Davies would allow. Everything in Paul's thought points to the extraordinary breach he believed the death and Resurrection of the Christ had brought to the normative Jewish way of structuring existence. When Paul wrote of Christ crucified and risen as a *"skandalon"* to the Jews, I think he understood clearly how profoundly Judaism had been "stood on its head" by the paradox of the crucified and resurrected Messiah. Jewish scholars have rightly pointed out that nothing in the dietary rituals of Judaism is as taboo as the drinking of blood, even symbolically. Hence the drinking of wine as Christ's true blood represented an incredible transformation; that which had been most taboo in Judaism now became most sacred in Christianity. This should occasion no surprise. *The unique singularity of both the taboo and the sacred are such that they can be transformed into each other, especially in a religious revolution in which the paradoxical and the impossible overthrow the day-to-day world, as did the "good news" of the crucified Messiah.* I find nothing in Paul's writings to suggest that he shrank from the uttermost consequences of the religious revolution he helped to create.

Furthermore, everything we have studied about Paul points to his extraordinary capacity to make manifest the unmanifest. We have seen this in his interpretation of baptism; we shall also see it in his doctrine of Christ as the Last Adam. We see it in his understanding of the elements of the Lord's Supper. There was a very obvious anticipation of the identification of wine with blood in the biblical description of wine as *dam anavim,* the blood of the grape. The very redness of the wine and its capacity to intoxicate, thereby weakening the defenses of the ego, were reminiscent of blood. Wine was sacred to Dionysus, and his devotees ripped the god to pieces while intoxicated. Neither the Semitic nor the Hellenistic worlds of Paul's time were very far removed from an archaic sensibility in which blood and wine were comingled in sacrificial violence. On the contrary, even the rabbis were aware of the equation of wine and blood. If one can classify religious movements as Apollonian and Dionysian, the Judaism of the Pharisees can be regarded as profoundly Apollonian. Not surprisingly, the rabbis manifested a certain distrust of wine and, on occasion, they equated it with blood. Their awareness of the Dionysian aspects of wine were especially apparent in some of their homilies concerning Noah. They were especially critical of Noah as the founder of viticulture because of his drunkenness. One Palestinian rabbi went so far as to assert that the tree that caused Adam's downfall was the vine.[28]

Strong taboos, such as the rabbinic taboo against drinking blood, are seldom necessary save as a defense against exceedingly strong temptation. When a taboo is so strong that it defines the appropriate way to prepare meat to this day, there is very good reason to suspect that the taboo is a defense against a powerful though repressed temptation to drink blood that finally surfaced and came to symbolic expression in the awesome rite of the Lord's Supper.

When we ask what could have driven archaic man to lust after blood, we are reminded of the biblical conception that the life of a man or an animal, the soul of the creature, is to be found in the blood.[30] Men lusted after blood for its life-giving qualities. Implicit in Paul's equation of the wine of the Lord's Meal with the blood of Christ is the idea that no blood is truly life-giving save the blood that redeems from death. This belief was consistent with Paul's often-expressed idea that Christians are redeemed by becoming one with the Risen Christ. The idea that blood is life-giving was also related to another conception in biblical Judaism that had an impact on early Christianity. In biblical religion the blood of the sacrificial animal was reserved for God's consumption alone.[31] He who dared to consume such blood was guilty of one of the gravest of all trespasses: He placed himself in God's stead by partaking of His portion. We have already noted that the quest to become immortal through identification with the Risen and immortal Christ was in reality the quest for the godlike omnipotence already attained by him. To consume sacrificial blood at the Lord's Meal was thus another expression of the yearning for omnipotence that manifested itself in early Christianity in identification with Christ and ultimately with God in and through the Christ.

Scholars who look for Greek memorial feasts or "pagan" sacrificial rituals in searching out the origins of the Eucharist often pay too little attention to the extent to which primitive Christianity was an expression of fulfilled messianism within Judaism (C. H. Dodd has used the term "realized eschatology"). They also do not seem to have perceived how thoroughly the men of the early Church, and most especially Paul of Tarsus, intuitively grasped the full depth-psychological meaning of the transformation that had occurred in and to them. While there is an admitted element of abstraction in utilizing such terms as *ego, id,* and *superego* to describe religious cultures, there is some merit in regarding Christianity as a religious community that permitted the resurfacing of the archaic wisdom of the unconscious among its believers to a far greater extent than did Judaism. In contrast, the Judaism of the Pharisees can be regarded as a community that acculturated its members in such a way that the superego was more likely to hold sway. This does not mean that Pauline Christianity owes nothing to the Hellenistic world. On the contrary, the explosion of primary process images that had been repressed within Judaism made it possible for the new level of consciousness (Christianity) to integrate Hellenistic elements when it developed into its own unique religious culture. Furthermore, we have noted that Pauline Christianity did not involve the total abolition of the reality principle among Christians; that would only have been possible had the Messiah come in glory and completed once and for all his task. It was the genius of Christians like Paul that they were able to permit some of the archaic contents of the unconscious to surface, for the Messiah had in part abolished reality's limitations by overcoming his own death; nevertheless, the pleasure principle was not permitted to become entirely regnant, since the Messiah's return in glory and the final abolition of the reality principle and death lay yet in the future. In the meantime, Christians could only defeat death by becoming one with the Messiah. There was no more total identification with Christ than that achieved by feasting on his body.

Feasting on the body of the Messiah was also a restoration of archaic beginnings both for the individual and the group. For the individual, it restored the oldest method of achieving union with another being. For the group, it involved restoring one of the oldest modes of participatory worship. From the very beginning Jesus' death was associated with the Passover, the most archaic of Israel's festivals. There is disagreement on whether the Last Supper took place on the first evening of Passover or on the night before. Whenever the exact time, the events of the Last Supper and the Crucifixion took place at the Passover season and the meal was speedily assimilated to the Passover meal. The association of the redemptive acts of the Christian faith with Passover brought forth a wealth of images of enormous religious and emotional power, which included the contrasts between the new messianic world and the world Christianity claimed to have supplanted, between the aborted redemption achieved by Moses and the perfect redemption achieved by Christ, between the old and the new covenants, the old and the new Israels, and the contrast between the imperfect animal sacrifice of the old dispensation (the paschal lamb) and the perfect self-sacrifice of the Messiah (the true lamb of God), to name but a few.[32]

The contrast between the paschal lamb of Judaism and Christ as the perfect "lamb of God" is especially interesting. It is also relevant to some of the archaic aspects of the Lord's Meal. When Paul identified Christ as "our Passover" which has been "sacrificed," (I Cor. 5:8), he was undoubtedly following a tradition that had already established itself in the primitive church (cf. John 1:29 and I Peter 1:19–20). Christ as the "lamb of God" was thus identified with the most archaic sacrificial offering in Judaism. According to W. O. E. Oesterley, Passover originated long before the nomadic Israelites settled in Canaan and adapted themselves to agricultural life. Passover may originally have been a night, spring, and full moon festival of desert nomads.[33] Other scholars distinguish between an original Canaanite agrarian feast of unleavened bread and the sacrifice of the paschal lamb, which was probably an offering of desert herdsmen.[34] Oesterley believed that the ancient sacrifice was probably initially in honor of the moon god in order to insure the fertility of the flock and the herd.

The archaic character of the Passover offering is apparent in the account in Exodus:

> In the tenth day of this month they shall take to them every man a lamb. . . . Your lamb shall be without blemish, a male of the first year: And ye shall keep it up until the fourteenth day of the same month: and the whole assembly of the congregation of Israel shall kill it in the evening. And they shall take of the blood, and strike it on the two side posts and on the upper door posts of the house, wherein they shall eat it. And they shall eat the flesh in that night, roast with fire, and unleaven bread; and with bitter herbs they shall eat it. Eat not of it raw, nor sodden with fire; his head with his legs and with the purtenance thereof. And ye shall let nothing of it remain until morning; and that which remains of it until the morning ye shall burn with fire (Exod. 12:3–10).

The whole community took collective responsibility for the sacrificial slaughter, and all were required to take part in the consumption of the victim. Even the head and the genitals had to be eaten. Of all the sacrifices of ancient Israel, this best fits Freud's description of a totem meal.

Another indication of the archaic character of the paschal sacrifice can be found in the fact the Passover festival contains traces of a time when it involved the sacrificial killing of the first-born of men.[35] Exodus 13:2 contains the injunction that "whatever opens the womb among the children of Israel, both of man and beast" is to be "sanctified" unto God. According to the Danish scholar Johannes Pedersen, the verse originated at a time when the first-born of Israel were actually slain.[36] In the biblical account, the tenth plague visited upon the Egyptians was the slaughter of their first-born sons. God is depicted as commanding the Israelites to smear the blood of the paschal lamb on their doorposts lest they too suffer the fate of the Egyptians (Exod. 12:13, cf. 12:39). The biblical account clearly indicates that without this blood the Israelite first-born would have met the same fate as the Egyptian young.

In the ceremony of smearing the doorposts with the blood of the paschal lamb, it is as if the Israelites were saying to God, "We have slaughtered the lamb on your behalf. As evidence, we have smeared its blood on our doorposts. Accept the blood of the lamb in place of our children." When Paul said that Christians are "justified" by means of Christ's "blood" (Rom. 5:9), I think that he regarded Christ as the perfect paschal lamb (I Cor. 5:8). For Paul the difference between the old paschal lamb and Christ was that Christ truly redeemed all identified with him from the finality of death whereas the older sacrifice only redeemed the first-born of Israel from God's attack upon the Egyptians.

So there were, in fact, links between the Passover sacrifice and infanticidal sacrifice in archaic times. Paul's identification of Christ with the paschal lamb thus completes the circle. There should be no surprise that the Eucharist was speedily assimilated to the imagery of Passover. The real intent of the paschal sacrifice as a surrogate for human victims resurfaces in Christianity. When Paul referred to Christ as "our Passover," he provided yet another link with the most ancient sacrificial aspect of Passover. The old paschal lamb is no longer the surrogate; the divine-human victim reappears. Christ becomes the perfect paschal lamb whose blood redeems humanity from its ultimate peril.

Both ancient and modern authorities have also noted a parallel between the paschal lamb and the ram that God accepted in place of Abraham's son. In both sacrifices an animal took the place of a human victim. Shalom Spiegel, a Jewish scholar of exceptional insight and authority, has pointed out that *Jewish tradition often treated Isaac as if he had actually been slain by Abraham*.[37] Some of the traditions cited by Spiegel even claimed that after having been slain, Isaac was resurrected from the dead.[38] There are important parallels between Isaac and Jesus in these traditions. Isaac's trustful obedience even unto death is often stressed, and he is frequently treated as a vicarious atonement for Israel's sins. On Rosh Hashannah and Yom Kippur, God is implored to forgive rather than to slay the household of Israel because of the merits of Isaac's self-sacrificing obedience on Mount Moriah.[39] Spiegel explicitly rejected the notion that Jews took up the theme of Isaac's sacrifice as a vicarious atonement because of Christian influence. On the contrary, he maintained that the theme entered Christianity from Judaism and that Paul of Tarsus was the mediating link. Although the comparison is not explicit in Paul's extant writings, his insistence upon Christ as the perfect atonement for the sins of mankind suggests that for Paul as well as for those early fathers of the Church who explicitly take up the comparison, *Isaac's Akedah is an aborted Golgotha*[40]; Isaac is depicted as lacking the capacity to redeem mankind because he did not really die on his wooden pyre. Jesus is depicted as the perfect Isaac. In this contrast between Isaac and Jesus we again see an exemplification of Freud's contention that Christianity brings to manifest expression that which remains latent in Judaism.

Jesus' atoning death at the Passover season effects a convergence of redemptive themes. Jesus is the perfect lamb; he is also the perfect Isaac. His sacrifice is alone efficacious. Like the Law, Isaac anticipates redemption but can not achieve it. Jesus dies for all men's sins, but most especially for the sin of Adam. Jesus accepts death in order to undo the totality of God's infanticidal hostility toward man from the moment of Adam's first catastrophic disobedience to the small disobediences of ordinary men in Paul's own era.

Nevertheless, Jesus' atoning death can not save men from their sins unless it is in some sense their death. That is one of the most powerful reasons why the impulse to identify with Jesus by eating his very substance in the Lord's Meal became so overwhelming. We have already noted two other reasons for the impulse: the disciples' yearning for Jesus to be a present reality and their desire to achieve the reward of his perfect sacrificial obedience, namely, resurrection and immortality. It was the genius of Paul to express the redemptive yearnings of his contemporaries. He also helped them to find their way back to mankind's oldest and most effective method of becoming one with a beloved person or object. We do not know to what degree Paul's interpretation of the Lord's Meal as the loving consumption of the body and blood of the perfect sacrificial offering was original and to what extent it was an expression of the Christian religious and psychological revolution of which he was part. We do know that his insistence on the real presence of Christ in the Eucharist as well as his insistence on its superlative character as the perfect sacrificial meal is consistent with his other religious and psychological perspectives. It is my conviction, which is admittedly beyond proof, that Paul's understanding of the Eucharist was original with him.

On the surface, it might appear that Freud erred in his hypothesis that the Eucharist represents a resurfacing and a reenactment of the primal crime. Nevertheless, the reiteration throughout both Testaments of the theme that God requires the death of the Egyptian first-born, the *Akedah* and finally Calvary suggests that we ought not to dismiss Freud's hypothesis too hastily.

Biblical religion reflects an enormous amount of intergenerational ambivalence. The story of Abraham is typical. He yearns for the blessing of an heir to carry on his line, yet when the heir is on the point of manhood, Abraham is tempted by a heavenly voice to sacrifice his only son. The story of Jepthah and his daughter reveals a comparable ambivalence with a sorrier outcome. Sons, especially first-born sons, had good reason to fear parental anger. Undoubtedly the constantly repeated perception of the confusing mixture of parental love and hostility goes a long way to explain the image biblical man had of his God. In addition to being the beneficent progenitor, the Heavenly Father was a wrathful infanticide. When one measures the miniscule offense that brought the death sentence upon Adam and his progeny against the severity of the retaliation, there is no other way to regard the biblical God—unless somewhere in the recesses of the biblical man's psyche was lodged the memory of a crime great enough to cause men to believe they had reason to fear the inordinate retaliatory violence of the Heavenly Father. *Such a memory need not have been based on fact.* In the unconscious, there is no distinction between fact and fantasy; it could easily have been based upon fantasy, each man's fantasy of wanting to kill his own father or his latent hatred of the God whom he obeyed at the cost of his instinctual freedom. Both Judaism in the *Akedah* tradition and Christianity in the Golgotha tradition were convinced that nothing less than a filial victim or his surrogate would satisfy God's punitive cravings.

The perceptions of Freud and Paul concerning the Eucharist can be unified if we interpret the consuming of Christ's substance as the believer's way of uniting with the Son-as-victim in order to share in the Son's obedience unto death for the original crime against the Father. Nevertheless, such is the irony of human existence that the sons could only be quit of the original crime by replicating it. Here we have another instance of the convergence of the sacred and the sacrilegious we have already noted in the drinking of the wine of the Lord's Meal as Christ's blood. If Freud's myth presents an accurate psychological portrait, it was Paul's achievement to bring to the surface the persistent, latent sense of intergenerational strife and fear of retaliation that plagued biblical man. Paul was able to interpret intuitively the ritual of the Eucharist so that it became a way of dramatically replicating a crime that may seldom have been committed in fact but that was most assuredly committed over and over again in fantasy. Furthermore, the very act of dramatic representation became the means by which the psychological effects of the original crime were at least temporarily undone.

It is exceedingly difficult for most men to face frankly their com-

plex feelings of cannibalistic love and hatred toward their progenitors. If we ask ourselves what personal and social needs are met when
men gather together on their most solemn occasions and in their most
sacred precincts to eat the true body of the redeeming Son of God,
Freud's strange hypothesis at least helps us to understand some of
these needs. *Human solidarity is profoundly sensuous.* By partaking
of "one loaf" men achieve the most sensuous form of solidarity; they
become "one body." Both Freud and Paul understood human solidarity
as rooted in primordial criminality; by partaking of Christ, the true
"tree of life" at the Lord's Meal and thereby becoming "like God,"
men confess, repeat, and re-present the original crime, the crime of
sacrilegious consumption, which Freud, Paul, and the author of
Genesis regard as the primal source of human disorder. Finally, by
reenacting the "original crime" against the resurrected "victim" who
is both food and feeder, yet beyond all possible harm, men are able
dramatically to re-present the crime without incurring further guilt.

By consuming the body of the indestructible, life-giving redeemer,
the believer reenacts his craving to cannibalize his parental life-giver
without harming either himself or others. On the contrary, he does
much good, for he achieves a solidarity of shared complicity, aspira-
tion, and hope that is the basis of any viable human community.

Sacrificial worship is the most perfect form of human worship. It
effects a convergence of the destructive and the loving, the sinful
and the hopeful, the latent and the manifest in human consciousness
and experience. Furthermore, in true sacrificial worship the believer
achieves at least momentarily the goal that men will only achieve decisively if and when they return to the Garden, *an end of repression.* In
sacrificial worship little, if anything, is repressed: the life-giving
originator is consumed, the yearning for omnipotence expressed,
and the ultimate goal of true sexual union is achieved in that men
cease to be their separate selves and become, if only momentarily,
"one body."[41] Yet, while repression is momentarily ended, the order
of things continues as it must if there is to be a human future.

Paul's abiding influence cannot be ascribed to his excellence as a
theologian alone. The Pharisee could not have become the Apostle

apart from a profound emotional revolution. As with Luther, the convergence of Paul's personal emotional upheaval with that of millions of less articulate men helps to explain his extraordinary impact. Nowhere is that emotional revolution more visible than in Paul's understanding of the Lord's Meal. As with all religious and emotional upheavals, it was both profoundly conservative and radically progressive at the same time. The Eucharist looks back to the ironic beginnings of human social structure when men actually became one by eating each other and the hostility between the generations was enacted in titan-like violence. Such a backward glance to the archaic beginnings of the race enabled individual men to recollect the loving and destructive elements which were present in their own infancy. The Eucharist is also forward-looking. It terminated to some extent the need to handle archaic cravings by sublimation or repression, which had been characteristic of Judaism. It thus permitted the formation of a new community based on an old-new synthesis of the destructive, the loving, and the hopeful in intimate human experience. By his capacity to move backward to the beginning, Paul enabled his followers to move forward toward the End.

Chapter VII

The Apostle and
The Seed of Abraham

a. Apostle of the Messiah or Turncoat?

In the twentieth century Jewish students of the New Testament
such as Martin Buber, Leo Baeck, and Hans Joachim Schoeps have
sought to revise the negative evaluation that characterized the age-
old Jewish attitude toward Jesus of Nazareth. They have tended to
regard Jesus as a representative of the prophetic tradition. Buber has
even referred to Jesus as a brother. Nevertheless, as Günther Bornkamm has observed, Paul is still regarded as a stranger outside of the
mainstream of Jewish life of his time.[1] Whether Paul is seen as a
Hellenistic Jew alien to the authentic traditions of the Palestinian
heartland or as more pagan than Jewish, he is usually regarded as
one of the personalities most responsible for the Judeo-Christian split.
There is also a very strong tendency to ascribe to Paul a large measure
of responsibility for the religiously inspired anti-Semitism that has
brought so much sorrow to the Jewish people. "Jesus, yes; Paul,
never!" would seem to be the watchword of much of the thoughtful
Jewish New Testament scholarship in modern times.

I have never been able to share that judgment. It seems to me
that the issues to which Paul addressed himself arose entirely within
the religious and symbolic universe of the Judaism of his time and
that he never ceased to regard himself as a believing, faithful Jew
rather than as an apostate. The fundamental issues dividing Paul
from the Pharisees were the questions of whether Jesus was in fact

114

Israel's Messiah and whether his Resurrection had ushered in that period known as the "Days of the Messiah." In a word, the issue was what C. H. Dodd has called "realized eschatology." Paul had no doubt that the Messianic Age had commenced. His argument with his own people revolved around the question of how men ought to comport themselves in this new eon. He did not reject the belief that God had made known his will to the prophets, teachers, and sages of Israel. Without belief in God's revelation, his theology would have been meaningless. Paul's quarrel was over the question of where men stood in God's timetable for the salvation of mankind. He was convinced that the redemption his people had longed for had begun and that what they had seen obscurely could finally be understood clearly in the light of the Messiah's redemptive activity.

Paul was a Jewish messianist, not an anti-Semite.[2] Unfortunately, when men dwell in radically different "worlds" they are likely to regard each other with great hostility.[3] Each correctly perceives the other's "world" as a challenge to the integrity of his own. When brothers find themselves in such opposing spheres, as did Paul and the Pharisees, fraternal feelings are likely to become fratricidal.

Paul wrote some extremely harsh things about his fellow Jews after they ceased to share a common world (cf. I Thes. 2:14–16). His harshness was not unlike that of the members of the Community of the Scrolls.[4] When Paul wrote that his fellow Jews had proven faithless to their God, he was speaking of his own kin in what he regarded as a family dispute. Things are often said within the family that have a very different meaning when repeated by outsiders. It was not Paul but some of his spiritual heirs who interpreted his writings so that they contributed toward the climate of opinion that permitted Auschwitz.[5] Paul could not have anticipated the development of anti-Semitism, nor can he be held responsible for it.

Paul never ceased to love his people in his own way. When he declared: "For I would willingly be *Anathema* and cut off from Christ if it could help my brothers of Israel, my own flesh and blood" (Rom. 9:3), he expressed his concern for what he honestly believed to be Israel's salvation. Admittedly, Paul's conception of what constituted

Israel's salvation was not one that most of his Jewish contemporaries were prepared to accept. Nevertheless, there is no hint of malice in his attitude. He is impatient, harsh, at times furiously angry, but his negative feelings are based upon his inability to understand why his fellow Jews cannot see what he has seen and believe what he has come to believe: that God has redeemed both Israel and the gentiles through the death and Resurrection of Jesus of Nazareth.

We must not confuse Paul's impatience and anger with the degrading attempts to force conversion upon the Jews in the Middle Ages. Paul did not betray his own people, as did the apostates of a later time, by joining a larger, more powerful community. He left the stronger, established Jewish community to join a fragile, persecuted sect that made claims for itself that the civilized world, when it deigned to take notice, regarded as folly (I Cor. 1:18–29).

To this day, it is exceedingly difficult for thoughtful Jews to see Paul as other than an apostate and a betrayer, applying to him the kind of animus Jews have understandably felt toward members of their community who became Christian in medieval and modern times, and who often became malevolent persecutors of their own people. When Rabbi Solomon Ha-Levi (Saul) converted (c. 1390) and ultimately became Don Pablo de Santa Maria (Paul), bishop of his native city, Burgos, he proved to be one of the most violently hostile anti-Semites in all of Spanish history. In our own time, Reinhard Heydrich's Jewish grandmother was undoubtedly a factor in his infamous role as S. S. Obergruppenführer and author of the "final solution." The experience of the Jewish community with turncoats has been incredibly bitter. Jews have tended to interpret Paul's conversion and his denunciation of the Synogogue in that light, and, as a result, Paul has often been regarded as the prototype of all Jewish turncoats.

Understandable as such feelings may be, they do not do justice to Paul. The Apostle can only be judged against the religious and cultural background of his own rather than a later time. In Paul's time the Jewish world was divided into a number of sects, each of which claimed that it alone was faithful to God's word as revealed in

Sacred Writ.[6] Today, the heirs of the Pharisees have won the spiritual battle within Judaism; their interpretation of Judaism is regarded as authentic and normative. The Pharisees were already exceedingly powerful and influential in Paul's day, but they were by no means unchallenged. Then, rejection of Pharisaism was not equivalent to rejection of Judaism. Other groups, including the followers of Jesus, considered themselves loyal and faithful Israelites, although they offered competing interpretations of God's covenant with Israel. Paul offered one such interpretation.

Though the competing sects possessed irreconcilable differences, they did start out from certain common assumptions about God's dealings with Israel. Paul, the Pharisees, the Sadducees, the Community of the Scrolls, and the Jerusalem Church shared a common religious world based upon the biblical theology of covenant and election. Paul did not reject that theology either before or after his conversion. After his conversion, he placed a radically novel interpretation on what was meant by Israel's election and God's redemptive activity. Just as the Community of the Scrolls believed that only those faithful to its norms were the truly elect community, Paul and his fellow Christians were convinced that the people of God now consisted solely of those who were "in Christ." Paul's exclusivism paralleled that of the Community of the Scrolls. Paul did not reject the Scripture as the vessel of God's word to his people, but he did insist that it had to be interpreted in the light of the Messiah's death and Resurrection.

Even in his radical reinterpretation of Scripture, Paul was indebted to his rabbinic teachers. His belief that Scripture could only be understood in the light of the Messiah's career was in some respects derived from the rabbinic doctrine of the twofold Law. According to the Pharisees, the true meaning of the *written text* of Scripture could only be apprehended in the light of their own interpretative traditions, which they designated as the *oral Law*.[7] They insisted that the written and the oral Law were completely in harmony. However, they were frequently at odds with the Sadducees, who contended that the written text alone yielded an authoritative understanding of God's will. Thus the Sadducees rejected the doctrine of the resurrection of the dead because they saw no evidence for it in Scripture. In contrast, the Pharisees interpreted the Law by means of their oral traditions so that it yielded the doctrine of resurrection (although one searches Scriptures in vain for explicit evidence of this belief). When Paul contrasted the "letter" and the "Spirit" of the Law (II Cor. 3:6), he was pursuing an interpretative strategy that had been suggested by his rabbinic teachers.

By interpreting Scripture in the light of their own experience, the Pharisees made it a living document for their community while preserving a sense of continuity with the past. *This is exactly what Paul, the former Pharisee, did in the light of his own experience.* Paul's vision of the Risen Christ became the prism through which all of life took on new meaning. He never asserted, "I reject the Law and the covenant because of Jesus Christ." The sacred traditions of his people never ceased to be divinely inspired for the Apostle. His problem was that of harmonizing a tradition he regarded as holy with his own experience. Things would have been very different had Paul really thought of himself as an apostate or believed that he was creating a new religion. He did what any other religious Jew at the time might have done had he been similarly affected. Admittedly, Paul's experience involved so radical an alteration in his spiritual cosmos that the new meanings he ascribed to Scripture seemed to his former peers and their successors to be a total rejection of Israel's sacred traditions.

Both Paul's fidelity to his Damascus experience and the Jewish claim that the Apostle was deluded exemplify one of the most agonizing problems faced by any religion of revelation. When men believe that God reveals his will to them, a potential conflict is introduced between those religious institutions that claim a monopoly of interpretative authority and those charismatic individuals who claim that God has bypassed the institutions to reveal his will directly to them. Institutions tend to limit God's revelation to the distant past. They look with the gravest suspicion on "latter-day saints" and personalities like Paul. Nevertheless, there is absolutely no logical reason why God's revelation must be confined to any time, place, or person. Nor are there irrefutable criteria by which a claim such as Paul's can be judged to be less credible than the claim of Moses or Isaiah. There are, of course, practical reasons why institutions are compelled to reject latter-day revelations. Once an institution has become routinized, to use Max Weber's language, it can only regard the bearer of a new revelation as a disturber of the peace.[8]

Paul was such a disturber of the peace. He understood, of course, the profound contrast between his revelation experience and the traditions of the Pharisees (cf. I Cor. 1:18–28). Ironically, he felt compelled to be faithful to his encounter with the Risen Christ because of the very conception of a revealing God that he had received from his Jewish teachers. After Paul's time, and perhaps in reaction to Paul, the rabbis were to express the direst warnings about heeding "heavenly voices."[9] They also were to insist that prophecy had long since departed from Israel.[10] In Paul's time, however, the situation still retained a measure of fluidity. Since God had made known his will to other Israelites before him, Paul may have asked himself whether there was any possible basis for rejecting what had been so overwhelmingly revealed to him. He resolved the conflict between tradition and experience in favor of his own experience.

An echo of Paul's conflict may be discerned in II Corinthians: "Not that we are capable, of ourselves to put anything to our credit; for *our qualification comes from God.* He it is who empowered us to be *servants of a new covenant,* not of the letter, but of the Spirit. For the letter kills, but the Spirit gives life" (II Cor. 3:5, 6; italics added).

Paul understood the encounter with Christ at Damascus as well as his subsequent revelations to be gifts of the Holy Spirit. They had completely transformed his understanding of God's covenant with Israel, so much so that it had become "a new covenant." When He asserted "the letter kills, but the Spirit gives life," there was an implied biographical reference. By "letter" Paul undoubtedly meant Scripture as interpreted by the Pharisees in spite of their doctrine of the twofold Law. Before Damascus, Paul had known only the "letter" as his fundamental religious guide; after Damascus, his understanding of Scripture had been radically transformed by the gift of the Spirit, his vision of the crucified Messiah.

Nevertheless, Paul did not at any time question the Law's abiding holiness. Even his negative comparison of Moses with himself was not inconsistent with his view of the Law. To traditional Jews, Paul's assertion of his own superiority over Moses has the aura of the worst kind of arrogance if not blasphemy, yet Paul was moved by no such intent. He wrote to the Corinthians: "Now if the *ministry of death, engraven letter by letter on tablets of stone* appeared surrounded by such glory that the children of Israel could not fix their gaze upon Moses' face because of its glory (although it was only transient) how much more glorious will be the ministry of the Spirit. . . . for if the transient ministry had its time of glory, how much more is the enduring ministration glorious!" (II Cor. 3:7–11) (italics added).

No Jew can read Paul's characterization of Moses' leadership as a "ministry of death" without initial offense. The characterization became even more offensive when these words were used at a later time by non-Jews to further anti-Semitic violence. In fairness to Paul, it must be recognized that his harsh epithets were motivated by his belief that the God who had appeared to Moses had revealed himself more completely to the Apostle. Paul was convinced that Christ as Messiah had placed the giving of the Law in its proper perspective. He saw Moses as having presented an obscure, distorted version of God's revelation that could not bring salvation. He regarded his contemporaries who remained faithful to the old understanding of the Law as blind to its true import:

> We do not act as Moses did, who put a veil over his face (so that the people of Israel could not perceive the ultimate significance of that which was to be abolished). But their minds became hardened (and that is why) the same veil remains drawn, even today (in spite of everything) at the reading of the Old Covenant. But until

> today, every time that Moses is read, a veil lies over their minds. It cannot be removed because it is only through Christ that it is abolished (II Cor. 3:13–15).

The text is difficult. The imagery is rich. Paul contended that what had been veiled over in pre-messianic Judaism had been unveiled by Christianity. This would accord with the Freudian conception, which I accept, that the Christian religious revolution brought to the surface unconscious feelings about divine-human figures that had been repressed or sublimated in Judaism.

In any event, Paul wanted to contrast the old and the new way of understanding God's Law. That is very different than rejecting the Law entirely. Furthermore, although Paul strenuously objected to the circumcision of non-Jewish Christians, he did not normally object to the observance of the Law by Jews or Jewish-Christians.[11] Paul himself apparently remained to a degree an observant Jew. He submitted to the punishment of thirty-nine stripes inflicted upon him by Jewish officials five times (II Cor. 11:24). Had he really broken with his people he would not have submitted to this punitive discipline. The extent of Paul's observance of traditional Jewish Law remains a matter of scholarly debate, but he apparently maintained a semblance of observance when he was among Jews: ". . . to the Jews I was like a Jew, to gain the Jews. To those who live under the Law, as if I were under the Law—although I am not under the Law—to gain those who live under the Law" (I Cor. 9:20). Of course, no Pharisee could have written that he lived "*as if* I were under the Law . . . . to gain those who live under the Law," but the fundamental issue was the question of where men stood in the divine timetable. Paul behaved "as if" he were under the Law because he did not wish to give initial offense to religiously compliant Jews. His ultimate object in dealing with them was to reveal the Good News of the coming of the Messiah.

In reality it was not Paul but Jesus who instituted the irreparable breach with established Judaism.[12] The conflict between the claims of charisma and the authority of tradition that Paul's career elicited were far less intense than that produced by the career of Jesus. The often-repeated assertion that the Jerusalem Church was largely traditional save for its belief in Jesus as the Messiah can only be maintained if one assumes that Jesus' own disciples were ignorant of the extent to which Jesus himself was in conflict with established Judaism.[13] Jesus' extraordinary assertion of his own authority over that of the Law, especially as interpreted by the Pharisees, rendered any religious consensus with established Judaism unthinkable. When Jesus claimed the priority of his own authority in the Sermon on the Mount ("You have heard how it was said . . . but *I* say unto you. . . ."), and when he asserted that "The Son of Man is Lord of the Sabbath" (Matt. 12:8), he was claiming that he was the Lord of the Law. Jesus' followers regarded him as the absolute authority for their understanding of what obedience to God's Law truly involved. Within the sphere of a religion of revelation, claims such as those Jesus made for himself are either true or totally blasphemous. Jesus' contemporaries were compelled to take sides when confronted by his claims. From the point of view of established Judaism, Jesus was an *am ha-aretz*, one ignorant of the intricacies of traditional Law, who had the incredible audacity to claim an authority greater than Israel's wisest men. Neither the Pharisaic nor the Sadducean parties were prepared to accept his claims. It is a little silly for contemporary Jewish scholars to regard Jesus as one of Israel's greatest teachers. Within the context of Judaism as a revealed religion, he was either much more or much less.

Those who minimize the break between established Judaism and the primitive Church tend to interpret Paul's relations with the Church, and especially with Peter, in terms of mutual antipathy.[14] The Jerusalem Church has been depicted as committed to circumcision and the observance of the Law as preconditions for entry into the new community. It was supposed to have sent out emissaries to discredit Paul's work among the Gentiles, especially his opposition to the circumcision of Gentile converts to Christianity. Paul's "Judaizing" opponents are pictured as Jews zealous for the Law, whether or not they were actually emissaries of Jerusalem. What is at stake in this interpretation is the question of Paul's relations with his own people. Those who stress his hostility to the Jewish Christians usually picture him as turning his back on his own kin and creating a rival Gentile religion that was destined to maintain an antagonistic posture not only toward Judaism but even toward Jewish Christianity. This view is consistent with the image of Paul as the turncoat and founder of Christian anti-Semitism.

In all probability, the conflict between Paul and the Jerusalem Church and Paul and Peter has been exaggerated. On Paul's first visit to Jerusalem three years after his conversion, he stayed with Peter for fifteen days (Gal. 1:18). We have no record of their discussions, but it is difficult to imagine them ignoring the Christian religious revolution and they must have compared ideas. At a later date, Paul recognized Peter's mission to the Jews as somehow paralleling his own mission to the Gentiles (Gal. 2:27). There is reason to believe that Peter shared Paul's conviction that Christ was the "end of the Law." Peter is known to have dispensed with the dietary laws in his encounter with Cornelius the Roman centurion (Acts 10:1–48) and at the church at Antioch (Gal. 2:12).[15] While it is true that Paul criticized Peter bitterly for having withdrawn from table fellowship with Gentile Christians when "certain friends of James" arrived on the scene, the basis of Paul's criticism was that Peter was acting out of expediency rather than principle (Gal. 2:12–14). Paul does not suggest that there were theological differences between them either in Galatians or in Corinthians (cf. I Cor. 1:12ff.). Furthermore, at the Apostolic Council described in Acts 15:7–11, Peter is pictured as taking a position similar to Paul's with regard to the sufficiency of baptism without circumcision for the admission of Gentile converts. Hence there is no need to draw too great a contrast between Paul and Peter.

Similarly, the contrast between the Jerusalem Christians and Paul has probably been overdrawn.[16] Paul was of course insistent upon his independence with regard to the Jerusalem Church, but independence must not be seen as opposition. Paul's autonomy vis-à-vis the Jerusalem Church was based on the same conviction that motivated his independence over against the Pharisees. Paul believed that he had received both his commission as an Apostle and the content of his Gospel "through a revelation of Jesus Christ" (Gal. 1:12). At the Apostolic Council he was anxious not to cause a breach in the unity of the Church of Christ, but there is little doubt that he would have done so had the leaders rejected his position on the mission to the Gentiles. Even when Paul wrote that the leaders of the Church accepted his position, he quickly added that it was of little consequence to him that the "pillars" were regarded as leaders "since God has no favorites" (Gal. 2:6). The fundamental issue for Paul at the time of conversion and in the presence of the Jerusalem leaders was the word of God versus the word of man. No worldly preeminence could give any man the authority to add or detract from what God had revealed to Paul.

Although Paul was insistent about his independence of all human authority, his account of the Apostolic Council in Galatians emphasized the Council's agreement that "the Gospel of the uncircumcision" was commited to him. Paul described that accord: "And when they perceived the grace that was given to me, James and Cephas and John, who were reputed to be pillars, gave to me and Barnabbas the right hand of fellowship, that we should go to the Gentiles and they to the circumcised" (Gal. 2:9). There are some differences between the meeting described in Acts 15 and the one Paul described as an eyewitness in Galatians 2.[17] It is possible that we have the record of two meetings rather than one. In any event, both Acts and Galatians agree that Paul and the leaders of the Jerusalem Church arrived at a viable accord after a serious discussion of the issues between them. When Paul prepared to return to Jerusalem at the conclusion of his final missionary journey, he regarded that agreement as still binding (Romans 15).

We know, of course, that there was bitter opposition to Paul throughout his career. Some of it came, understandably enough, from the leaders of established Judaism. Much of it may have come from overzealous Gentile converts. According to Johannes Munck, the "Judaizing" antagonists at Galatia, who demanded the circumcision of Gentile converts, were not Jewish Christians but Gentiles who had become overly zealous for the observance of the traditions of the "old" Israel after they had entered the "new" Israel.[18] We need not dwell at length on Munck's arguments; they have been debated by scholars since their publication.[19] What is significant here is Munck's contention that there was a far smaller gulf between Paul and the Jerusalem Christians than most scholars had previously conceded. There was, of course, a major difference in emphasis. The Jerusalem Church was primarily interested in bringing the Gospel to Israel; Paul's concern, at least initially, was to proclaim the Good News of Israel's Messiah to the Gentiles. While this placed him in a very different sphere of activity, neither Paul's letters nor Acts suggest that Paul and the "pillars" of the Jerusalem Church were at odds on this division of labor or on the requirements for entry into the Church.

There were probably practical reasons for the division of labor. Paul may have been an embarassment and a danger to the primitive Church. Their situation was precarious enough, as the stoning of Stephen had demonstrated. The Pharisaic party in Jerusalem could hardly have felt well disposed toward a man they regarded as a turncoat. According to Walther Schmithals, the Jerusalem Church was as convinced as Paul that the Law was no longer necessary for salvation even for Jews.[20] However, they were compelled to maintain at least the appearance of being observant Jews. Living in Jerusalem, the leaders of the Church realized that they could not challenge the observance of the Law by Jews and remain free from persecution. Their attitude was probably similar to Paul's when he testified that he lived "as if" under the Law in order to win his people to the Gospel (I Cor. 9:20). They too lived "as if" under the Law. They had little choice if they were to remain in Jerusalem.

Perhaps the best way to describe the attitude shared by Paul and Jerusalem concerning the Law is that both were indifferent to its observance by Jews or Jewish Christians as long as those who observed it understood that salvation came from Christ, not the Law. Paul wrote to the Corinthians urging both the circumcised and the uncircumcised to "remain in the state (*klēsis*) in which he was when he was called" (I Cor. 7:18–20). Paul argued that "circumcision is nothing and uncircumcision is nothing" (7:19), by which he meant that there was nothing good or bad about observing or failing to observe the details of the Law. The Law was no longer the path to salvation. Whether it was observed or not in the Age of the Messiah was a practical rather than a religious matter. One might say that Paul intuitively understood the difference between religious and sociocultural motives for observing the Law. For the Christians of Jerusalem, observance was a matter of prudence. Such considerations could be justified theologically. The Church could not have been free to win souls for Christ in Jerusalem had it openly challenged the Law. Nevertheless, both Paul and the leaders of the Church agreed that outside of Palestine gentile converts need not accept the Law. Paul's counsel that both the circumcised and the uncircumcised ought to continue as they were before conversion was relevant to the situation of the Church. It is also evidence that he understood and approved of the stand of the Jerusalem Christians on the Law; it is very likely that they understood and approved of Paul's doctrine that Christ was the *telos* of the Law.

Paul could not have maintained relations with the Jerusalem Church that contained important elements of accord if, as some of his harsher critics have suggested, he had been a disloyal apostate. Admittedly, there must have been tension, but no matter how uncomfortable the men of Jerusalem may have felt with Paul, they must have understood something of what had happened to him. The irreparable breach with established Judaism had occurred the moment the Lordship of Jesus supplanted all other authorities within the Jewish community. Both Paul and his peers had been overwhelmed by the same redemptive experience; all believed that they had entered a radically new eon; all were convinced that God's Word could not possibly be understood as it had been before Christ's career. And all knew how extraordinarily difficult it was to communicate what they had received to the "unredeemed" among their own kin. Willy-nilly, they had been irrevocably wrenched out of all that had been customary in the "unredeemed" world.

Nevertheless, though he was estranged from the world of established Judaism, Paul cannot justly be regarded as in any sense lacking loyalty to his own people. He may have been deluded in believing that the Age of the Messiah was dawning, but there was neither malice nor infidelity in his commitment. Unfortunately, there was tragedy, because equally sincere men were convinced that to follow the Christian way would be to explode the very foundations of God's covenant with his people. Living in two very distinct worlds, Paul and his erstwhile rabbinic colleagues were condemned to become irreconcilable enemies, for each believed that what the other regarded as simple faithfulness was in reality gross rebellion against the Lord of Creation.

b. Israel's Conversion and Mankind's Salvation

In spite of the agreement at the Apostolic Council that Peter would "preach to the circumcised" and Paul to the "uncircumcised," Paul never ceased to hope that his own kin would accept Jesus as their Messiah. Although Paul regarded the mission to the Gentiles as his own distinctive calling, his desire to bring about the conversion of the Jews was at least as powerful as that of the Jerusalem Christians. Recent Pauline scholarship has suggested that the Apostle had his own plan for Israel's conversion that differed radically from the more direct methods of proclaiming the Christian message used by the Jerusalem Church. Paul believed that the success of his mission to the Gentiles was a precondition for the conversion of the Jews, who would only accept Christ *after* the conversion of the Gentiles. Thus Paul's conception of himself as Apostle to the Gentiles involved his hopes for his kin as well.

Paul's description of his call to be Apostle to the Gentiles (Gal. 1:15) was reminiscent of similar calls to Isaiah (49:1–6) and

Jeremiah (1:4), in which God designated his servants from the womb to be his messenger unto the nations: "Then God, who had specially *chosen* me while I was *still in my mother's womb* called me through his grace and chose to reveal his Son in me, so that I might preach the Good News about him to to the Gentiles" (Gal. 1:15–16). The italicized words are apparently quoted from Isaiah 49:1. Jeremiah had a somewhat similar conception of his own commission: "Now the word of the Lord came unto me saying 'Before I formed you in the belly I knew you and before you came forth out of the womb, I sanctified you and appointed you a prophet to the nations" (Jer. 1:4). Not only did Paul regard himself as greater than Moses, but he saw God's call to the prophets as an anticipation of his own commission as Apostle. There were, of course, differences in the message, the time and the manner of delivery. Nevertheless, Paul regarded himself as God's "chosen instrument" to carry Christ's name before the Gentiles (cf. Acts 9:15f.; 22:14f.; 26:16–18).

Paul's assertion that he had been designated for his role from his mother's womb is yet another example of his symbolic consciousness. Long before psychoanalysis gave conceptual expression to the fact that our lives are powerfully influenced by unconscious forces that have their inception in the history of the race and begin to express themselves in us *in utero,* Paul was aware of some of the archaic forces that had impelled him to his vocation. Again we note Paul's capacity to give religious expression to some of mankind's most profound emotional intuitions. It can, of course, be argued that Paul's use of the phrase was stylistic and dependent upon the usage of the prophets. There are, however, too many instances in which we have found Paul's symbolic consciousness at work for it to be likely that he was merely resorting to a literary convention. On the contrary, it is more likely that he used the symbolic conventions of his time to express the intuition that the forces that had impelled him to his role were at least as old as he was. One wonders whether this was one of the passages Freud had in mind when he referred to the "dark traces of the past" that lay ready to break forth into consciousness in Paul's soul.

According to Munck, Paul was convinced that Christ would not return to complete the work of salvation until he had first completed his labor of carrying the Gospel to the Gentiles and then brought about the conversion of the Jews.[21] He thus regarded his commission as Apostle to the Gentiles as part of a greater work, the redemption of both Jew and Gentile in Christ. If Munck is correct, Paul believed that the final consummation of the Messiah's labors depended upon him!

Paul's dream of a united mankind in which tribal and creedal differences would finally be obliterated was consistent with a compelling strain in Jewish thought that has persisted from the days of the prophets to our own time. Nowhere is Paul more prototypically Jewish than in his strenuous pursuit of this universalist vision. Perhaps the very stringency of Judaism's definition of itself over against the "gentiles" helped to generate the vision of a unified mankind. When carried to an extreme, Jewish particularism flies in the face of a profound yearning for union and community that has frequently moved men. That yearning may be utopian, but it remains powerful to this day. Among men such as Paul, it was probably intensified. One might speculate that the more particularistic a group becomes, the more likely it is to generate a universalistic ideology as a way out of its own isolation.

It is possible that Paul's upbringing in Tarsus influenced his desire to unify humanity in Christ. Living as a member of a minority in a predominantly non-Jewish city, Paul was probably more sensitive to the pain of ethnic and religious division than he would have been had be been reared in Jerusalem. There are profound differences between minority and majority group cultures.[22] Minority groups live on the sufferance of their hosts. This fact conditions their social and economic status, their behavior, and their self-perceptions. The difference between minority and majority group psychology is visible today in the differences between Diaspora Jews and native Israelis.[23] It would be foolish to suggest that Paul shared many of the complex psychological attitudes that have beset Diaspora Jewish identity in the twentieth century. The settings are radically different. Nevertheless, Paul's overriding concern for the ultimate unity of Jew and Gentile has had parallels throughout history among those Diaspora Jews who have dreamed of the unification of mankind as a way out of their own isolation as Jews.

Paul's dream of the unity of mankind "in Christ" was not one that the majority of his own kinsmen were able to share. Throughout Paul's missionary career, he encountered bitter and often violent antagonism from his own people. Acts is full of reports of Jewish opposition to Paul's missionary work (Acts 9:22–25, 29; 13:50; 14:2, 4–6, 19; 17:5–10; 18:4, 6; 18:12–17; 19:8–9; 20:18–35). Usually Paul preached in the local synagogue when he came to a new community. With predictable regularity the synagogue authorities were hostile and compelled him to establish his own churches. In some communities the traditionalists sought to kill him; in others they incited the populace and the authorities against him. As we have noted, wherever he preached, Paul was painfully aware of the immense gulf between himself and his kinsmen.

A typical incident is depicted in Acts 17. After Paul and Silas arrived in Thessalonika, he preached in the synagogue for "three consecutive sabbaths." He developed his arguments "from Scripture . . . proving how it was ordained that the Christ should suffer and rise from the dead" (2–3). Some Jews were convinced as were some Greeks. Paul's success and the controversial character of his preaching soon impelled the Jewish authorities to stir up the populace against him. Their complaint as recorded in Acts has a ring of truth about it: "The people who have been turning the whole world upside down have come down here. . . . They have broken every one of Caesar's edicts by claiming that there is another King, Jesus" (6–7). To the extent that the special circumstances of Paul's startling conversion became known, the opposition of the Jewish community must have been further aggravated.

The hostility between Paul and his kinsmen was mutual. Perhaps the most savage expression of Paul's anger is to be found in Thessalonians. Paul wrote to the Church at Thessalonika, apparently at a time of persecution:

For you, my brothers, have been like the churches of God in Christ Jesus which are in Judaea, in suffering the same treatment from your countrymen as they have suffered from the Jews, the people who put the Lord Jesus to death and the prophets too. And now they have been persecuting us, and acting in a way that cannot please God and makes them enemies of the whole human race, because they are hindering us from preaching to the Gentiles and trying to save them . . . but retribution is overtaking them at last (I Thes. 2:14–16).

In a later generation Jews were to be regarded by anti-Semites as "enemies of the whole human race" without qualification. In Paul's outburst, their enmity consisted in impeding his mission to the Gentiles. Since Paul was convinced that nothing less than the salvation of mankind was at stake, it is not surprising that he regarded any opposition to his work as enmity against mankind.

Paul's bitter condemnation of his own people in I Thessalonians lacks any moderating qualification. In fairness to Paul, we must remember that his hostility was entirely consistent with his people's way of handling religious conflict in that era.[24] The same methods are still often employed today by those Jews and non-Jews alike who are convinced that their special point of view is privileged before God.

Nevertheless, Paul's anger reveals only one aspect of his complex feelings towards his kinsmen. In spite of his anger, Paul fully expected "Israel after the flesh" to be converted to faith in Christ. Furthermore, Paul expected to play a crucial role in this conversion. In order to understand Paul's role as he projected it, we must consider the very special significance Paul ascribed to the collection of money he had gathered from the churches of Greece and Asia Minor to present to the Church in Jerusalem.

Romans 15 was written by Paul after he had gathered the collection from the Gentile churches and before he set out from Greece, presumably from Corinth, to journey to Jerusalem. He wrote that he expected to present the collection on behalf of the "poor among the saints" (Rom. 15:26) (i.e., the "saints" within the Church), upon arriving in Jerusalem. This chapter is one of our best sources for understanding Paul's preoccupations immediately before he set out with the all-important gift for the Jerusalem Church.

It is evident from Romans 15 that Paul feared for his own safety in Jerusalem. He asked his readers to pray that he might "escape the unbelievers in Judaea." He also asked that they pray that the gifts he brought be "accepted by the saints" (15:31). Paul was well aware of the hazards of his enterprise.

In view of the variety of interests Paul had challenged, as well as the unfortunate example of the stoning of Stephen, the visit to Jerusalem was indeed a precarious venture. Nevertheless, Paul felt compelled to make the journey because of the decisive importance he attached to collection. Both Nickle and Munck stressed the fact that the collection was no mere gift of earthly valuables. *It was to be Paul's proof to all in Jerusalem, Christian and Jew alike, that the Gentiles had found salvation in Christ.* Paul had gathered the collection with difficulty over a period of several years. The venture had met with opposition in Corinth and perhaps in Galatia (cf. II Cor. 8:1–9:15; I Cor. 16:1; Gal. 2:10). According to Acts, at least eight companions representing the Gentile Churches accompanied Paul (20:4f.). Munck believed that the presence of so large a delegation was Paul's way of making the delivery of the collection "an unconcealable public affair."[25] Paul wanted all Jerusalem to learn of the mighty deeds wrought by Christ for the salvation of mankind by the conversion of the Gentile world.

Both Munck and Nickle argued that Paul believed that the presentation of the collection would be one of the culminating acts in the drama of mankind's salvation preceding Christ's glorious return. Paul believed that the Messiah had appeared in Jerusalem. The city remained for him even after conversion what it was for his rabbinic contemporaries, the *omphalos,* the navel of the universe, the very center of the cosmos.[26] It was in Jerusalem that the final acts in the drama of salvation would unfold. As Isaiah and Micah had prophesied, it was to Jerusalem that the nations would come in the last days and it was from Jerusalem that the word of the Lord would finally flow (Isa. 2:2f.; Mic. 4.1f.).

According to both Munck and Nickle, Paul saw his arrival in Jerusalem accompanied by the representatives of the Gentile churches as the fulfillment of Isaiah and Micah's prophecy.[27] He was convinced that God had designated him to be the "light unto the nations" whom the prophets had anticipated. Paul saw the delivery of the collection as a demonstration of the love of the converted nations for their Jewish brethren in Christ. And he believed that when he returned in triumph, all Jerusalem would know by the gift that God had bestowed his saving grace upon the Gentiles. The Jews would thereupon be converted and God would do the rest!

I find the Munck Nickle hypothesis extremely plausible although it has been challenged by some very distinguished scholars.[28] It rings true psychologically. Consider Paul's situation after his conversion: He had turned his back on everything he had previously known and believed. He was undoubtedly regarded by his former teachers and colleagues as either a madman or an apostate. Even his new colleagues were less than unanimous in their approval. Many rejected his claim to be an Apostle. Others offered a host of ungenerous comments about him. Even the leaders of the Jerusalem Church were probably more comfortable with him in faraway Greece and Asia Minor than in Judaea. Paul's extraordinary sensitivity to the underlying dynamics of the Jewish religious world was paralleled by his awareness of the way others reacted to him. His apologia in II Corinthians 10:1–13:10 exhibits his acute sensitivity to the opinions of others. Only one conviction permitted him to transcend that sensitivity: He believed his authority came directly from Christ (Gal. 1:1; 1:11; cf. I Cor. 1:1; II Cor. 1:1; Rom. 1:1). It had been used to "build up" rather than "pull down" his followers (II Cor. 10:8). Even if the entire world rejected his message, Paul would have persevered.

Nevertheless, no man who worked as tirelessly for the conversion of others—literally for the conversion of all mankind—could have been without hope of vindication. Paul may have anticipated that the delivery of the collection would be the occasion of his final vindication. One psychoanalyst views the journey to Jerusalem with its predictable perils as evidence of Paul's masochism, but there is no reason to regard the enterprise as unduly masochistic.[29] Paul's quest for vindication and the belief that he would ultimately achieve it sufficiently explain why Paul not only ignored the dangers but spent so much time assembling the collection and preparing to return to Jerusalem.

Rejection of the wisdom of his teachers was more serious for Paul than rejection of his natural father. The importance of fidelity to what had been transmitted was so great in rabbinic Judaism that long lists of successive rabbinic traditionaries were often cited in establishing the authority of a tradition. Paul's rejection of his teachers' authority and his assertion of the priority of his own authority even over that of Moses must have created an enormous conflict within him. To the extent that there was a corner of his psyche which never ceased to be a Pharisee, Paul must have retained some feelings of guilt for having departed from what he had received. Such feelings would have been emotionally akin to the guilt parricide might engender. To reject the authority of the fathers is in a way to kill them, especially in a religious system in which the spiritual fathers were more important than one's natural father.

It must be remembered that the teacher-pupil relationship in Judaism transcended even the father-son relationship. There is a rabbinic tradition that if a son finds both his father and his teacher in mortal danger, he must first rescue the teacher. In Jewish teaching, the father brings the son into this world; the teacher brings him into the World-to-Come.[30] The teacher's act of paternity is thus the greater.

Paul was only able to "kill" his old fathers emotionally after he had found a "new obedience" in Christ.[31] Although I have avoided comparisons between Paul and Luther, both men were able to free themselves of the injunctions of their old fathers—in Luther's case Father Hans, in Paul's his rabbinic teachers and perhaps his natural father—because they had found a new submission, Luther as a monk and Paul as Christ's Apostle. Nevertheless, I believe that Paul never ceased to yearn for a reconciliation with his old teachers, not on their terms, of course, but on his own. Paul hoped the day would come when his former colleagues would acknowledge that he had been right. Just as he expected humanity to achieve its true unity through the obliteration of the old distinctions of Jew and Gentile, he may also have hoped that his teachers' conversion would release him from a gnawing sense of guilt that he had betrayed them. I believe Paul hoped to find a way to be loyal to *both* his old and his new fathers. One of the virtues of the Munck-Nickle hypothesis, that Paul saw delivery of the collection as the event that would finally bring about the conversion of the Jews, is that it fits together with a plausible reconstruction of Paul's motivations for making a journey so fraught with hazard.

At first glance, Paul's expectation that the presence of non-Jewish Christians laden with gifts would bring about Israel's conversion seems startlingly overoptimistic, especially in view of the fact that neither Jesus nor the preaching of the "saints" had achieved this end. Objectively Paul was mistaken, but, as we shall see, his expectation was not without a certain psychological plausibility. The key to Paul's optimism can be found in his conception of the conflict between the Church and the Synagogue: The imagery that Paul utilized to describe that conflict was *fraternal strife.*

Paul introduced the theme of fraternal conflict in Romans 9–11 after expressing his sorrow that Christ had been rejected by his own "flesh and blood" (Rom. 9:5). He held that God would only bestow salvation on those who are truly worthy to be reckoned among Abraham's seed. Paul argued that mere physical descent from Abraham is not sufficient for inclusion among those God has destined for salvation. Paul used a series of Christian *midrashim* or homilies to make his point. He cited the examples of Isaac and Jacob to reinforce his point that physical descent from the first patriarch by itself was insufficient for membership in God's elect community. Both patriarchs were *chosen by God* to be "true" descendants of Abraham, although each had a brother who might have inherited

Abraham's blessings. In Paul's homilies, Isaac and Jacob became prototypes of the Church, whereas the rejected brothers, Ishmael and Esau, became prototypes of the Synagogue. The Church was the chosen brother; the Synagogue was the rejected brother (Rom. 9:6–13).

Paul marveled at what he believed to be God's choice of the Gentile Christians to become the true "Israel." He saw in it a fulfillment of Hosea's prophecy: "I will say unto them that were not my people, 'Thou art my people' and they shall say, 'Thou art my God'" (Hosea 2:23; cf. Rom. 9:25–26). For Paul, the people who "were not my people" were the non-Jews who said "Thou art my God" by their faith in Christ. According to Paul they were called "children of the living God" (Rom. 9:26). Thus election has passed from Abraham's descendants "according to the flesh" to those who were his spiritual descendants (cf. Rom. 4:13–17). For Paul only Christians were spiritual descendants of Abraham and, as such, the favored sons. The "unbelieving" Jews were, of course, the rejected offspring.

From the Jewish point of view, the most controversial aspect of these homilies was Paul's radical reinterpretation of the doctrine of the election of Israel so that uncircumcised Gentiles were regarded as Abraham's true descendants. Paul's identification of Jewish "unbelief" with Pharaoh's enmity toward both God and Israel was even more startling to religious Jews. Paul argued in another *midrash* that just as God had his hidden reasons for hardening Pharaoh's heart, he now had his reasons for treating Israel as he had once treated Pharaoh (Rom. 9:14–18). The hardening of Pharaoh's heart was necessary so that God could display his mighty deeds of redemption against Egypt; so, too, God had hardened Israel's heart against belief in her Messiah so that the Gentiles might first be redeemed (Rom. 11:12).

Pharaoh was, of course, regarded by Jews as the archetypal enemy, who sought to exterminate the entire people. Paul's identification of the "unbelieving" Synagogue with Pharaoh was therefore a matter of profound offense. The offense was compounded when Paul also identified the "old" Israel with the worshipers of Baal who killed the prophets, broke down the altars, and attempted to slay the prophet Elijah (with whom Paul identified himself) (Rom. 11:3–6).

Paul's picture is clear. The "old" Israel has become God's enemy. The enmity will not last forever, although it can only be terminated by the "old" Israel confessing Jesus Christ as Lord. If Jews fail to make this confession, they deserve and can expect no better fate than that which befell Pharaoh, the followers of Baal, Sodom and Gomorrah (Rom. 9:29), or any other enemy of God.

Because of its enormous emotional power, Paul's image of Israel as the unfaithful brother rejected by God has strongly influenced both the Church's self-understanding and her interpretation of the Synagogue. One of the most depressing aspects of my research on Paul has been the dreary regularity with which even well-meaning Christian commentators, following in the spirit of Paul's interpretation of the conflict, have seen Israel's inability to accept Jesus as the Messiah as deliberate, willful offense against God. Thus C. K. Barrett wrote of Israel's "defection," calling Israel "an apostate people."[32] Those Jews who remained faithful to their own sacred traditions were designated by Barrett as mired in "Jewish apostasy."[33] The same tendency is visible in Munck, who wrote of Israel's "guilt" and "impenitence" in rejecting Christ.[34] The examples could be multiplied endlessly. What is so sad about this point of view is that even the more liberal Christian commentators seem unable to regard Judaism as a distinctive religion with its own autonomous integrity; instead, they look at it as an apostate form of Christianity.

This interpretation of Judaism is a direct corollary of Paul's insistence that the Church is the true Israel and that the "old" Israel could only be saved by conversion to Christ. The effect of this interpretation of Israel's "unbelief" has been to widen immeasurably the gap between the Church and the Synagogue. To be a Jew faithful to one's own traditions was for Paul to be in willful enmity, rebellion, and apostasy against God.

In fairness to Paul, I must again say that there was no special malice involved in his point of view. When, for example, Paul likened Israel to Sodom and Gomorrah, he merely quoted Isaiah

1:9, in which the prophet offered a comparable denunciation of Israel in his own time (Rom. 9:29). On the contrary, Paul was trying to be as generous toward his spiritual adversaries as the logic of a religion of revelation could permit. My own dissent from that kind of religious ideology is motivated by a desire to accept the integrity of every man's sacred traditions. It is my conviction that there are no false gods, that all gods are true, at least in the sense that the sacred traditions of mankind are functional expressions of the life and the values of the peoples who maintain them. This position arises very largely out of my horror at the exclusivism of biblical religion.

Paul's insistence that the "old" Israel has become like Ishmael (Rom. 9:6–9; cf. Gal. 4:21–31) can also be seen as yet another example of the working of Paul's symbolic consciousness. The idea that the conflict of the "descendants" of Isaac and Ishmael or Jacob and Esau was largely a matter of fraternal rivalry was already implicit in the original biblical narratives. In rabbinic Judaism the conflict between Rome and Judaea was often depicted symbolically in terms of the strife between Jacob, the studious, contemplative brother, and Esau, the ruddy, violent hunter.[35] Of course, the oldest and most tragic fraternal conflict in Scripture is that of Cain and Abel. It would be difficult for a psychoanalyst to fault Paul when he interpreted the rivalry between Church and Synagogue as fraternal. The projection of sibling rivalry onto religious strife is by no means the only component in the age-old Judeo-Christian conflict, but it is an important one, particularly when the conflict is focused, as it was for Paul, on the question of who was God's beloved child.

At a later date, the psychological power of these images was immensely strengthened when the Crucifixion was regarded as a deicide. Jews were then seen as veritable murderers of God. Behind the twin assertions that the Church was the true Israel and that the "old" Israel had been cast off as Christ-killers was the implied assertion, "We Christians are the Father's favorites. You Jews have been rejected by the Father. You tried to murder Him."[36]

Such an accusation translates the emotions of religious conflict into the emotions of family strife. Admittedly, there is more involved in religious conflict than family strife. Nevertheless, the oldest and most abiding sources of both love and hate are to be found within the context of the nuclear family. It is therefore not surprising that the conflicts of great religious communities have replicated the emotional conflicts of the family on a grand scale. Norman O. Brown has suggested that ultimately all fraternal conflict is over the father's inheritance and perhaps even his body, at least at the level of the underlying emotional content.[37] This description is certainly in harmony with Paul's symbolic representation of the Judeo-Christian conflict.

We can now understand why there was a certain psychological plausibility to Paul's belief that the conversion of the Jews would begin in earnest when he arrived in Jerusalem with the collection. Paul believed that by stirring his own kinsmen to envy the Gentile Christians he would move them to adopt the new faith. Paul asserted that God's ultimate purpose in making him Apostle to the Gentiles was to make the Jews jealous of the "new" Israel thereby to move some to conversion. Thus Paul saw his mission to the Gentiles as the prelude to his culminating task, that of winning over the Jews. According to Paul, God's purposes would not be fulfilled until Jew and Christian became one people of God. He expressed his purpose as Apostle to the Gentiles: "I have been sent to the Gentiles as their Apostle, and I am proud of being sent, *but the purpose of it is to make my own people jealous of you, and in this way save some of them"* (Rom. 11:14; italics added).

Envy or jealousy hardly seems an appropriate motive for religious conversion until one reflects on the extent to which Paul interpreted the Church-Synagogue conflict in terms of fraternal strife. The source of fraternal rivalry is almost always envy lest the parents bestow a greater measure of love on the rival sibling. Paul's plan to stir his kinsmen to jealousy was psychologically consistent with his underlying intuition of what the rivalry between Church and Synagogue was all about. Although we lack any way of validating the conjecture, it is reasonable to assume that Paul's perception of the nature of the conflict reflected his own experience. We know that he had a sister living in Jerusalem (Acts 23:16). Although we have few other details concerning his family background, it is possible that as a Pharisee Paul experienced the very same kind of envy of Christians, perhaps subliminally, that as a Christian he hoped to stir up in his kinsmen.

Mutual envy probably plays an important role in the Judeo-Christian encounter to this day. In spite of their insistence on the unique destiny of Israel before God, traditional Jews often envy non-Jews their greater security and liberation from nonfunctional behavioral constraint. It would also seem that non-Jews often envy Jews by taking seriously Israel's pathetic delusion of somehow being God's favored child, yet claiming that the election has passed to the Christian Church. Hannah Arendt observed that both the Pan-Slav and the Pan-German forms of tribal nationalism that flourished in the first decades of the twentieth century claimed that God had elected their respective tribes and had ordained the tribe's right to dominate its neighbors. She claimed that much of the extraordinary virulence of the anti-Semitism of the Pans was due to their envious fury at Israel's older claim to be the elect of God.[38] Paul's apparently naïve desire to move his kin to jealousy is fully consistent with the profound psychological depth the Apostle manifested elsewhere in his letters.

Paul was convinced that Israel's jealousy would be followed by conversion and that conversion would lead to the general resurrection and the final salvation of mankind: "Since their rejection meant the reconciliation of the world, do you know what their acceptance will mean? Nothing less than life from the dead!" (Rom. 11:15). Thus *Paul saw Israel's conversion as the supreme event within God's redemptive plan.* Once Israel was "saved," at least representationally, the final sequence of eschatological events would commence. Christ would return. The dead would be resurrected and Christ would hand over the kingdom to God the Father, "having done away with every sovereignty, authority and power" (I Cor. 15:25).

It should be obvious that, whatever the merits of Paul's eschatological vision, it was not the expression of an apostate's malice. Rightly or wrongly, Paul regarded himself as playing a role in the redemption of both his own people and mankind second only to Jesus.

If this interpretation of Paul's conception of his role and Israel's place in the divine economy has merit, one must ask whether there was not something inflated, grandiose, and perhaps even megalomanic in Paul's extraordinary conception of himself and his idea of what he believed he could accomplish. There is, of course, the possibility that Paul's identification with Christ was so complete that he willingly set in motion the chain of events leading to his own martyrdom (cf. II Cor. 5:8ff.; 12:10f.; Phil. 1:21–26). In any event, things did not turn out as Paul had anticipated. When he arrived in Jerusalem, his kinsmen were stirred to anger rather than jealousy and conversion. He was attacked in the Temple and taken into custody for his own safety by Roman soldiers, and the events leading to his eventual death were initiated.

Paul's mission to convert his own people ended in failure. Nevertheless, the Apostle cannot be regarded as a deluded visionary whose pretensions were finally destroyed by a contemptuous world. In the light of history, Paul's perception of himself as Apostle to the Gentiles proved correct to a degree that exceeded his most grandiose expectations. No other figure in the history of the Church has been as influential in interpreting the meaning of the Christian message from generation to generation. Nor is it likely that Christendom will ever again know an interpreter of comparable authority and influence. Ironically, Paul's rabbinic teachers provided their pupil with much of the training he used to argue so persuasively against them. The Pharisees were the foremost interpreters of Scripture and taught Paul the interpreter's skills and methods. Paul's spiritual gifts, especially his symbolic consciousness and his ability to make manifest the unmanifest, were, of course, his own. Where the Pharisees taught Paul how to unveil the deeper meanings embedded in the text of Scripture, he sought to uncover the deeper meanings to be discovered in the life, death, and Resurrection of the one he believed to be Israel's Messiah. Yet, Paul could only build on what he had received.

In discussing the factors that led to my interest in Paul, I remarked that I had titled this book *My Brother Paul* with considerable sadness. I recognize Paul as a brother; I concur in his judgment that the Judeo-Christian encounter is fraternal. Regrettably I cannot pretend that I find fraternity devoid of fratricide. There has always been a fratricidal element in the meeting of Church and Synagogue. I find no malice in Paul's identification of the Synagogue as the wayward, unfaithful brother. Nevertheless, I believe the identification has had predictable results from which Paul would have shrunk in horror. Paul's insistence that before God men are divided into collectivities of faithful and perfidious brothers, an insight he had perhaps acquired from his rabbinic teachers and the biblical doctrine of Israel's election, helped to release fratricidal emotions that thereafter became regnant in Judeo-Christian relations.

The sorry story of Christian violence and Jewish contempt (for Christian violence reinforced the negative opinion Jews had of their brother religion as well as their own sense of chosenness) ultimately derived from the fact that human beings are born incomplete and seek throughout life to replicate the protective enclaves they knew in infancy.[43] Men apparently find it exceedingly difficult ever to leave behind the loves and hatreds of the world of childhood. Paradoxically, it was Paul's greatness that he repressed that world less than did his former peers among the Pharisees. Where men find no familial relationships, they must apparently create them lest they be stricken with the terrifying sense of their own hopeless solitude in an unfeeling cosmos. They project the fantasy of a Heavenly Father who chooses among brothers as the protective capacities of their earthly fathers diminish in credibility. Their fratricidal conflicts are the quests of the insecure for paternal potency. They turn fellow men into brothers so that they can war over the illusory patrimony of earthly or heavenly progenitors. In every age they repeat the tale of Cain and Abel, Isaac and Ishmael, Jacob and Esau, and Joseph and his brothers. Even the sacrificial death of Jesus may contain an element of fratricide. After all, "the first born of many brothers" must endure death's perils so that the younger brothers may live.

Was Paul's dream of one humanity united in Christ a hopeless illusion? Not entirely. Paul maintained that the final end to fraternal strife was inseparable from overcoming suffering and mortality. Like most apocalyptic visionaries, Paul's dream was based on a thoroughly realistic assessment of the world he lived in. He was, of course, far more optimistic about the imminent abolition of the world of the Old Adam than the evidence of history would seem to justify. Two thousand years after the Apostle's career, the world of suffering and mortality continues to hold sway. Furthermore, fraternal strife exists within the "body of Christ" as well as between the Church and other religious communities. Nevertheless, I believe Paul was absolutely correct in feeling that fraternal discord would cease when the drama of human history was terminated, when death was overcome, and when God would become "all in all." Before strife and suffering can come to an end, the Old Adam must give way to the new. Thus Paul was indeed right that fratricidal strife would last as long as mankind as we know it endures.

Chapter VIII

The Last Adam

Paul shared with many of his Jewish contemporaries the belief that human existence is profoundly exilic in character and that the goal of all things is restoration to their original, unflawed condition. In the imagery of the apocryphal, pseudepigraphical, and rabbinic writings, Adam is the first exile; each of his descendants recapitulates in his own way the original father's fate. Exilic existence will not end until Adam's progeny return to Eden out of which they have come. Once restored to the Garden men will enjoy the deathless felicity God originally intended for mankind. Insofar as the Messiah is regarded as the decisive agent in the process of cosmic restoration, as he was by Paul, his function is to undo the damage done to creation by Adam and to restore Adam's heirs to his condition before the Fall. Paul therefore designated the one he regarded as the Messiah as the Last Adam.

We have observed that the heart and center of Paul's existence after conversion was to be found in the simple but awesome proclamation that "Christ is risen."[1] In view of his faith that Christ was in the process of defeating "the last enemy" (I Cor. 15:26), it is not surprising that he meditated extensively on the origins of death. We have noted that Paul did not regard either death or physical suffering as purely natural events. For Paul, as for his Jewish contemporaries, human existence was a drama of exile and return, of sin and redemption, played out before mankind's Heavenly Father. To the extent that twentieth-century scholars can still make a meaningful distinction between the Hellenistic and Jewish components of first-century Christianity, Paul's conviction that human mortality ultimately derived from Adam's rebellious behavior reflected the Jewish component. When Paul asserted that death and corruption entered the world as a consequence of Adam's sin, he was very much within the world of first-century Jewish theology.

In recent years Christian scholars such as W. D. Davies, Robin Scroggs, and C. K. Barrett have studied the relevance of rabbinic speculation concerning Adam in order to understand Paul's theology. Scroggs, in particular, has pointed to the importance of both rabbinic and apocryphal speculation (if indeed the two tendencies can be separated) concerning the Fall of Adam for an understanding of Paul's interpretation of Christ's role as "the Last Adam" who reverses the condemnation brought upon the race by the first Adam.

According to Scroggs, rabbinic tradition maintained that (1) before sinning Adam enjoyed *royal prerogatives* over all of creation: Just as God is king on high, Adam's original destiny was to be king below. (2) Adam originally possessed *superlative wisdom,* far greater than that of the angels. (3) Adam was truly made in the *image* (*eikon*) *of God.* Adam therefore resembled God himself rather than the angels, who were originally inferior to him. (4) Adam possessed a *glorious nature.* The ball of his heel outshone the sun. Adam thus partook of the very glory of God insofar as was possible for a created being. (5) Finally, *Adam possessed cosmic dimensions.* He was reduced to the size of mortal men only after his disobedience.[2]

Scroggs' categories summarize conveniently and accurately rabbinic speculation about Adam before the Fall. I concur with his estimate of the significance of these speculations: The rabbinic-apocryphal picture of Adam before the Fall resembles that tradition's image of what man will be like in the World to Come. The deathless, glorified, felicitous existence enjoyed by Adam before sinning is the kind of existence that awaits the righteous in the Age to Come. Adam originally enjoyed the kind of existence God intended all men to savor. When the corruptions of the present era are finally undone, Adam's progeny will be restored to the felicitous existence their primal father was meant to enjoy. Although there is an elusive and an ambiguous character to rabbinic speculation concerning the World to Come, which makes it exceedingly difficult to assert that any doctrine represents the rabbinic consensus, it would seem that there was at least agreement that the dead would be resurrected and that those found acceptable by God would enjoy some kind of bliss. My caution in suggesting more than this reflects the admonition implied in the well-known saying of R. Joḥanan, a second-century Palestinian teacher: "R. Joḥanan said: Every prophet prophesied only for the days of the Messiah, but as for the World to Come (i.e., the last age after the final judgment of mankind), 'Eye has not seen nor ear heard what God has prepared for those who wait for Him.' (Isa. 64:4)" (Berakhoth 34b). It is possible that Joḥanan's comment reflected a rabbinic reaction to the increasingly successful Christian movement. Nevertheless, there was a link in rabbinic myth between the felicity that awaits the righteous and the immortality lost by Adam at the Fall. The rabbis frequently utilized the term *gan 'eden,* the Garden of Eden, to refer to the paradise to come. Even the English language cannot avoid a certain linguistic concurrence in this idea; the same word is used for both the Paradise to be regained and the Paradise lost.

Although no single rabbinic reflection on the World to Come can be taken as authoritative, there is one statement by Rab, a third-century Babylonian authority, which may be relevant to our study of Paul. According to Rab,

> The World to Come is not like this world. In the World to Come there is neither eating nor drinking; there is no begetting of children or business; no envy or hatred or strife; but the righteous sit enthroned with their crowns on their heads and enjoy the lustre of the Shekhinah, as it is written, "And they beheld God, and ate and drank" (Exod. 24:11)—they were satisfied with the radiance of God's Shekhinah; it was food and drink to them (Berakhoth 17a).

This saying resembles Jesus' reply to the Sadducees concerning the marital status of a woman who had successively married several brothers according to the law of levirate marriage. Jesus said: "When they rise from the dead men and women do not marry; no, they are like the angels in heaven" (Mark 12:24; cf. Matt. 22:30, Luke 20:34-36). Behind the sayings of Joḥanan, Rab, and Jesus, it is possible to discern a common conviction that the order of things as we know it offers few hints concerning existence in the Age to Come. As we shall see, Paul shared this conviction (cf. I Cor. 15:46-50).

There is, however, a link between the rabbinic traditions concerning the World to Come in which "there is neither eating nor drinking" and the traditions concerning Adam's original condition. Among the most interesting are those that maintained that Adam possessed cosmic dimensions before the Fall.[3] According to these traditions, before sinning Adam extended from one end of the world to the other. Afterward he was so reduced in size that he could hide himself "among the trees of the garden" (Gen. 3:8). Adam is thus depicted as originally coextensive with the entire created order.

When we ask whether there is any biological state that might correspond to Adam's primal condition as described in these traditions, we can point to the prenatal state. In the womb there is neither dichotomy between subject and object nor any experienced interval between craving and gratification. *Prenatal existence is the closest approximation to absolutely effortless, timeless felicity men ever experience.* Insofar as the religious images of the Garden of Eden, Adam's Fall and the World to Come possess any biological counterpart, they can be seen as symbolic expressions of the contrast between prenatal and postnatal existence. We have all experienced a catastrophic "fall." Something in each of us craves to return to the "Garden." Nor is the imagery of the Garden inappropriate. We were "planted" in the womb of the mother. We remained rooted there for nine months through the umbilical cord, our lifeline for nurture and growth.

Originally, the totally gratified fetus has no way of experiencing otherness. The fetus is all there is in its own experience. Actually, language fails when we attempt to describe its condition of inclusiveness and sufficiency. In order to have a sense of discrete identity, one must confront a domain of otherness. The fetus encounters no such domain. It experiences neither time, effort, nor limitation. In comparison, postnatal existence, with its anxieties, stress, and limitation, seems like a catastrophic fall from grace.

There have been many attempts to picture the "order" of things at the end of time. Some involve the idea of a restoration of the primordial beginning, others some kind of improvement upon it. If we ask what biological reality might correspond to the Age to Come, insofar as its ambiguous and imprecise outlines in the literature permit such associations, we must conclude that the biological counterpart of the bliss that awaits the righteous is none other than that which they "experienced" in the womb. I stress the question of the biological counterpart of the religious imagery because *I think that eschatological speculation is meaningfully and functionally related to human experience*. Those who assert that the original and the final felicity have absolutely no biological counterpart remove these religious images from the domain of human meanings.

According to both Paul and his Jewish contemporaries, biological death was not the only catastrophe that entered the world as a result of Adam's sin. The authors of the apocalyptic writings considered human mortality a reflection of the very nature of things. They regarded the consequences of Adam's disobedience as cosmic as well as human: Although man was originally destined to rule over both the angels and the elemental powers of the created order, the original order dominated by man was overturned as a result of Adam's sin.[4] Both mankind and creation were subjugated to all manner of demonic powers. W. L. Knox has pointed to the very widespread belief in Paul's time in the subjugation of both men and the natural order to astral powers.[5] When this belief was synthesized with the doctrine of the Fall, the subordination of men to astral and demonic powers was interpreted as a consequence of Adam's sin. Death ceased to be regarded solely as a punishment inflicted by God against a rebellious humanity. It was seen as one of the most powerful of the usurping powers that gained dominion over creation after the Fall.

It became the demonic "last enemy," which, according to Paul, God would finally destroy (I Cor. 15:26).

The belief that creation had gotten out of hand, was now subordinated to hostile powers, and yearned for redemption had in all probability many sources. Innumerable scholars have tried to identify them. One source of the conviction that creation had become disarranged was undoubtedly the unstable situation of Palestinian Jews under the military and political domination of Rome. Another was the inevitable limitations and obstacles *any* life must meet. Given the special stresses the Jews of Palestine were compelled to endure as well as the fact that the symbols available to them for speculation on the human condition were largely rooted in the imagery of the Bible, it is not surprising that thought on the origin of human disorder took the form of reflection on the Fall of Adam. Adam's fate was biologically and perhaps even existentially replicated in the career of every man. Those who regarded the cosmos as flawed by demonic domination saw redemption as essentially the liberation of the cosmos from that domination. Redemption was also seen as the liberation of mankind from the limitations of mortality. The two aspects of redemption were in reality two sides of the same coin. Apocalyptists such as Paul intuitively understood that human mortality was related to the entire matrix out of which life arises.[6] No fundamental alteration of the human condition was possible without a concomitant rectification of its encompassing matrix. Paul and his contemporaries used the symbolic language of their time and culture to make their point, but it would be a mistake to underestimate the existential realism underlying their analysis of the predicament of Adam's progeny.

After Damascus Paul became convinced that the related flaws in creation, disobedience, mortality, and the subjugation of the cosmos to the elemental powers were in the process of being overcome. He expressed this conviction in many places. Those most germane to our topic are his reflections on the first and Last Adam in Romans 5 and I Corinthians 15. In Romans 5 Paul began with a reflection on the origin of death. "Well, then, sin entered the world through one man, and through sin death, and thus death has spread through the whole human race because everyone has sinned" (Rom. 5:12). Few passages in the New Testament have been commented upon as extensively as this. As we have seen, Paul's twin assertions that death is the result of sin and that sin entered the world "through one man" are entirely in keeping with the mythic speculations of his Jewish contemporaries. Romans 5:12 rests in the final analysis upon the authority of Genesis 3:17ff. In this passage Paul also seems to hold that men die because they replicate Adam's sin, not because of Adam's sin. However, Paul's Jewish contemporaries could not have agreed with Paul as he continued his reflection on the two Adams: "Adam prefigured the One to come, but the gift itself outweighed the fall. If it is certain that through one man's fall so many died, it is even more certain that divine grace, coming through one man, Jesus Christ, came to many as an abundant free gift" (Rom. 5:15).

The "abundant free gift" that comes through Christ is, of course, an end to mortality. In this verse Adam is depicted as the antitype of Jesus. There is some scholarly debate concerning the meaning of "the One to come." According to Barrett, "the One to come" is the eschatological Christ who will be fully revealed at the Last Day.[7] Just as the fruit of Adam's sin is death, so through Christ's superlative righteousness many will receive "divine grace" as "an abundant free gift" (Rom. 5:16). Paul elaborates on this theme in the next verse: "If it is certain that death reigned over everyone as the consequence of one man's fall, it is even more certain that one man, Jesus Christ, will cause everyone to reign in life who receives the free gift that he does not deserve, of being made righteous." The undeserved "free gift" that Christ makes available is the opposite of the penalty brought upon mankind by his antitype. Adam brings death; Jesus brings eternal life.

Paul also describes Jesus as reversing the "condemnation" brought about by Adam and bringing in its stead "justification" (Rom. 5:16). Justification has a very explicit meaning for Paul. When God justifies the unworthy sinner, he pronounces a verdict of acquittal upon him and bestows upon him the gift of eternal life. From the time of Martin Luther until the beginning of the twentieth century, Protestants have tended to regard the doctrine of justification by faith as the heart and center of Paul's theology. This estimate of Paul's theological positions has been challenged by a number of modern scholars of great authority.[8] I do not wish to enter this controversy directly. Nevertheless, I believe that one aspect of the doctrine of justification by faith must remain central to any interpretation of Paul: We must not lose sight of the decisive importance of *the fruit of God's justification of the sinner* as understood by Paul. *The fruit of justification is eternal life.* In Romans 6:23 Paul explicitly contrasts the fruits of sin and justification: "For the wage paid by sin is death; the present given by God is eternal life in Christ Jesus. . . ." Adam paid the price of sin; through Jesus the unearned gift of justification is bestowed.

The centrality of eternal life as the fruit of justification is emphasized with great force in Paul's discussion of Adam and Christ in I Corinthians 15. Scroggs has observed that the themes of Romans 5:12–21 and I Corinthians 15 "are related but not identical."[9] In I Corinthians 15 Paul is primarily interested in rendering credible to the skeptical Corinthians the Christian hope that those who are "in Christ" will ultimately be resurrected as was Jesus. By resurrection Paul meant the resurrection of the body, as did his Jewish contemporaries. Apparently there was considerable skepticism in Corinth concerning the future resurrection of the bodies of the dead even among those who believed in Jesus' Resurrection.[10] Paul confronted this skepticism by arguing that "Christ has in fact been raised from the dead as the first fruits (*aparche*) of all who have fallen asleep" (I Cor. 15:20). According to Jean Héring, the word *aparche* is almost synonymous with the Hebrew *arrabon,* which is an earnest or a deposit.[11] Paul's meaning is that Christ's Resurrection anticipates the resurrection of his followers, who will some day share his glorious destiny.

Having asserted that resurrection awaits the believer, Paul returned to the theme of the first and Last Adam: "Death came through one man. Just as all men die in Adam, so all men will be brought to life in Christ. . ." (I Cor. 15:21–22).

Paul's emphasis in I Corinthians is on the perfected, eternal life that awaits the believer in Christ. A second discussion of Adam and Christ follows Paul's reply to a question he himself poses rhetorically: "How are dead people raised, and what sort of body do they have when they come back?" (I Cor. 15:35). Paul answered by distinguishing between earthly and heavenly bodies. The earthly body dies; the heavenly body "is raised imperishable" (I Cor. 15:42). The two Adams partake respectively of two very different realms: "The first man, being from earth, is earthly by nature; the second man is from heaven" (I Cor. 15:47). This reflection can be seen as a Christian *midrash* or homily on Genesis 2:7: "The Lord God formed man of the dust of the ground and breathed into his nostrils the breath of life; and Adam became a living soul." Paul commented on this verse: "The first Adam, as scripture says, 'became a living soul.'" (I Cor. 15:45). Paul then observed that "the last Adam has become a life-giving spirit" (*pneuma zōopoioun*) (I Cor. 15:45). As "a living soul" the first Adam is earthly and perishable; so too are all who share in his nature. As a "life-giving spirit" the Risen Christ imparts his nature to those who become one with him. That nature is incorruptible, imperishable, and glorious.

Christ's resurrected nature is that of a *soma pneumatikon,* a "spiritual body." We have already noted that the spiritual body is not immaterial. On the contrary, it alone truly exists for Paul. Paul's reference to the heavenly nature of the Last Adam need not be understood as a reference to a Gnostic myth of Christ's heavenly origin but to the special character and dignity of his incorruptible body after Resurrection.[12] A miraculous transformation must take place before men can share Christ's resurrected nature with him: "Flesh and blood cannot inherit the kingdom of God: and the perishable cannot inherit what lasts forever" (I Cor. 15:50). When the transformation occurs, all things will be changed. The perishable world will be redeemed. Death, corruption, and demonic domination will be forever defeated.

Paul's assertions about Christ's extraordinary power to redeem man and the cosmos leads to the question of why Christ had the superlative merit to be "the first fruit of all who have fallen asleep" as well as the fount of eternal life for a resurrected humanity. Before attempting a response, it is necessary to consider Paul's conception of the nature of sin. In an important sense, both Paul and his Jewish contemporaries were convinced that *disobedience was the only sin.* Since Judaism regarded all of the commandments as expressions of God's will, every commandment presented men with the agonizing choice of obedience or rebellion against the all-wise and all-powerful Father. It made no difference whether or not a commandment was opaque to human understanding. It was a supreme act of arrogance for a man to judge for himself what to obey and what not to obey. It might in fact be argued that obedience to seemingly inconsequential or irrational commandments was of greater consequence than obedience to commandments whose purpose could be understood. The real issue was whether a man submitted to or rebelled against his Creator. Furthermore, the Creator was always in the right since the very structure of reality was the fruit of his will.

The supreme importance of obedience in biblical religion was well illustrated by Herman Melville in Father Mapple's description of Jonah's sin in the famous sermon in *Moby Dick*:

> As with all sinners among men, the sin of the son of Amittai was *his wilful disobedience of the command of God—never mind what that command was, or how conveyed*—which he found a hard command. But all the things that God would have us do are hard for us to do. . . . And *if we obey God, we must disobey ourselves*; and it is in this disobeying ourselves, wherein the hardness of obeying God consists (Italics added).

It has been argued that Father Mapple's God is the God of an especially rigid form of Calvinism and not the true God of biblical faith.[13] Nevertheless, Father Mapple is correct when he observes that in biblical religion man's primary duty is to subordinate his own inclinations to the will of God. In biblical religion a man who decides for himself which of God's commandments he will obey puts himself in God's place, asserting the priority of his own judgment.

He judges what God alone can judge and, by so doing, arrogates to himself a preeminence God alone rightfully possesses. There is no place in this system for the modern ideal of the autonomous man who regards his own actions as entirely within his ethical competence.

Paul asserted that Adam committed the archetypal sin of biblical religion, disobedience. Because of Adam's disobedience in not fulfilling a single commandment death entered the world. By contrast, Christ alone was so perfectly obedient that he even regarded his own life as of no account whatsoever against the majestic framework of God's wisdom. As Paul regarded Adam as the paradigmatically sinful man, he saw Christ as the only truly righteous man. For Christ's obedience extended even to the extraordinary agony of death as an unblemished innocent on the cross. Although Paul offers many suggestions as to why Christ's death brought about the liberation of mankind from the consequences of Adam's sin, Paul is most explicit in asserting that Christ was a "life-giving spirit" because of his obedience: "As by one man's disobedience many were made sinners, so *by one man's obedience* many will be made righteous" (Romans 5:19; italics added).

In his first letter to the Corinthians, Paul reminded them that he had handed on to them the Good News that he had received: "I taught you what I had been taught myself, namely that Christ died for our sins" (I Cor. 15:3). This is one of the earliest statements of the Christian *kerygma*.[14] It has often been interpreted as a reference to Christ's death as a vicarious atonement for the sins of mankind. There can be little doubt that Paul maintained that Christ's death was sacrificial in character (cf. Romans 3:21–28; 5:1–2; I Cor. 5:7). Freud stressed this conception of Christ's death in *Totem and Taboo* and *Moses and Monotheism*. Nevertheless, even if we accept the thesis that Paul regarded Christ's death as a vicarious atonement, we have yet to identify the superlative merit possessed by Christ that made such atonement possible. Others died without so fortunate a result; what was unique about Jesus? Paul answered that question in the passage we have cited, Romans 5:19. *Christ's merit consisted in his superlative obedience.* Christ, in his innocence, had more justification for rebellion against the fate meted out to him than any man. Nevertheless he submitted in perfect obedience to unmerited death on the cross. According to Paul, Christ alone was unblemished by any trace of rebellion against the Father. Paul's logic was in keeping with that of his Jewish contemporaries, for a prevalent Jewish speculation was that were a man totally without sin—that is, perfectly obedient—he would not be condemned to death.[15] Unlike his Jewish contemporaries, Paul was convinced that there was one such man, Christ, and that the merit of his flawless obedience was sufficient to bestow life on others as well as himself.

Paul's stress on Christ's perfect obedience and innocence is related to his belief that Christ was victorious over the angelic powers. In his polemic against the Law in Galatians, Paul asserted that these powers rather than God delivered the Law to Israel at Sinai. God's purpose in permitting this was "to specify transgressions" (Gal. 3:19), thereby causing men to look beyond the Law to Christ as the way to salvation. The imposition of the Law on Israel was holy in that it fulfilled God's plan. Nevertheless, Paul believed that, apart from God's larger intentions in Christ, the Law could by itself only intensify the domination of the angels.

Had Christ been tainted with even a trace of sinfulness, the powers to whom dominion had fallen after Adam's transgression would have been within their legitimate right in claiming Christ as their victim. Under the Law, their Law, the wages of sin are rightfully death. Happily for mankind, the cosmic powers did not recognize Christ as the sinless obedient Son of God. Christ permitted them to exceed their proper sphere when they condemned him to crucifixion. By his perfect obedience to the Father's wise and mysterious plan, Christ tricked the "rulers of this age" (*hoi archontes tou aiōnos toutou*) (I Cor. 2:8), and thereby deprived them of their dominion over mankind. Christ thus reversed what Adam had sadly initiated.

This interpretation of Christ's role rests upon Paul's argument in Galatians that the Law was given by angels rather than God and his assertion in I Corinthians and Colossians that by his death Christ defeated the ruling powers of the cosmos: "He disarmed the principalities and powers and made a public example of them, trampling over them in him (or, 'in it', the cross)" (Col. 2:15). "The hidden wisdom of God . . . is a wisdom which none of the rulers of this age have ever known, or they would not have crucified the Lord of Glory" (I Cor. 2:7–8).

Héring has argued persuasively in his commentary on I Corinthians that "the rulers of this age" to whom Paul referred are angelic powers rather than political rulers within the Roman Empire.[16] J. L. Houlden in his commentary on Colossians offered a concurring judgment that the passages in Colossians and I Corinthians refer to Christ's victory over the unknowing elemental powers. Houlden cited Ignatius, Justin, and Athanasius, all of whom alluded to a tradition in which Christ hoodwinked the devil and his angels into acting beyond their proper sphere by crucifying God's innocent Son.[17] Christ thereby deprived the elemental powers of their death-dealing dominion over mankind. Houlden conceded that the myth is not completely developed in the extant letters of Paul. Nevertheless, he concurred with Albert Schweitzer in feeling that Paul utilized this myth as one of his most important explanations of how Christ by his perfect obedience defeated death.[18]

The tendency to objectify hostile powers is not unknown in paranoia. When groups objectify hostile powers, such as the punitive rulers of mankind, it is very likely that some shared anxiety has been given a "local habitation and a name." With his myth of Christ's liberation of mankind from the hostile powers, Paul made a further contribution to mankind's self-liberation. The shared paranoia implicit in the pervasive conviction that the world was dominated by essentially hostile spirits was not invented by Paul. One of the major controversies of scholarship has been over the question of the extent to which the myth of Christ defeating the elemental powers was of Gnostic origin. That question cannot be solved here, but it is important to note that the conviction that the world was thus menaced was maintained both by apocalyptic Jews, who saw the threat as a consequence of the Fall, and by pagan Greeks, who undoubtedly arrived at the same pervasive feelings of threat from a common existential albeit a divergent cultural source.[19] What is impressive in Paul is the way in which he interpreted the crucifixion so that it became an expression of the partial liberation of mankind from these threatening powers as well as the internal anxieties out of which fear of the elemental powers derived.

If we interpret Paul's myth of Christ's reversal of the subjugation of Adam and his progeny to the elemental powers in terms of metaphors of paternity and filiation, we observe that Paul claimed that Christ is in effect the truly obedient Son who liberated mankind from the primal wretchedness of the disobedient son. Christ proved his obedience by foregoing all pretension to the status of the Father (Phil. 2:5–11) and by accepting in his absolute purity a condemnation he in no wise deserved. Furthermore, by insisting that men could only be saved by faith in the good Son rather than through their own works, Paul assures the other sons that they were not required to achieve the good Son's perfect obedience in order to be accepted by the Father. Once the good Son overwhelmed the hostile powers through his innocence, it became possible for the Father freely to render unto the less virtuous brothers the fruits of the good Son's impeccable righteousness. Having been made like unto him in spite of themselves, they could share in his glorious destiny.

There is at least one further aspect of this scheme that is worthy of comment. The elemental powers represented in all likelihood the displacement of an original fear of the infanticidal Progenitor (or Progenitrix). In Paul's system the Father retained ultimate authority throughout the entire drama. The cosmic powers only reigned at his pleasure. They were incapable of withstanding his rule or his superlative wisdom. By displacing fear of the Father onto hostile cosmic powers and ascribing all injury to their agency, an attempt was made to dilute the fear of the infanticidal Progenitor. Nevertheless, even these obviously subordinate cosmic powers could only be overcome by the death of the virtuous Son. In one way or another the Son had to die; only through his death would the infanticidal Progenitor's thirst for an offspring-victim be sated.

There is also evidence that Paul saw Adam's disobedience as an expression of the sinner's quest for godlike omnipotence. This theme is dealt with in Philippians 2:6–11, one of the most difficult passages in the New Testament. There has been much debate concerning the authorship of Philippians. However, recent commentators have tended to assert its authenticity as a genuine letter of Paul.[20] Bearing in mind that this passage can yield no more than the most tentative results, let us examine it:

> Though he was in the form of God
> He did not count as a thing to be grasped
> Equality with God,

> But emptied himself,
> Taking the form of a servant,
> Being born in the likeness of men.

> And being found in human form
> He humbled himself
> And became obedient unto death,
> Even on a cross.

> Therefore God has highly exalted him
> And bestowed on him the name
> Which is above every name,

> That at the name of Jesus,
> Every knee should bow,
> In heaven and on earth and under the earth,

> And every tongue confess
> That Jesus is Lord
> To the glory of God the Father.

I have arranged these verses as suggested by Ernst Lohmeyer.[21] In 1927 Lohmeyer advanced the view that the passage was poetic in form and that it was actually a primitive Christian hymn. This view has been almost universally accepted although the arrangement and interpretation of the verses has been widely debated.

Lohmeyer's interpretation leads to the question of who composed the hymn. Did Paul or a member of his circle compose it or did Paul quote the hymn because he agreed with its contents and knew the Philippians would be familiar with it? Paul may have taken a contemporary hymn and reworked it for his own purposes. Modern scholarship has demonstrated that Paul frequently used formulas and traditions that he had received from others and edited them to conform to his own meanings.[22] For our understanding of Paul, it would make little difference whether he actually composed the hymn or used a version he had edited. Presumably, Paul would not have commended religious ideas to the Philippians with which he did not concur.

It is widely believed that the Adam-Christ contrast is presupposed in this hymn, in spite of the fact that Adam is not explicitly mentioned.[23] When Paul (for the sake of economy we shall refer to Paul as if we were certain that he was the original author) wrote:

> Though he was in the form (*morphe*) of God,
> He did not count as a thing to be grasped
> Equality with God,

he seems to have the contrast of Christ and Adam very much in mind. According to Genesis 1:26, Adam was created in the "image" of God. Although the Septuagint translates "image" as "*eikon*," there is considerable warrant for regarding Paul's use of *morphe* as suggesting that both Adam and Christ originally bore the divine image. There are, of course, differences. Adam comes into existence only when God initiates his earthly career; Christ seems to have enjoyed a heavenly preexistence before assuming his servant role on earth (cf. Col. 1:15–20). This contrast accords with Paul's treatment of Adam and Christ as the earthly and heavenly men respectively in I Corinthians 15.

In these verses in Philippians the meaning of *harpagmos* is problematic. I have accepted the translation "thing to be grasped" used by Houlden in his commentary. The word is rare and again any interpretation must be tendered cautiously. The description of Christ implied in this passage seems to be that in spite of his original status as possessing "the form of God," he did not grasp at God's preeminent place in the order of things. Barrett has suggested that the meaning of the passage is multifaceted: Paul asserts that (1) as eternal, preexistent Son of God, Christ had equality with God, but, in perfect obedience to his Father, he emptied himself of his divine status and accepted the status of the most despised and rejected of men. This would accord with the translation in the Catholic Jerusalem Bible, "he did not cling to his equality with God but emptied himself." (2) As the new Adam, that is insofar as he was man rather than Son of God, Christ had no such equality with God and made no attempt to seize it, as did the first Adam. Instead he freely accepted the role of obedient, dependent, perfectly submissive creature that God had originally inended for all men.

This description of Christ contrasts with what we know of Adam. Like Christ, Adam found himself originally in a most felicitous environment. Adam was given royal prerogatives in the earthly sphere as was Christ in the heavenly domain. All that was required of him was that he live in submission to his Creator. The test of Adam's obedience was that he obey a single commandment, hardly a matter requiring great effort. Obedience would not have been burdensome. God asked almost nothing of Adam and was prepared in return to reward him with both eternal life and absolute dominion over the created world.

The test of obedience was inconsequential; the consequences of disobedience were enormous. The passage in Philippians offers greater insight into why disobedience is so horrendous an offense than the passages in Romans 5 and I Corinthians 15. If Christ's obedience involved his refusal to grasp at "equality with God," *any* disobedience must have involved precisely such a grasping at equality. Although Adam is not mentioned explicitly, the Adam-Christ contrast would seem to be implied. Adam's real sin was not merely partaking of the fruit of the forbidden tree; it was his attempt to achieve "equality with God." Such equality would have involved ridding himself of God, for he who enjoys equal status has no further need of the Creator.

At this point we can understand the crucial significance of Adam's disobedience in bringing about the downfall of the cosmos and Christ's obedience in effecting its restoration. In biblical religion disobedience is more than an act of insubordination. Fundamentally, disobedience reflects the desire to be rid of God so that one might enjoy his prerogatives. Above all, behind disobedience lies the quest for omnipotence. The Serpent's enticement of Eve suggests this insight: "For God knows that in the day that you eat thereof your eyes will be opened, and *you shall be as gods. . .*" (Gen. 3:5). The idea is expressed more explicitly by Paul in the hymn in Philippians we have quoted: "He did not count as a thing to be grasped,/ Equality with God."

The image may be mythic, but it depicts the sinner's profound yearning for omnipotence, his desire to be rid of God so that he alone can be the unimpeded master of both his fate and his world. Paul is at one with his Jewish contemporaries in regarding this yearning as the original human flaw.[24] The hymn in Philippians presupposes a view of Adam as anticipating the sin of Lucifer, prince of this world, who is depicted as saying: "I will ascend above the heights of the clouds: I will be like the Most High" (Isa. 14:14). In our hymn Christ, "though in the form of God," rejects Adam's attempt at omnipotent self-exaltation by emptying himself and "taking the form of a servant." Where Adam sought a status that was too high for him, Christ voluntarily lowered himself to the condition of an absolutely obedient servant. The cross, which was once a stumbling block impeding Paul's faith in Christ, is here regarded as the ultimate test of Christ's obedient servitude. In contrast with Adam's Promethean attempt at riddance of the divine, Christ "became obedient unto death, Even death on a cross."

If we take Philippians as representative of Paul's thought, whether or not he actually composed the hymn, we observe that Paul and Freud had points of convergence and divergence in their estimate of the sin that brought about mankind's Fall. Both Paul and Freud agree that civilization as we know it began with an original act of rebellion and that the deed was an attempt to snatch the prerogatives of the Father. Freud is more specific than Paul in insisting that the sons desired to eliminate the Father altogether. Freud and Paul differ on the nature of the original crime. Freud maintained that the sons sought the sexual prerogatives of the Father; Paul insisted that Adam sought the omnipotent condition that belonged to the Father alone.

Or did the prerogatives belong to the Father? Both Freud and Paul stress mankind's rebellious strivings against the Father. Both have little or nothing to say about strife with a female Progenetrix. Could it be that Freud and Paul were participants in a Jewish culture that maintained as one of its abiding elements of millennial continuity a fear of the female element in religion and culture which was so immense that both were silent about the religious significance of their feelings toward the parent who is the source of the oldest and most consuming of anxieties, the mother? Paul's silence is perhaps stranger than Freud's because he labored in a pagan world that had yet to suppress its female deities. Although Paul and Freud both avoided the religious problems involved in mankind's exceedingly complicated feelings about female deities and the human mothers they presuppose, Paul's analysis of the motives for mankind's original disobedience (i.e., the quest for a godlike omnipotence) uncovers an older and a deeper level of the reasons for intergenerational strife than does Freud's hypothesis that the rebellious sons were moved by sexual rivalry.

Throughout this book, I have maintained that much that was repressed in Judaism was brought to conscious expression by Paul. There is, however, at least one area in which Paul carried over Judaism's repression of the emotional roots of human action. Paul's view of the divine-human encounter was distorted by an overly masculine orientation he had probably inherited from rabbinic Judaism. His religious images rest upon the model of the warfare of the *brothers,* the atoning death of the *Son,* and the gracious forgiveness of the *Father.* Although Catholicism found a limited place for the feminine element in the adoration of the Virgin at a later time—as did Jewish mysticism with its conception of the feminine nature of God's Holy *Shekhinah*—there is no hint of this development in Paul.[25]

We have noted several times that both Paul and the Judaism of his time agreed that the fundamental religious problem was to achieve an appropriate relationship with the Father. If our images of God largely reflect conflicts with earthly progenitors, such a view of religion presupposes a very serious repression. The quest for the right relationship with the earthly father is, of course, of great importance, but it is by no means as fraught with anxiety and conflict as the older and more decisive problem of achieving a relationship with the mother and, in later life, with adult females. In an earlier work, I suggested that rabbinic Judaism's repression of the female deities arose out of fear, as does all repression, and that the distorted emphasis on masculinity that disturbs and distorts both Judaism and all other biblically derived religions to this day stem from the male's inability to acknowledge openly or cope with his extraordinarily powerful fear of women.[26]

Nevertheless, Paul did not entirely ignore the problem of the feminine aspect of divinity. As we have noted, if the image of a "return to the Garden" has any biological counterpart, it is return to the maternal matrix. Paul's vision of the final consummation as return to the Garden can therefore be understood as *reunion with the mother*. Paul seemed to be saying that when men achieve the right relationship with the Father, it will finally become possible for them to be reunited with the Mother. When we translate the theology of restoration into the images of human biology, exile is seen as exile from the mother; return is, of course, reunion with her. Nor is it entirely accidental that from the earliest Semitic nomads to the Protestant nomads who subdued the American continent, wanderers have always fled from women psychologically if not physically. Both ancient Jews and modern Americans have found male companionship easier to handle, as Leslie Fiedler has observed.[27] There was simply too much conflict involved in achieving a satisfactory relationship with a woman. Men wanted to lose themselves in her, and that was too threatening. As a result, from prebiblical times to our own, they ran away but never gave up hope that in the end they would find her again.

Paul's images express symbolically the insight that restoration is ultimately a return to the maternal matrix and the lost omnipotence of the womb. They have been reformulated in the language of contemporary theology by Thomas J. J. Altizer. He observed that the transcendence of God is a "consequence of the fall."[28] Altizer linked the Fall of Adam with "the loss of the primordial All." He observed that God does not become a transcendent Other over against man until that loss takes place. Although Altizer used the language of contemporary theology, his imagery can be related to both the psychoanalytic understanding of the meaning of the Fall and to Paul's myth of the Last Adam. Altizer's insight greatly resembles Norman O. Brown's comment that "separateness, then, is the fall— the fall into division is the original lie."[29] For Altizer the ultimate term in the human drama is "the actualization of New Jerusalem." Altizer insisted that the attainment of New Jerusalem involved the transformation of the "primordial All," out of which the cosmic process originated, and that the attainment of the eschatological Totality would involve "the eschatological realization of Nirvana." Altizer reminded us that "Nirvana is one of a number of Oriental names and images for a total and primordial bliss."[30] Altizer thus regarded the goal of all existence as the recovery of the primordial Totality. He saw the New Jerusalem as both the historical actualization and "the dialectical reversal" of the original All. Nevertheless, Altizer insisted that the attainment of New Jerusalem involves the primordial bliss of Nirvana and that its final consummation will involve the recovery of Nirvana. In spite of Altizer's insistence that the final Totality is a "dialectical reversal" of the original Totality, there is a sense in which the attainment of the New Jerusalem is a recovery of the old Eden from which mankind was exiled at the Fall. Furthermore, both the original and final Totality may involve the primordial bliss that orientals have named Nirvana. In Altizer's myth, the world moves forward to return to its original bliss.

It is startling to see a distinguished Christian theologian link oriental and Christian themes and to insist upon the identity of Buddha and Christ and the New Jerusalem and Nirvana. Nevertheless, it is my conviction that Altizer's insights do justice to the theology of the Fall and that they unify psychoanalytic, phenomenological, and theological insights about its meaning. Furthermore, I believe that Altizer's insistence on the equivalence of Eden, the New Jerusalem, and Nirvana is in accord with Paul's myth of Christ as the Last Adam.

Let us return to the statement in Philippians that Christ did not grasp at "equality with God" and its corollary that such radical self-exaltation constituted Adam's initial flaw, but let us bear in mind Altizer's observation that the transcendence of God was not an original given but a consequence of the Fall. If we further recall the apocalyptic-rabbinic tradition, which Paul apparently accepted, that before sinning Adam enjoyed a condition of perfect felicity, Adam's condition of primordial bliss can also be named Nirvana, as Altizer has suggested. If it be objected that there are differences between the biblical and oriental images, there is an obvious response. Both images attempt to express in words and symbols a condition that is incapable of adequate verbal or conceptual expression. The orientals utilized their verbal traditions to give inadequate expression to a contentless, desireless state that eludes description. Paul, the rabbis, and the apocalypticists utilized their own symbols and legends to express imperfectly the same reality. Furthermore, it is not accidental that psychoanalysts have regarded both Nirvana and the original Eden as religiomythic images for the bliss of the prenatal state.[32] Prenatal existence is, as we have suggested, the only biological state to which these images could apply. This is especially true in Buddhism, where the bliss and emptiness of Nirvana is explicitly distinguished from the absolute nothingness of death. Furthermore, the same distinction between Adam's primordial bliss and the nothingness of death is implicit in the fact that the biblical tradition treats the Garden as part of the created order. Adam's bliss is not primordial chaos.

Admittedly, our discussion concerns mythic images that cannot be pressed too far. In the Garden myth the creation of Eve as Adam's sexual companion as well as the injunction to Adam to enjoy dominion reflect a situation in which the subject-object dichotomy has already become manifest. I would concur with the observations of Altizer and Brown that the moment Adam became aware of otherness, the Fall had taken place. The subject-object dichotomy necessarily involves an end to bliss. Any limitation on the self involves some measure of negation and frustration. The initiation of the subject-object dichotomy must therefore have been coterminous with the Fall. This would accord with Altizer's observation that the most important of all subject-object dichotomies, the transcendence of God, was consequent upon the Fall. This is, of course, not the way the biblical story is told. Nevertheless, if the biblical story has any counterpart in human experience, Adam's bliss must be prior to the subject-object dichotomy.

If Adam's bliss did precede the subject-object dichotomy, we may, without intending the slightest irreverence, ask why God didn't simply leave Adam alone instead of giving him even a single commandment he was destined to reject? One might argue that Adam's Fall occurred as soon as he became aware of God as the opposing Other rather than when he disobeyed him. The moment negation and differentiation entered Adam's world, his primordial bliss was at an end. Paul seems to have understood this at least in part when he observed: "I should not have known what sin was except for the Law. . ." (Rom. 7:7). and "Once, when there was no Law, I was alive; but when the commandment came, sin came to life and I died. . ." (Rom. 7:9). Paul does not explicitly apply this description to Adam. Nevertheless, in Romans 5 Paul distinguished between the sin of Adam, who rejected a single divinely ordained commandment, and the generations between Adam and Moses, who sinned though they received no actual commandments (Rom. 5:12–14). Adam's sin involved rejection of a specific prohibition imposed upon him. As such, his situation was like that of the Israelites after Moses who had received the Law rather than that of the generations between Adam and Moses. Paul's description of the way in which the Law engenders rebellion thus applies to Adam.

*Adam's attempt to achieve "equality with God" can thus be inter-
preted as an attempt to deny the divine-human split engendered by
the intrusive and unanticipated appearance of God to Adam as the
opposing Other.* Another way of expressing the same idea is to suggest
that by his disobedience Adam attempted to overcome the first consequence of the Fall, the transcendence of God. Adam sought to restore
the undisturbed bliss that preceded God's intrusive commandment.
One might argue that poor Adam was destined to lose no matter what
strategy he elected. Had he obeyed God, he would have been compelled to acknowledge the abiding supremacy of the transcendent
Other; by refusing servitude in the hope of negating the transcendent
God and restoring the blissful *status quo ante,* Adam only succeeded
in intensifying the Deity's sovereign transcendence and condemning
himself and his progeny to a life of rebelliousness, suffering, travail,
and death. Admittedly, Paul nowhere offers this interpretation, but
the myth of the first and Last Adam is so rich in its interpretive sug-
gestiveness that I offer it as not inconsistent with the fundamental
thrust of Paul's vision.

We have already suggested that the quest for omnipotence, the
oldest of mankind's yearnings, is in reality the quest to restore the
undisturbed tranquility of prenatal existence.[33] Thus Adam's attempt
to achieve an omnipotent "equality with God" (Phil. 2:6) can be
interpreted as his quest to restore the condition that preceded the
subject-object dichotomy. In the language of oriental religion, Adam's
goal can be seen as the restoration of primordial Nirvana.

It is also possible to argue that God was as much the victim of
the original catastrophe as Adam. Adam's presence confronted God
with an intruding Other as Adam was by God's. If subjectivity can
meaningfully be ascribed to God, it can be suggested that, as a consequence of the Fall, God exchanged a primordial bliss in which he was
"all in all" for a problematic dominance and transcendence over his rebellious creatures.

The problem of the Fall from God's side had been dealt with
explicitly within the Jewish mystical tradition, especially Lurianic
Kabbalism. In that tradition the Fall was regarded as the catastrophic
point at which God's Holy *Shekhinah,* his Divine Presence, was

exiled from the primordial Divine Ground.[34] The goal of all existence in this system was regarded as the termination of cosmic exile and the restoration of the cosmos to its source, the aboriginal *Urgrund*. Thus the reversal of Adam's Fall in Lurianic Kabbalism would ultimately involve a restoration of God to God so that once again God could undividedly be "all in all." If again we turn to the language of the orient, God's goal is the same as Adam's, the restoration of primordial Nirvana and return to the originating Womb of all existence.

I believe that Paul shared something of this imagery and that it lies behind his myth of Christ as the Last Adam, especially his related apocalyptic vision of God's final victory (I Cor. 15:20–28). Paul stressed the fact that Christ as the Last Adam is a "life-giving spirit" (*pneuma zoopōioun*) (I Cor. 15:45). In contrast to the first Adam, the Last Adam will bring "life." Furthemore, the "life" that the Last Adam brings is, as we have observed, no more like the life we know than Adam "the man made of earth" (I Cor. 15:47) was like Christ, "the man from heaven" (I Cor. 15:48). When Paul asserted that "Flesh and blood cannot inherit the kingdom of God, nor can corruption inherit incorruptibility" (I Cor. 15:30), he was warning that nothing in our fallen existence without Christ can give us a hint as to what true "life" would really be like with him.

Paul's doctrines of the Resurrection and the Last Judgment seem to suggest initially that the life to come partakes of discrete identity in which the subject-object dichotomy will be maintained. Nevertheless, there are indications that this was not really the way Paul envisaged matters. As we have seen, Paul's insisted upon the radical incommensurability of spiritual existence after the Resurrection with the fallen existence that preceded it (I Cor. 15:42–50). However, the most important indication that Paul had another way of understanding the life to come is to be found in his apocalyptic vision of God's final recovery of all things from the disorder of the Fall:

But in truth, Christ is risen from the dead in the forefront of the departed. For since it was through a man

(Adam) that death supervened, the resurrection of the dead likewise took place through a man. For as all die because of their link with Adam, so all shall be restored to life through their link with Christ. But each in his own rank. The first fruit is Christ, then will come those who are of Christ at the time of the Parousia; *then—it will be the end, when he returns the kingdom to God the Father, after utterly destroying every rule and every authority and power.* For he (Christ) must reign until he has put all enemies beneath his feet, and *the last enemy which will be destroyed is death.* Indeed "God has subjected all the universe under his feet." But when it is said: "All is subjected," it is clear that it is with the exception of him who made the universe subject to him. *And when the universe has been subject to him, then the Son himself will submit to the one who made the universe* subject to him, *so that God may be all in all* (I Cor. 15:20–28; italics added).

In this translation I follow Héring save in verse 28, where I accept the Jerusalem Bible and the traditional translation. In Paul's apocalypse Christ as the Last Adam is depicted as totally reversing the consequences of the Fall. He is the "first fruit." After he is restored to life, those "of Christ" are to be resurrected. Then the "end" (*telos*) will come. Christ will be finally victorious over the elemental powers, "every rule and every power and authority" to which the world was subjugated as a consequence of the Fall. Finally, the worst consequence of the fall will be overcome by Christ's victory over death. In Paul's apocalypse death is no longer a punitive affliction to which God condemned an unworthy mankind. Death has become the most potent of the elemental powers to which mankind was subject after the Fall. Death is "the last enemy" to be defeated in Christ's work of reversing the Fall.

Ernst Käsemann has observed that for Paul "the Lordship of Christ is limited and provisional. It only serves the end of making way for the sole lordship of God."[35] When Christ completes his task he will, according to Paul, commit one final act of filial obedience. He will finally subordinate himself to God the Father to whom all things in heaven and earth are now perfectly subject. Héring has observed that Paul may have wanted to distinguish Christ the obedient Son, from the Greek son-gods who displaced, castrated and destroyed their progenitors.[36] Had Freud paid more attention to this apocalypse, it is likely that he would have been somewhat more reticent in asserting that Christianity is a "son religion" in which the Son ultimately triumphs over the Father. *At the very last, Paul depicted the Son as submitting totally to the Father.* According to Héring, Christ's final submission is so complete that it even involves "the extinction of the dignity of *Kurios* to which he has been raised" (Phil. 2:9).[37]

Héring does not believe that at the very end Paul envisaged Christ as losing his nature as the Son and Image of God. This raises the question of the terminal condition of the cosmos at its ultimate restoration. Following the traditional texts, I have accepted the translation "that God may be all in all" (I Cor. 15–28) for Paul's description of the eschatological completion of the cosmic drama. Héring objected to this translation. In its place he offered the phrase, "that God may be present in the whole universe and completely."[38] He claimed that Paul looked forward at the end to "the total and visible presence of the Kingdom of God.[39] Nevertheless, I think that the traditional translation comes closer to Paul's meaning and the final thrust of his theology. If the transcendence of God is a consequence of the Fall, and if the subject-object dichotomy is a decisive manifestation of God's transcendence, then the only way the Fall could be reversed would be to obliterate the subject-object dichotomy. *It is precisely the distinction between God as subject and the cosmos as object that is terminated when God becomes "all in all."* Furthermore, only by God becoming "all in all" could all of the original cosmic exiles, man's exile from Eden, the Shekhinah's exile from God, and the cosmos' exile from its Source be terminated in the final restoration of all things to their Originating Ground. One might say that *Christ as the Last Adam is seen by Paul as the cosmic agent through whom the eschatological return of the cosmos to its originating Sacred Womb is finally attained.*

Beneath the metaphors of exile and return, Source and Ground, we can discern feminine images of maternity and the yearning of the maternal offspring to return to their originating Matrix. Even God's omnipotence after the Fall is limited by his transcendence. *Both* God and man must therefore be in quest of the very same primal omnipotence that could only be attained by the reunion of God, man, and the cosmos in the seamless web of perfectly unified, undifferentiated Being. As we have noted, these religious images can be interpreted psychologically and biologically. We have also observed the parallelism if not the identity of these images with the oriental conception of Nirvana. Nor ought we to be surprised if contemporary scholars find parallels between oriental, Christian, and Jewish mystical images. All of these images have been nurtured by a common participation in the human condition.

Before we conclude this discussion, we might ask whether the Judeo-Christian experience of time is really linear, as Oscar Cullmann and other scholars have suggested.[40] If a circle is big enough it may appear to be a line. Nevertheless, if there is any merit to our interpretation of Paul's vision of the final consummation, the Judeo-Christian conception of time may in fact be circular rather than linear. The goal of God, man, and the world, in both Judaism and Pauline Christianity (which can legitimately be regarded as a revolutionary Jewish mysticism), may be the restoration of the primordial undifferentiated unity out of which all three have arisen. The difference between Judaism and Pauline Christianity would be over the related questions of whether the process of primordial restoration had commenced, and if so, by whose agency. Judaism in both Paul's time and ours would insist that mankind's exile from its original Totality has yet to be overcome. God must therefore appear in normative Judaism as the transcendent Law-giver who seeks to guide fallen men through the wasteland of the exile. Paul and those who share his faith insist that Christ has initiated the cosmic return and that in faith men can already anticipate the final restoration of all things to their seamless Matrix. Paul might further insist that through the Risen Christ, the Last Adam, mankind has the glorious assurance that its exile from God, and hence its distinctive existence as mankind, will soon be terminated. That is why Christ is both the *Last Adam* and the first *God-man*. When all is restored to God, mankind and God will become one and God will truly be the flawless, limitless, absolutely unimpeded Divine Unity who encompasses within himself all that is and ever has been. As "all in all," God will become the absolute perfection of what Christ the God-man anticipates and acts to bring about. Paul's *kerygma* looked forward to the last age when in and through Christ all things would arrive at the termination of their cycle of craving and rebirth: the final restoration of God, man, and the world to each other and the primordial bliss the orientals have named Nirvana.

Paul's final vision thus transcended even his own faith and offers a universal vision that is parallel to if not identical with the culminating wisdom of Freud's metapsychology, Jewish and Christian mystical theology, and oriental religion. Paul's vision of God's final triumph as "all in all" is not unlike Hegel's vision of the end of the process by which the World Spirit comes to know itself as Spirit:

> nur—
> aus dem Kelche dieses Geisterreiches
> schäumt ihm seine Unendlichkeit.

> Only
> The chalice of this realm of spirits
> Foams forth to God His own Infinitude.

Although many attempts have been made in both Jewish and Christian circles to diminish the preeminent standing of this extraordinary man in the religious life of mankind, Paul's wisdom has had a pheonix-like capacity to outlive the reservations of all his detractors. Paul has been controversial for two thousand years, but the debate surrounding him has been testimony to his greatness. No man could have done so much to make manifest that which was unmanifest in the religious life of mankind without enduring great personal travail and eliciting the hostility of those who were unprepared to follow him on his excruciatingly painful journey. The yearnings of childhood arise out of too much pain and anxiety for any man to win unanimous praise for giving them a local habitation and a name in the religious life of mankind.

Almost two thousand years before the depth psychology that his religious imagination helped to make possible, Paul of Tarsus gave expression to mankind's yearning for a new and flawless beginning that could finally end the cycle of anxiety, repression, desire, and craving—the inevitable concomitants of the human pilgrimage. Paul made of that yearning a force for the spiritual unification of the majority of men in the western world. Admittedly, Paul's faith could not overcome the limitations that Almighty *Ananke*, Goddess of Limit and Necessity, has imposed upon her children. Nevertheless, His faith enabled *Ananke's* children to express their most perilous and inextinguishable yearning, the quest for omnipotence, so that the quest could become the basis of sanity and shared fellowship for his spiritual heirs rather than a divisive, solipsistic force rending asunder all hope for human community between them. Paul's influence transcends the heritage of insight and imagination he bequeathed to his heirs. His attempt at self-liberation—for that in the final analysis is what his conversion was all about—is of such universal relevance that even in an age in which the symbols of religion have become functionally transparent to many of its most insightful scholars, Paul stands revealed as a man whose life and thought still have much to teach us.

NOTES

Chapter I

1. Sigmund Freud, *Moses and Monotheism*, trans. Katherine Jones (New York: Alfred A. Knopf, 1939), p. 110.
2. Karl Menninger, *The Theory of Psychoanalytic Technique* (New York: Basic Books, 1958), pp. 77–98; and Freud, "Observations on Wild Analysis," in *Collected Papers* (hereafter referred to as *CP*), vol. II, pp. 297–304; Freud, "Further Recommendations on the Technique of Psychoanalysis," *CP*, vol. II; Adolph Stern, "On the Counter-Transference in Psychoanalysis," *Psychoanalytic Review*, XI (1924).
3. Sören Kierkegaard, *Concluding Unscientific Postscript*, trans. David F. Swenson (Princeton: Princeton University Press, 1941), pp. 119–47. Cf. James Collins, *The Mind of Kierkegaard* (Chicago: Henry Regnery, 1953), pp. 98–136.
4. William James, *The Varieties of Religious Experience* (Garden City, N. Y.: Doubleday Dolphin Books, undated), pp. 155, 159. James specifically cites Paul as an example of a twice-born man. On the twice-born phenomenon, see Erik H. Erikson, *Young Man Luther* (New York: W. W. Norton & Co., 1958), p. 118.
5. See Béda Rigaux, *The Letters of St. Paul*, trans. Stephen Yonick (Chicago: Franciscan Herald Press, 1968), pp. 45–51. This book is indispensable for the study of Paul. Karl Barth maintained that "the passages refer to that timeless age to which all

men belong" in *The Epistle to the Romans*, trans. by Edwin C. Hoskyns from the 6th ed. (Oxford: Oxford University Press, 1933), p. 249. Cf. W. G. Kümmel, *Römer 7 und die Bekehrung des Paulus* (Leipzig, 1929); Rudolf Bultmann, "Römer 7 und die Anthropologie des Paulus," in *Imago Dei: Festschrift für G. Krüger* (Giessen, 1932), pp. 53–62; Hans Joachim Schoeps, *Paul* (Philadelphia: Westminster Press, 1961), p. 184. Schoeps concurred with Kümmel, who rejected the thesis of Romans 7 as autobiographical. Günther Bornkamm also rejects the autobiographical thesis in *Paul*, trans. D. M. G. Stalker (New York: Harper & Row, 1971), p. 125. A scholar of a previous generation, Adolf Diessmann, argued that Romans 7 was autobiographical in *Paul: A Study in Social and Religious History*, trans. W. E. Wilson (New York: Harper & Bros., 1957), pp. 91ff. Lastly, Martin Buber regarded Romans 7 as autobiographical in *Two Types of Faith*, trans. Norman P. Goldhawk (London: Routledge & Kegan Paul, 1951), p. 147.

6. Freud, *Group Psychology and the Analysis of the Ego*, trans. James Strachey (London: International Psycho-Analytical Press, 1922), p. 95.

7. Freud, *loc. cit.*

8. Cf. John Knox, *Chapters in a Life of St. Paul* (London: A. & C. Black, 1954), pp. 30–43.

9. Gershom Scholem, *On the Kabbalah and Its Symbolism*, trans. Ralph Mannheim (New York: Schocken Books, 1965), p. 14.

10. Krister Stendahl, "The Apostle Paul and the Introspective Conscience of the West," *Harvard Theological Review*, 56 (July 1963): 199–215.

11. Peter Berger, *A Rumor of Angels* (Garden City, N. Y.: Doubleday & Co., 1970), pp. 28–48.

12. Cf. Philip Rieff, *The Triumph of the Therapeutic: Uses of Faith after Freud* (New York: Harper & Row, 1966).

Chapter II

1. Albert Schweitzer, *The Mysticism of Paul the Apostle*, trans. William Montgomery (London: A. & C. Black, 1953). Cf. W. D. Davies, "Paul and Judaism Since Schweitzer," in Davies,

Paul and Rabbinic Judaism: Some Rabbinic Elements in Pauline Thought (New York: Harper Torchbooks, 1967), pp. vii-xv. For contrasting views, see Hans Conzelmann, "Current Problems in Pauline Research," and Edward Schweitzer, "Dying and Rising With Christ," in Richard Batey, ed., *New Testament Issues* (New York: Harper & Row, 1970).

2. Schweitzer, *op. cit.,* pp. 52–74.
3. Cf. Schweitzer, *op. cit.,* pp. 116–25.
4. On this verse, see Schoeps, *op. cit.,* p. 192, who argued that Paul sought to demonstrate from within the Law that Christ had brought the Law to a fulfilling end.
5. I accept J. L. Houlden's view that Ephesians is Pauline in spirit rather than an authentic letter by Paul. The verse cited is in Paul's spirit, whether written by him or a disciple. Cf. Houlden, *Paul's Letters From Prison* (Harmondsworth, Middlesex· Penguin Books, 1970), pp. 235–56.
6. John A. T. Robinson, *The Body: A Study in Pauline Theology* (London: SCM Press, 1952), p. 51.
7. Robinson, *loc. cit.*
8. Robinson, *op. cit.,* p. 9.
9. Freud, *Group Psychology and the Analysis of the Ego,* p. 46.
10. Freud, *op. cit.,* p. 47.
11. Freud, *loc. cit.*
12. Freud, *op. cit.,* p. 51.
13. Otto Fenichel, *The Psychoanalytic Theory of Neurosis* (New York: W. W. Norton & Co., 1945), pp. 394f.; cf. Franz Alexander, *The Fundamentals of Psychoanalysis* (New York: W. W. Norton & Co., 1963), pp. 92f., 116f.
14. Theodore Reik, *Myth and Guilt* (New York: George Braziller, 1957), p. 264.
15. The classical statement is biblical: "Ye shall be holy as I the Lord your God am holy" (Lev. 19:2); cf. *Sifra ad. loc.* (ed. Weiss), f. 57b; *Mekilta, Shirah* (ed. Friedmann), 3, f. 37a. Although identification with God was absolutely proscribed, imitation of his moral attributes was enjoined.
16. Rudolph Schnackenberg, *Baptism in the Thought of St. Paul,* trans. G. R. Beasley Murray (Oxford: Basil Blackwell, 1964), pp. 133, 136.
17. I am indebted in large measure to Norman O. Brown, *Love's*

Body (New York: Random House, 1966), for my appreciation of the extent to which Paul's rich symbolic consciousness was operative in his religious thought and experience. Brown, in turn, is perhaps indebted to Freud's discussion of primary process thinking; cf. Freud, *The Interpretation of Dreams*, trans. James Strachey (London: George Allen & Unwin, 1954), pp. 588–609.

18. I am indebted to Bakan for his formulation of the parallel between psychoanalysis and religion in *The Duality of Human Existence* (Chicago: Rand McNally, 1966), pp. 5ff.
19. Freud, *Civilization and Its Discontents*, trans. James Strachey (New York: W. W. Norton & Co., 1961), p. 15.
20. Cf. Fenichel, *op. cit.*, pp. 415–52.

Chapter III

1. Barth, *The Resurrection of the Dead* (London, 1933), p. 107.
2. For a summary of current debate on Paul's conversion, see Rigaux, *op. cit.*, pp. 40–67 and notes.
3. Joseph Klausner, *From Jesus to Paul*, trans. William F. Stinespring (Boston: Beacon Press, 1961), pp. 326ff.
4. Cf. Erikson, *op. cit.*, pp. 93f., who maintains that both Paul and Luther "were shaken by an attack involving both body and psyche . . . in more or less pathological states." Erikson has a judgment similar to Klausner's on the question of Paul's alleged epilepsy. According to Erikson, Paul reported symptoms that definitely suggest the syndrome of epilepsy (*loc. cit.*).
5. Cf. Sidney Tarachow, "St. Paul and Early Christianity," in Warner Muensterberger and Sidney Axelrad, eds., *Psychoanalysis and the Social Sciences* (New York: International Universities Press, 1955), vol. 4, p. 234.
6. Reik, *op. cit.*, p. 343. Although Reik was a psychoanalyst, he regarded Paul's conversion as "a mystery." Schoeps rejected a psychological explanation of the conversion, *op. cit.*, pp. 54f., as did Johannes Munck, *Paul and the Salvation of Mankind*, trans. Frank Clarke (Richmond: John Knox Press, 1959), p. 24.
7. Cf. Gershom Scholem, *Major Trends in Jewish Mysticism* (New York: Schocken Books, 1941), pp. 287–324.

8. Gershom Scholem, *On the Kabbalah and Its Symbolism*, p. 95.

9. Freud, *Group Psychology*, p. 81.

10. Cf. Gershom Scholem, *The Messianic Idea in Judaism* (New York: Schocken Books, 1971), pp. 1–36, 78–141, and W. D. Davies, *Torah in the Messianic Age and/or The Age To Come* (Philadelphia: Society of Biblical Literature, 1952).

11. Freud, "On Narcissism—An Introduction," in CP, Vol. IV, p. 48.

12. Brown, *op. cit.*, pp. 141ff.

13. I am indebted to Schoeps, *op. cit.*, pp. 168ff. However, I do not accept the idea that Paul saw the conflict but the Jerusalem Church did not. For a similar distinction between the Age of Torah and the Age of the Messiah, see Leo Baeck, "The Faith of Paul," in Baeck, *Judaism and Christianity*, trans. Walter Kaufmann (Philadelphia: Jewish Publication Society, 1958), pp. 139–70.

14. Cf. Schoeps, *op. cit.*, pp. 171–75.

15. Cf. Schoeps, *op. cit.*, p. 192.

16. Cf. Bultmann, *Theology of the New Testament*, trans. Kendrick Grobel (New York: Charles Scribner's Sons, 1951), vol. 1, pp. 308f.

17. Cf. Diessmann, *op. cit.*, pp. 85–95; but for a contrasting view, cf. Martin Dibelius, *Paul*, ed. Werner Georg Kümmel, trans. Frank Clarke (London: Longmans, 1953), pp. 46–66. Arthur Darby Nock saw sexual conflicts as the source of Paul's conviction that the Law had "failed" in *St. Paul* (New York: Harper & Bros., 1938), pp. 70f.

18. Stendahl, *op. cit.*

19. Cf. *Midrash Tehillim*, ed. S. Buber (Vilna, 1891), 92, 412. Eng. trans., *The Midrash on Psalms*, trans. William G. Braude (New Haven: Yale University Press, 1959), vols. 1 and 2, Shabbat 55a-b. For a list of rabbinic sources on the origin of death, cf. Louis Ginzberg, *The Legends of the Jews* (Philadelphia: Jewish Publication Society, 1909–13), vol. 5, pp. 128–31, n. 142.

20. Cf. Schoeps, *op. cit.*, pp. 134–41; Davies, *op. cit.*, pp. 274ff. But Klausner denies the presence of the idea of a suffering Messiah in the Tannaitic period in *The Messianic Idea in Israel*, trans. William F. Stinespring (New York: The Macmillan Co., 1955), p. 405.

21. On the relationship between eschatological fantasies and group, class, or national degradation, see Norman Cohn, *The Pursuit of the Millennium* (New York: Harper & Bros., 1957); Yonina Talmon, "The Pursuit of the Millennium: The Relation Between Religious and Social Change," *European Journal of Sociology*, 3 (1962): 125–48; and Reik, *Masochism in Modern Man* (New York: Farrar, Straus and Cudahy, 1941), pp. 321ff.

22. Cohn, *op. cit.*, and Talmon, *op. cit.*

23. Reik, *Masochism in Modern Man, loc. cit.*

24. Cf. Davies, *op. cit.*, pp. 263ff. For a convenient summary of rabbinic thought on martyrdom, see C. G. Montefiore and H. Loewe, *A Rabbinic Anthology* (Philadelphia: Jewish Publication Society, 1960), pp. 233–71; and George Foote Moore, *Judaism in the First Three Centuries of the Christian Era* (Cambridge: Harvard University Press, 1954), vol. 2, pp. 105ff. It is important to note that while martyrdom was praised, the Jew was admonished not to seek it unnecessarily.

25. Cf. Schoeps, *op. cit.*, pp. 134–41; and Davies, *op. cit.*, pp. 274ff.

26. For a discussion of rabbinic ambivalence, see Richard L. Rubenstein, *The Religious Imagination* (Indianapolis: Bobbs-Merrill, 1968), pp. 151–70.

27. If Knox is correct in his hypothesis that Paul visited Jerusalem for the first time after his conversion, Paul would have had no direct connection with Stephen. Knox relies heavily on the passage in Galatians in which Paul declared that when he went to Jerusalem for the first time as a Christian, "I was still not known by sight to the churches in Judaea; they only heard it said, He who once persecuted us is now preaching the faith he once tried to destroy" (Gal. 1:22f.). Knox, *op. cit.*, p. 36.

28. For a brief discussion of current scholarly debate over the literary and textual problems involved in understanding Acts, cf. Paul Feine and Johannes Behm, *Introduction to the New Testament*, ed. Werner Georg Kümmel, trans. A. J. Mattill, Jr. (Nashville: Abingdon Press, 1966), pp. 112–33.

29. Cf. Schnackenberg, *op. cit.*, pp. 61, 133, 136; and Robinson, *op. cit.*, pp. 51f.

30. Robinson, *op. cit.*, p. 58.

31. Cf. Rubenstein, *op. cit.*, pp. 101–16.

Chapter IV

1. Cyril of Jerusalem, 'Cat. Myst,' *Monumenta eucharistica et liturgica vetustissima,* collegit J. Quasten (Floril. Patr. VII, 2), (Bonn, 1935), 84, 15–16. I am indebted to Schnackenberg, *op. cit.,* p. 59, for this source. However, he does not seem to have noted its significance for a depth psychological understanding of Paul.
2. Schweitzer, *op. cit.,* pp. 13–15.
3. Cf. Bernard J. Bamberger, *Proselytism in the Talmudic Period* (New York: K'tav Publishing House, 1968), pp. 63f. According to the Talmud, "Λ convert is like a new born child" (Yebamoth 22a, 62a, 97b). Bamberger commented that this statement was one of "the most important legal generalizations" on the subject by the rabbis.
4. Cf. Schnackenburg, *op. cit.,* pp. 13 f.
5. Cf. Bamberger, *op. cit.,* pp. 42ff.
6. Cf. G. Vermes, *The Dead Sea Scrolls in English* (Baltimore: Penguin Books, 1968), pp. 45, 50.
7. Cf. Schnackenberg, *op. cit.,* p. 136.
8. Cf. Schnackenberg, *op. cit.,* pp. 8f.
9. Cf. Oscar Cullmann, *Baptism in the New Testament,* trans. J. K. S. Reid (London: SCM Press, 1950), pp. 10ff.
10. This was probably true of the Qumran community; cf. Schnackenberg, *op. cit.,* pp. 16f.
11. Sandor Ferenczi, *Thalassa: A Theory of Genitality,* trans. Henry A. Bunker (New York: W. W. Norton & Co., 1968).
12. Ferenczi, *op. cit.,* pp. 45f.
13. Freud, *Beyond the Pleasure Principle,* trans. James Strachey (New York: Bantam Books, 1967), p. 67.
14. Freud, *op. cit.,* p. 68.
15. Freud, *op. cit.,* p. 70.
16. Cf. Mircea Eliade, *Birth and Rebirth,* trans. Willard R. Trask (New York: Harper & Bros., 1958).
17. Eliade, *op. cit.,* p. xiii.
18. On Jesus' attitude toward the family, see David Flusser, *Jesus,* trans. Ronald Walls (New York: Herder and Herder, 1969),

pp. 20–22. Cf. William E. Phipps, *Was Jesus Married?* (New York: Harper & Row, 1970), who has, of course, a contrasting view. On Paul and marriage, cf. J. J. von Allmen, *Pauline Teaching on Marriage* (London: Faith Press, 1963).

19. Bultmann, *Theology of the New Testament,* vol. 1, p. 309.
20. Bornkamm, *op. cit.,* p. 208.
21. Cf. Jean Héring, *The First Epistle of Saint Paul to the Corinthians,* trans. A. W. Heathcote and P. J. Allcock (London: Epsworth Press, 1962), p. 45.
22. There is disagreement about the meaning of this passage. I have followed Héring, *op. cit.* The Roman Catholic Jerusalem Bible has "these present times of stress."
23. Tarachow, *op. cit.*
24. Freud, "Family Romances," in *CP,* vol. 5, pp. 74–78, and *Moses and Monotheism,* p. 9.
25. Bakan, *op. cit.,* pp. 205–7. Cf. E. Wellisch, *Isaac and Oedipus* (London: Routledge & Kegan Paul, 1954).
26. Cf. Melanie Klein, *Contributions to Psycho-Analysis 1921–1945* (London: The Hogarth Press and the Institute of Psycho-Analysis, 1948), p. 148.
27. Cf. Rubenstein, *op. cit.,* pp. 69–100.
28. Cf. Klausner, *op. cit.,* p. 331, who pointed out that it was easier to win female converts to Judaism because only ritual immersion was required of women, whereas circumcision was required of men. While I reject the idea that circumcision was abolished because it made proselytism easier, Klausner's argument has a certain strength insofar as the effect of the abolition was to strengthen Christianity's position as a missionary religion.
29. Bruno Bettelheim, *Symbolic Wounds* (Glencoe, Ill.: The Free Press, 1954, pp. 46–48, 105–14.
30. Cf. Rubenstein, *op. cit.,* pp. 94–100. On the Great Mother Goddess, cf. Erich Neumann, *The Great Mother,* trans. Ralph Mannheim (New York: Pantheon Books, 1955), and *Ernanos Jahrbuch* (Zurich, 1938). The entire issue of the 1938 *Ernanos Jahrbuch* is devoted to the problem of the Mother Goddess.
31. Schnackenberg, *op. cit.,* pp. 67f. I am mindful of the scholarly debate over whether Colossians is an authentic letter of Paul. This passage seems to me to be completely within the spirit of Paul's thought.

32. Freud, *Moses and Monotheism,* p. 113.
33. Cf. Reik, *Ritual: Psychoanalytic Studies* (London: The Hogarth Press and the Institute of Psycho-Analysis, 1931), pp. 69–89.

Chapter V

1. Freud, *Totem and Taboo,* trans. James Strachey (New York: W. W. Norton & Co., 1962).
2. Cf. Rubenstein, *op. cit.,* pp. 1–21.
3. Cf. *supra,* chap. 2, pp. 8ff.
4. Freud, *Totem and Taboo,* p. 143.
5. W. Robertson Smith, *The Religion of the Semites* (New York: Meridian Press, 1956).
6. On Canaanite sacrifices, cf. Theodore H. Gaster, "The Service of the Sanctuary: A Study in Hebrew Survivals," in *Melanges Syriens offert à M. R. Dussaud,* 2 (Paris, 1939): 577–82; Roland de Vaux, *Ancient Israel: Its Life and Institutions,* trans. John McHugh (New York: McGraw-Hill, 1961), pp. 438–46.
7. Freud, *Moses and Monotheism,* p. 174, and *Totem and Taboo,* p. 154.
8. Freud, *Totem and Taboo,* p. 155.
9. Cf. *supra,* chap. 2, pp. 1f., 19.
10. G. W. F. Hegel, *The Phenomenology of Mind,* trans. J. B. Baillie (London: George Allen & Unwin, 1931), p. 233.
11. For a psychoanalytic discussion of the loving and aggressive aspects of Holy Communion, see Margaretta K. Bowers, *Conflicts of the Clergy* (New York: Thomas Nelson and Sons, 1963), pp. 41–70.
12. Cf. A. L. Kroeber, *American Anthropologist, New Series,* 22 (1920): 48.
13. Freud, *Group Psychology and the Analysis of the Ego,* p. 69.

Chapter VI

1. Cf. Hans Lietzmann, *Mass and Lord's Supper: A Study in the History of Liturgy,* trans. Dorothea H. G. Reeve (Leiden: E. J. Brill, 1953–), p. 185. Cf. Héring, *op. cit.,* p. 115: "Our Epistle is

the oldest Christian document about the Lord's Supper." For a discussion of the priority of Mark 14 or I Corinthians 11, cf. Davies, *op. cit.,* pp. 242ff. Dom Gregory Dix regards Paul's account as older than Mark's. According to Dix, Paul's evidence is "about as strong as ancient historical evidence for anything at all is ever likely to be." *The Shape of the Liturgy* (Westminster, Md.: Dacre Press, 1945), p. 73.

2. Cf. Oscar Cullmann, *Early Christian Worship,* trans. A. Stewart Todd and James B. Torrence (London: SCM Press, 1962), pp. 10–15.

3. Freud, *Group Psychology and the Analysis of the Ego,* pp. 35–38.

4. Cullmann, *op. cit.,* p. 15.

5. Lietzmann, *op. cit.,* pp. 195–208; cf. also R. D. Richardson's introduction.

6. Lietzmann, *op. cit.,* pp. 204ff.

7. Cf. Schweitzer, *op. cit.,* pp. 249f., 270. Cf. Richardson, "A Further Inquiry into Eucharistic Origins with Special Reference to New Testament Problems," in Lietzmann, *op. cit.,* pp. 221ff. Cf. Ernest Käsemann, "The Pauline Doctrine of the Lord's Supper," in *Essays on New Testament Themes* (London: SCM Press, 1964), pp. 108–35. Cf. Cullmann, *op. cit.,* pp. 17ff., and Schoeps, *op. cit.,* pp. 117ff.

8. T. W. Manson, *Journal of Theological Studies, 46* (Jan.-Apr. 1945).

9. Cullmann, *op. cit.,* p. 19.

10. *Didache,* trans. Maxwell Staniforth, in *Early Christian Writings: The Apostolic Fathers* (Harmondsworth, Middlesex: Penguin Books, 1968), pp. 231f.

11. Cf. Héring, *op. cit.,* pp. 114–15. Cf. Maurice Goguel, *L'eucharistie des origines à Justin Martyr* (Paris, 1910), and F. Leenhardt, *Le sacramente de la sainte Cène* (Paris, 1948).

12. This is the opinion of J. Moffatt, *The First Epistle to the Corinthians* (London, 1938), p. 163. Cf. Héring, *op. cit.,* pp. 114ff. However, cf. Davies, *op. cit.,* pp. 247–50, who argued with much force that as a traditionary Paul handed down the fundamental intent of the Eucharistic tradition as he understood it rather than the tradition exactly as he had received it. Davies cited rabbinic practice to show that Paul's handling of Christian tradition resembled the way the rabbis handed down their traditions.

13. Lietzmann, *op. cit.*, p. 208.
14. *Tosefta,* ed. Zukermandel (Passewalk, 1880), p. 196, 1. 25 p. 197, 1. 1.
15. Héring, *op. cit.*, pp. 176f.
16. Käsemann, *op. cit.*, pp. 108–35.
17. Käsemann, *op. cit.*, p. 118.
18. Käsemann, *op. cit.*, p. 124.
19. Shalom Spiegel, "Prophetic Attestation of the Decalogue: Hosea 6:5, With Some Observations on Psalms 15 and 34," *Harvard Theological Review* (April 1934).
20. Ignatius, *Ad. Eph.,* XX; Eng. trans. *Ignatius: Epistle to the Ephesians,* in *Early Christian Writings: The Apostolic Fathers,* p. 20. Cf. Ignatius, *Epistle to the Romans,* in *op. cit.,* p. 106.
21. On the Mother Goddess, cf. Neumann, *op. cit.,* pp. 149ff. On the fear of being eaten, cf. Fenichel, "The Dread of Being Eaten," *International Journal of Psycho-Analysis, 10* (1929). Cf. Karl Abraham, "A Short Study of the Development of Libido," in *Selected Papers* (London: The Hogarth Press and the Institute of Psycho-Analysis, 1927); Joan Riviere and Melanie Klein, *Love, Hate and Reparation* (New York: W. W. Norton & Co., 1964), pp. 4–25.
22. Lev. 24:5ff. Cf. Johannes Pedersen, *Israel* (London: Oxford University Press, 1928–40), vol. 4, pp. 368f.
23. Lev. 2:13. Cf. Pedersen, *op. cit.,* vol. 4, p. 356.
24. Héring, *op. cit.,* p. 115
25. Bultmann, *Theology of the New Testament,* vol. 1, p. 146.
26. Davies, *op. cit.,* p. 259.
27. Davies, *loc. cit.*
28. Davies, *loc. cit.*
29. The rabbi was R. Meir. Cf. Tractate *Sanhedrin,* 70a; *Bereshith Rabba,* 36.4; and *Midrash Wa-Yikra Rabbah,* ed. M. Margulies (Jerusalem, 1933–58), 12.1. Cf. Rubenstein, *op. cit.,* pp. 58–68.
30. Deut. 12:23. Cf. Theodore Gaster, *Myth, Legend and Custom in the Old Testament* (New York: Harper & Row, 1969).
31. Cf. Pedersen, *op. cit.,* vol. 4, pp. 338–40.
32. Cf. Davies, *op. cit.,* who makes use of the contrasts between the "old" and the "new" throughout his work.
33. W. O. E. Oesterley, *Sacrifices of Ancient Israel* (London, 1937), pp. 99ff. Cf. Rubenstein, *op. cit.,* pp. 58–68.

34. Pedersen, op. cit.
35. Cf. Rubenstein, op. cit., pp. 60ff.
36. Pedersen, op. cit., pp. 313ff., 410.
37. Spiegel, The Last Trail, trans. Judah Goldin (New York: Schocken Books, 1970).
38. Spiegel, The Last Trial, pp. 33f., who cites Midrash Shibbole ha Leket, Inyan Tefillah, 18, ed. S. Buber, 9a. In this tradition Isaac is "reduced to ashes" as a burnt offering before God uses the dew of Mount Hermon to resurrect him.
39. The references are far too numerous to cite. E.g., "May the binding (Akedah) which our father Abraham bound his son Isaac on the altar appear before Thee, and as he (Abraham) subdued his feelings of mercy to do Thy will with a whole heart, so may Thy feelings of mercy remove Thine anger from upon us" High Holiday Prayer Book, ed. Morris Silverman (Hartford: Prayer Book Press, 1951), p. 165.
40. Spiegel, The Last Trial, p. 84. Cf. Schoeps, op. cit., pp. 141–49, for an excellent summary of rabbinic and patristic material of relevance to Paul's possible use of the Isaac-Christ typology, especially in Romans 8.
41. Cf. Bowers, op. cit., p. 59; Brown, op. cit., pp. 162–75. Ian D. Suttie, The Origins of Love and Hate (London: Kegan Paul, 1935), p. 145; R. S. Lee, Psychology and Worship (London: SCM Press, 1955), pp. 95–100.

Chapter VII

1. Bornkamm, op. cit., pp. 231ff.
2. Cf. Markus Barth, "Was Paul an Anti-Semite?" Journal of Ecumenical Studies, 5 (1968); and Stendahl, "Judaism and Christianity," Harvard Divinity School Bulletin, 28 (Oct. 1963).
3. I am indebted to Peter Berger, The Sacred Canopy (Garden City, N. Y.: Doubleday Anchor Books, 1969), pp. 3–51, for this insight.
4. Cf. Vermes, op. cit., pp. 38f.
5. Cf. Rubenstein, After Auschwitz (Indianapolis: Bobbs-Merrill, 1966), pp. 1–44; Rudolph M. Loewenstein, Christians and Jews

(New York: International Universities Press, 1951), pp. 89–106; Joshua Trachtenberg, *The Devil and the Jews* (New Haven: Yale University Press, 1943).

6. Cf. Vermes, *op. cit.*, pp. 34f., 53–67; Morton Scott Enslin, *Christian Beginnings* (New York: Harper Torchbooks, 1956), pts. 1 and 2, pp. 111–28.

7. Cf. Moore, *op. cit.*, vol. 1, pp. 251–62.

8. Cf. Max Weber, *Economy and Society*, ed. Guenther Roth and Claus Wittich (Totowa, N. J.: Bedminster Press, 1968), pp. 1111–62.

9. The classic tradition is the story of how R. Eliezer tried to validate his opinion in a discussion with R. Joshua by invoking a heavenly voice (*bat qol*). The heavenly voice did indeed declare that the Law (Halakhah) is according to the opinion of R. Eliezer, but R. Joshua rejected this opinion, declaring, "It is not in heaven" (Deut. 30:12). R. Jeremiah, who flourished two generations later, interpreted R. Joshua's position: "The Law was given to us from Sinai. (Since then) we pay no attention to heavenly voices . . ." *Baba Mezia*, 59b.

10. There was a tradition that after the death of Haggai, Zechariah, and Malachi, "the Holy Spirit ceased from Israel." Israel was nevertheless granted the privilege of hearing heavenly voices, but as we have seen, they had less authority by far than the rabbis. Cf. *Tosefta*, *Sotah*, 13, 2; Sanhedrin 11a; Sotah 48b; Yoma 9b.

11. Cf. I. Cor. 7:18–22.

12. Cf. Munck, *op. cit.*, pp. 247–81.

13. Munck, *op. cit.*, pp. 252f.

14. The problem is discussed by Munck, *op. cit.*, pp. 69–86, in a chapter entitled "The Tübingen School and Paul." He has shown that under the leadership of Ferdinand Christian Baur, the Tübingen School's hypothesis has dominated the interpretation of Paul's relations with the Jerusalem Church and his own people. For a detailed discussion of the history of New Testament interpretation, cf. Schweitzer, *Paul and His Interpreters*, trans. W. Montgomery (London, 1912).

15. This view has been challenged by John Bligh, who believes that the tradition that Peter was instructed by God in the vision of

the sail cloth to eat without regard to the Jewish dietary laws (Acts 10:9–16) is misplaced. According to Bligh, Paul rather than Peter had the vision. Bligh stressed the antagonism between Peter and Paul, but at the expense of the integrity of the received text. *Galatians* (London: St. Paul Publications, 1969), pp. 104–6.

16. This is, of course, Munck's thesis, which I accept. For a persuasive argument against Munck, see Bligh, *op. cit.,* pp. 31ff.

17. In Acts 15 the Apostolic Council ruled that all that was necessary for Gentile converts was to "abstain from anything polluted by idols, from fornication, from the meat of strangled animals and from blood" (Acts 15:20). In Galatians the agreement that Paul had been commissioned to preach to the "uncircumcised" and Peter to the "circumcised" is stressed. However, the fact that the accounts differ in emphasis does not necessarily mean that there were two meetings. Cf. Bligh, *op. cit.,* pp. 144ff. Munck saw the two accounts as "in agreement in essential details" in *The Acts of the Apostles,* rev. William P. Alright and C. S. Mann (Garden City, N. Y:. Doubleday & Co., 1967), p. lxviii.

18. Munck, *op. cit.,* pp. 87–134.

19. Cf. Davies, "A New View of Paul—J. Munck, 'Paulus und die Heilsgeschichte,'" in Davies, *Christian Origins and Judaism, A Collection of New Testament Studies* (London: Darton, Longman & Todd, 1962); Bligh, *op. cit.,* pp. 32ff.; Walter Schmithals, *Paul and James,* trans. Dorothea M. Barton (London: SCM Press, 1965), pp. 13–15. Cf. Rigaux, *op. cit.,* pp. 10–15, for a summary of discussion of Munck's thesis. Butlmann's critical review is also important: "Eine neues Paulus—Verständnis?" *Theologische Literaturzeitung,* 84 (Leipzig, 1959). For Schoeps' criticism of Munck, see Schoeps, *op. cit.,* pp. 50, 69. However, Schoeps concurred with Munck in his rejection of a "deep gulf" between Paul and James and Peter.

20. Schmithals, *op. cit.,* pp. 38–62.

21. Munck, *Christ and Israel, An Interpretation of Romans 9–11,* trans. Ingeborg Nixon (Philadelphia: Fortress Press, 1967), pp. 116–43.

22. Cf. Weber, *The Sociology of Religion,* trans. Ephriam Fischoff

(Boston: Beacon Press, 1963), pp. 95–137. On the relationship between aggression, class, and status, cf. Anthony Storr, *Human Aggression* (New York: Athenaeum, 1968). For a discussion of the ways in which Judaism responded to powerlessness and defeat after A.D. 70, cf. Rubenstein, *The Religious Imagination,* pp. ix-xvii.

23. Cf. Bettelheim, *Children of the Dream* (New York: The Macmillan Co., 1969); Rubenstein, "Homeland and Holocaust," in Donald R. Cutler, ed., *The Religious Situation: 1968* (Boston: Beacon Press, 1969).

24. The Community of the Scrolls was convinced that it alone constituted "the Children of Light." All the rest of Israel, not to say the rest of mankind, were consigned to moral and spiritual darkness. Cf. Vermes, *op. cit.*

25. Munck, *Christ and Israel,* p. 11. Nickle's thesis is presented in Keith F. Nickle, *The Collection: A Study in Paul's Strategy* (London: SCM Press, 1966).

26. Cf. Raphael Patai, *Man and Temple in Ancient Jewish Myth and Ritual* (London: Thomas Nelson and Sons, 1947), pp. 85, 132, 155.

27. Nickle did not refer specifically to the prophecies; Munck did. Cf. Nickle, *op. cit.,* pp. 127–43; Munck, *Paul and the Salvation of Mankind,* pp. 303f.

28. Cf. *supra,* chap. 7, n. 19.

29. Tarachow, *op. cit.*

30. *Baba Mezia* 33a.

31. Cf. Davies, *op. cit.,* pp. 177ff.

32. Cf. C. K. Barrett, *A Commentary on the Epistle to the Romans* (New York: Harper & Row, 1957), pp. 180, 194.

33. Barrett, *op. cit.,* p. 213.

34. Munck, *Paul and the Salvation of Mankind,* p. 300; *Christ and Israel,* p. 89. For another example of the inability of well-meaning Christians to accept the autonomous integrity of Judaism, cf. Käsemann, "Paul and Israel," in Käsemann, *New Testament Questions of Today,* trans. W. J. Montague (Philadelphia: Fortress Press, 1969), pp. 183–87.

35. Cf. Loewe and Montefiore, *op. cit.,* p. 686, n. 78; Moore, *op. cit.,* vol. 2, p. 371.

36. Cf. Freud, *Moses and Monotheism,* pp. 174–76; Rubenstein, *After Auschwitz,* pp. 1–44.
37. Brown, *op. cit.,* pp. 20f.
38. Hannah Arendt, *The Origins of Totalitarianism* (New York: Harcourt Brace, 1951), pp. 221–66.

Chapter VIII

1. Cf. *supra,* chap. 3, p. 1.
2. Robin Scroggs, *The Last Adam: A Study in Pauline Anthropology* (Philadelphia: Fortress Press, 1966), pp. 46–50.
3. *Midrash Bereshith Rabbah* 8:1, where a number of opinions are given concerning Adam as "filling the whole world." Cf. *Bereshith Rabbah* 12.6 and 19.9, where Adam's gigantic size is emphasized. Cf. Scroggs, *op. cit.,* pp. 49f., who also points out that Adam is described as a shapeless mass (*golem*) and that *golem* can also mean embryo. However, he apparently ignores the idea of Adam as an embryo extending from one end of the world to another as related to a conception of Adam as the primordial embryo within the cosmic womb. N. P. Williams, W. D. Davies, and C. K. Barrett see Adam's grandiose size as emphasizing the "seriousness of Adam's fall." None of these scholars attempt to offer a psychological interpretation. Cf. Norman P. Williams, *The Ideas of the Fall and of Original Sin* (London: Longmans, Green & Co., 1917); Davies, *Paul and Rabbinic Judaism,* p. 45; Barrett, *From First Adam to Last* (London: A. & C. Black, 1962), pp. 7f.
4. Cf. Scroggs, *op. cit.,* pp. 18–20.
5. W. L. Knox, *St. Paul and the Church of the Gentiles* (Cambridge: Cambridge University Press, 1939), pp. 99–106.
6. Cf. Käsemann, "On the Topic of Primitive Christian Apocalyptic," in Robert W. Funk, ed., *Apocalypticism* (New York: Herder and Herder, 1969), p. 133. Käsemann asserted that Paul's battle against the enthusiasts at Corinth was fought "under the banner of apocalyptic," p. 127. This viewpoint has been challenged by Gerhard Ebeling, "The Ground of Christian Theology," in Funk, *op. cit.,* p. 56. Cf. Käsemann, "The Beginnings of Christian Theology," in Funk, *op. cit.,* pp. 17–46.

7. Barrett, *op. cit.*, pp. 92–119.
8. For a brief discussion of the current problem, cf. Hans Conzelmann, "Current Problems in Pauline Research," in Batey, *op. cit.*, pp. 130–47. For contrasting views, see Davies, "Paul and Judaism Since Schweitzer," in Davies, *Paul and Rabbinic Judaism,* pp. vii-xv; and Scroggs, *op. cit.*, pp. 13–50.
9. Scroggs, *op. cit.*, p. 82.
10. I Cor. 15:12.
11. Héring, *op. cit.*, pp. 164f.
12. Bultmann, *Theology of the New Testament,* vol. 1, p. 174, saw the Fall of Adam as dependent on Gnostic mythology. One of the preeminent contemporary scholars on Gnosticism finds hardly any trace of the doctrine in Paul's writing. Cf. Robert Grant, *Gnosticism and Early Christianity* (New York: Columbia University Press, 1966), pp. 154–62.
13. Henry A. Murray, "In Nomine Diaboli," in Richard Chase, ed., *Melville* (Englewood Cliffs, N. J.: Prentice-Hall, 1962).
14. Héring, *op. cit.*, p. 158; Bultmann, *Theology of the New Testament,* vol. 1, p. 82.
15. Cf. Ginzberg, *op. cit.*, vol. 5, pp. 128–31, n. 142; Rubenstein, *The Religious Imagination,* pp. 43–47.
16. Héring, *op. cit.*, p. 16; Schweitzer, *op. cit.*, pp. 71f., saw Paul as preparing "the way to Gnosticism" in this passage. This is also Grant's opinion in *op. cit.*, p. 156.
17. Houlden, *op. cit.*, p. 190.
18. Houlden, *op. cit.*, p. 187. This theme hints at the theme of the Saviour as Trickster of the elemental powers. Cf. Ignatius, *Ad. Eph.*, 19.2; E. T., *op. cit.*, p. 81; Schweitzer, *op. cit.*, pp. 71–83.
19. At a later era, the idea that the Children of Light are menaced by the malevolent Powers of Darkness reappears in the theologies of the millennarian cults. Cohn, *op. cit.*, saw this phenomenon as an expression of group paranoia. Cf. Talmon, *op. cit.*
20. This is the opinion of Houlden, *op. cit.*, pp. 38–41, who accepts its authenticity but not its integrity as a single letter. F. W. Beare, *A Commentary on the Epistle to the Philippians* (London: A. & C. Black, 1959), p. 24, saw it as a compilation containing parts of three letters of Paul and an interpolated fragment (3:2–4:1), which Paul may have written to another group. For a discussion of the problem of the authenticity and integrity of Philippians

since Baur, cf. W. G. Kümmel, *Introduction to the New Testament,* founded by Paul Feine and Johannes Behm, pp. 235–37.

21. Ernst Lohmeyer, "Kyrios Jesus: Eine Untersuchung zu Phil. 2:5–11," *Sitzungberichte der Heidelberger Akademie der Wissenschaften, Phil. Hist. Klasse* (1928). For a bibliography of scholarship on the poem, cf. Beare, *op. cit.,* pp. 40–42.

22. On the origin of the hymn, cf. Lohmeyer, *op. cit.;* Frederick Hauk Borsch, *The Son of Man in Myth and History* (Philadelphia: Westminster Press, 1967), pp. 254f. On the use of tradition, cf. Martin Dibelius, *From Tradition to Gospel,* trans. Bertram Lee Woolf (New York: Charles Scribner's Sons, undated).

23. Cf. Barrett, *op. cit.,* pp. 14–17, 69ff.; Houlden, *op. cit.,* pp. 73–75; and Cullmann, *The Christology of the New Testament,* trans. S. G. Guthrie and C. A. M. Hall (Philadelphia: Westminster Press, 1959), pp. 174–81. Scroggs, *op. cit.,* was cautious, suggesting that the hymn might contain a "hint" of Paul's judgment on Adam, p. 89.

24. Cf. Rubenstein, *The Religious Imagination,* pp. 101–16.

25. Cf. Gershom Scholem, *Major Trends in Jewish Mysticism* (New York: Schocken Books, 1941), pp. 229–33.

26. Cf. Rubenstein, *The Religious Imagination,* pp. 96–100.

27. Leslie A. Fiedler, *Love and Death in the American Novel,* rev. ed. (New York: Dell, 1969).

28. Thomas J. J. Altizer, *The Descent into Hell* (Philadelphia: Lippincott, 1970), p. 189. For a discussion of Altizer's theological vision, cf. John Cobb, ed., *The Theology of Altizer: Critique and Response* (Philadelphia: Westminster Press, 1970).

29. Brown, *op. cit.,* p. 148.

30. Altizer, *op. cit.,* p. 191.

31. Altizer, *op. cit.,* p. 193. For an earlier statement of his views, see his *Oriental Mysticism and Biblical Eschatology* (Philadelphia: Westminster Press, 1961).

32. On the psychology of Nirvana, see Rune E. A. Johansson, *The Psychology of Nirvana* (London: George Allen & Unwin, 1969); cf. Frederick J. Streng, *Emptiness: A Study in Religious Meaning* (Nashville: Abingdon Press, 1970), pp. 79–81. According to Franz Alexander, "the end goal of Buddhistic absorption is an

attempt at psychological and physical regression to the condition of intra-uterine life." "Buddhistic Training as an Artificial Catatonia," in *The Scope of Psychoanalysis: 1921–1961: Selected Papers of Franz Alexander* (New York: Basic Books, 1961), pp. 74–89.

33. If not prenatal existence, at least the stage of primary narcissism. Cf. Fenichel, *op. cit.*, pp. 40f.; Ruth Munroe, *Schools of Psycho-Analytic Thought* (New York: Holt, Rinehart and Winston, 1955), pp. 178ff.

34. Scholem, *op. cit.*, pp. 244–86.

35. Käsemann, "On the Topic of Primitive Christian Apocalyptic," in Funk, *op. cit.*, p. 129.

36. Héring, *op. cit.*, p. 168.

37. Héring, *loc. cit.*

38. Héring, *op. cit.*, p. 165.

39. Héring, *op. cit.*, p. 169.

40. Cf. Cullmann, *Christ and Time* (London: SCM Press, 1951). On the question of whether the last things shall be like the first, cf. N. A. Dahl, "Christ, Creation and the Church," in W. D. Davies and D. Daube, *The Background of the New Testament and Its Eschatology* (Cambridge: Cambridge University Press, 1956). Dahl quoted Barnabas (VI:13), "God will make the last things like the first." See the classic study of Herman Gunkel, *Schöpfung und Chaos in Endzeit und Urzeit* (Göttingen, 1910), pp. 368–71. For two further views of the Adam-Christ tradition, cf. Karl Barth, *Christ and Adam* (Edinburgh: Oliver and Boyd, 1950), and Bultmann's reply to Barth, "Adam and Christ According to Romans 5," in W. Klassen and F. Snyder, *Current Issues in New Testament Interpretation* (New York: Harper & Bros., 1962).

A BIBLIOGRAPHICAL NOTE*

This book is an outgrowth of my earlier work *The Religious Imagination* (Indianapolis: Bobbs-Merrill, 1968; paperback ed., Beacon Press, 1971). Both the method employed and many of the themes discussed here have developed from themes dealt with in that volume.

Among the books that I have found most helpful were C. K. Barrett, *From First Adam to Last* (London, A. & C. Black, 1962), and *A Commentary on the Epistle to the Romans* (New York: Harper & Row, 1957). It was Barrett who taught me the crucial importance of Philippians 2:5–11 and sent me to Ernst Lohmeyer, "Kyrios Jesus: Eine Untersuchung zu Phil. 2:5–11, in *Sitzungberichte der Heidelberger Akademie der Wissenschaften, Phil. Hist. Klasse* (1928). No less helpful than Barrett was Robin Scroggs, *The Last Adam: A Study in Pauline Anthropology* (Philadelphia: Fortress Press, 1966). I first read Scroggs at the suggestion of Professor Jacob Neusner of Brown University, and I have read few books on Paul that I have found more enlightening.

Can anyone read Paul without attempting to understand that classic of twentieth-century theology, Karl Barth, *The Epistle to the Romans*, trans. Edwyn C. Hoskyns (Oxford: Oxford University Press, 1933)? I have been instructed by it since first reading it as a graduate student. Barth's *Christ and Adam* (Edinburgh: Oliver and

---

* This note does not list all of the books used in this book. The texts referred to here are those that have proven especially important to me in my work on Paul.

195

Boyd, 1956), was also helpful. Werner Georg Kümmel's revision of Paul Feine and Johannes Behm, *Introduction to the New Testament,* trans. A. J. Mattill, Jr. (Nashville: Abingdon Press, 1965), was especially useful in summarizing many of the issues about which scholars debate in their interpretations of Paul. Béda Rigaux, *The Letter of St. Paul* (Chicago: Franciscan Herald Press, 1968), performed the same service from the Roman Catholic point of view.

I have consulted many of the standard commentaries on Paul's letters, including the older commentaries of Luther and Calvin, but a few stand out as especially helpful. The most instructive one was J. L. Houlden, *Paul's Letters From Prison* (Harmondsworth, Middlesex: Penguin Books, 1970). Jean Héring, *The First Epistle of Saint Paul to the Corinthians* and *The Second Epistle of Saint Paul to the Corinthians,* trans. A. W. Heathcote and P. J. Allcock (London: Epsworth Press, 1962, 1967), were equally instructive. F. W. Beare, *Commentary on the Epistle to the Philippians* (London: A. & C. Black, 1959), is important not only as a commentary but because of its bibliography. There was much in John Bligh, *Galatians: A Discussion of St. Paul's Epistle* (London: St. Paul Publications, 1969), with which I profoundly disagree. Nevertheless, it is an important and richly suggestive work.

One of the most exciting articles I read on Paul was Krister Stendahl, "The Apostle Paul and the Introspective Conscience of the West," *Harvard Theological Review,* 56 (3, July 1963). I was compelled to rethink my understanding of Paul as a result of that article. John A. T. Robinson, *The Body* (London: SCM Press, 1952), and Albert Schweitzer, *The Mysticism of Paul the Apostle,* trans. William Montgomery (London: A. & C. Black, 1953), had a comparable impact on my thinking.

On the subject of Holy Communion, I read with great interest Hans Lietzmann, *Mass and Lord's Supper,* trans. Dorothea H. G. Reeve (Leiden: E. J. Brill, 1953); Dom Gregory Dix, *The Shape of the Liturgy* (Westminster, Md.: Dacre Press, 1945), and Oscar Cullmann, *Early Christian Worship,* trans. Floyd V. Filson (London: SCM Press, 1951). On the subject of baptism, my most important resource was Rudolph Schnackenberg, *Baptism in the Thought of Saint Paul,* trans. G. R. Beasley Murray (Oxford: Basil Blackwell, 1964). Cullmann's *Baptism in the New Testament,* trans. J. K. S. Reid (London: SCM Press, 1950), was also most informative.

Among the interpretations of Paul's life and thought I consulted were Arthur Darby Nock, *St. Paul* (New York: Harper & Bros., 1938); Martin Dibelius, *Paul*, ed. and completed by W. G. Kümmel, trans. Frank Clarke (London: Longmans, 1953); and John Knox, *Chapters in a Life of St. Paul* (London: A. & C. Black, 1954); and above all, Günther Bornkamm, *Paul*, trans. D. M. G. Stalker (Harper & Row, 1971). Although I find myself unable to accept a number of Bornkamm's conclusions, I believe that this book is one of the best and most authoritative contemporary studies of the Apostle. Rudolf Bultmann, *Theology of the New Testament*, 2 vols., trans. Kendrick Grobel (New York: Charles Scribner's Sons, 1951), must be studied diligently by any contemporary student of Paul.

My unreserved praise goes to W. D. Davies, *Paul and Rabbinic Judaism: Some Rabbinic Elements in Pauline Thought* (New York: Harper & Row, 1967). It is my belief that contemporary interpretations of Paul must build largely upon the foundations laid by Davies in this work. Another scholar whose interpretations of Paul must be studied with great respect is Ernst Käsemann. Two collections of his essays are available in English: *Essays on New Testament Themes*, trans. W. J. Montague (London: SCM Press, 1964), and *New Testament Questions of Today*, trans. W. J. Montague (Philadelphia: Fortress Press, 1969).

The crucial volume for understanding Paul's relations with his own people is Johannes Munck, *Paul and the Salvation of Mankind*, trans. Frank Clarke (Richmond: John Knox Press, 1959). His *Christ and Israel: An Interpretation of Romans 9–11*, trans. Ingeborg Nixon (Philadelphia: Fortress Press, 1967), offers the student an insight into how Munck arrived at his thesis.

By far the best and most authoritative Jewish study on Paul is Hans Joachim Schoeps, *Paul: The Theology of the Apostle in the Light of Jewish History*, trans. Harold J. Knight (Philadelphia: Westminster Press, 1961). There is much in this book with which I would take issue; there is nothing in it that would diminish my respect for the authority or the integrity of his scholarship. An older book of continuing relevance is Joseph Klausner, *From Jesus to Paul*, trans. William F. Stinespring (Boston: Beacon Press, 1961). Martin Buber, *Two Types of Faith*, trans. Norman P. Goldhawk (London: Routledge & Kegan Paul, 1951), ought to be read as a sample of Jewish interpretation of Paul and for what it reveals about Buber rather than Paul. I was surprised to find Leo Baeck's essay, "The Faith of Paul," in Baeck, *Judaism and Christianity*, trans. Walter Kaufman (Philadelphia: Jewish Publication Society, 1958), far more authoritative than Buber's effort. Another important work by Klausner is *The Messianic Idea in Judaism*, trans. William F. Stinespring (New York: The Macmillan Co., 1955).

One way of regarding Paul is to see him as a Christian Aggadist, that is, a Christian who utilized the rabbinic methods of homily and interpretation. The greatest treasury of information concerning the Aggadah in the English language is, to the best of my knowledge, Louis Ginzberg, *The Legends of the Jews* (Philadelphia: Jewish Publication Society, 1909–13). It is, I believe, an indispensable resource for the study of both rabbinic Judaism and Pauline Christianity. C. G. Montefiore and H. Loewe, *A Rabbinic Anthology* (Philadelphia: Jewish Publication Society, 1960), is a useful, convenient, and surprisingly complete collection of rabbinic literature. However, I take most emphatic exception to Loewe's observation in his introduction that "no one misunderstood Judaism more profoundly than Paul." On the specific issue of the sacrifice of Isaac and its relationship to Paul and Christianity, Shalom Spiegel, *The Last Trial* (New York: Schocken Books, 1970), is indispensable. However, Spiegel's book is more than that; it is a sheer delight and one of the finest works of contemporary Jewish scholarship.

The preeminent Jewish scholar of our times is Gershom Scholem. His interest in messianism, mysticism, and Gnosticism is especially relevant to the study of Paul. Anything Scholem writes merits serious study. For those who can read Hebrew or are willing to learn, his *Shabbat Zvi and the Shabbetaian Movement During His Lifetime* (Tel Aviv: Am Oved, 1967) is indispensable for an understanding of messianism as a perennial phenomenon in Jewish life. His *Jewish Gnosticism, Merkabah Mysticism, and Talmudic Tradition* (New York: Jewish Theological Seminary of America, 1960) contains an important observation on II Corinthians 12:2–4, in which Paul describes "a man in Christ" who was caught up into the "third heaven." Scholem's most recent work in English, *The Messianic Idea in Judaism*, trans. Michael Meyer and Hillel Halkin (New York: Schocken Books, 1971), and his *On the Kabbalah and Its Symbolism*, trans. *Ralph Mannheim* (New York: Schocken Books, 1965), are helpful for the insight they afford into the problem of the "end of the Law" and the coming of the Messiah in Jewish religious speculation. W. D. Davies, *Torah in the Messianic Age and/or the Age to Come* (Philadelphia: Society of Biblical Literature, 1952), deals with the same problem.

Sigmund Freud, *Totem and Taboo*, trans. James Strachey (New York: W. W. Norton & Co., 1962), taught me to understand the psychological truth of the biblical tradition that human civilization began with an act of primal rebellion against God. It also taught me the importance of sacrificial religion. His *Moses and Monotheism*, trans. Katherine Jones (New York: Alfred A. Knopf, 1939), interpreted Paul as the religious genius who brought to the light of consciousness the past's hidden secrets. Freud's interpretation of Paul is presupposed in this work, although I do not believe that a primal crime took place as a decisive act at the beginning of history. In *Group Psychology and the Analysis of the Ego* (London: International Psycho-Analytical Press, 1922), Freud illuminated the crucial importance of identification as the Christian's fundamental mode of relating to Christ. I hardly consider Theodore Reik, *Myth and Guilt* (New York: George Braziller, 1957), a scholarly work. Nevertheless, Reik understood the importance of Paul's doctrine of the Last Adam and saw how profundly this doctrine linked Paul with the Judaism out of which he came.

Otto Fenichel, *The Psychoanalytic Theory of Neurosis* (New York: W. W. Norton & Co., 1965); Franz Alexander, *The Fundamentals of Psychoanalysis* (New York: W. W. Norton & Co., 1963); and Ruth Munroe, *Schools of Psycho-Analytic Thought* (New York: Holt, Rinehart & Winston, 1955), offer excellent overviews of the theory and practice of psychoanalysis.

When I began this work, I was convinced that Erik H. Erikson, *Young Man Luther* (New York: W. W. Norton & Co., 1958), would offer a model for me. I was mistaken. Although I am indebted to Erikson, I am more indebted to Norman O. Brown, *Love's Body* (New York: Random House, 1966). Both in method and perspective it proved far more helpful for understanding Paul than Erikson's superb volume. Freud, *Beyond the Pleasure Principle*, trans. James Strachey (New York: Bantam Books, 1967), has always seemed to me to be a secularized, contemporary statement of the perennial vision of Jewish mysticism. Freud's view that we move forward to get back to where we came from is, of course, decisive for my interpretation of Paul. This vision was elaborated by Sandor Ferenczi in *Thalassa: A Theory of Genitality*, trans. Henry A. Bunker (New York: W. W. Norton & Co., 1968). He deepened my understanding of the motivational factors involved in baptism as well as Paul's vision of Christ as the Last Adam.

David Bakan's seminal work, *Sigmund Freud and the Jewish Mystical Tradition* (New York: Van Nostrand, 1958), and his observations on religion and the infanticidal impulse in *The Duality of Human Existence* (Chicago: Rand McNally, 1966) had an influence on my thinking that is visible throughout. Margaretta K. Bowers' work with clergy and her observations on the emotional importance of Holy Communion in their lives enlightened my understanding of the psychodynamics of that rite: *Conflicts of the Clergy* (New York: Thomas Nelson, 1963). Bruno Bettelheim, *Symbolic Wounds* (Glencoe, Ill.: The Free Press, 1954), offered an insightful interpretation of what is psychologically and culturally at stake in infant circumcision.

I believe that psychoanalysis can best be studied together with sociology. I found Peter Berger, *The Sacred Canopy* (Garden City, N. Y.: Doubleday Anchor Books, 1969), an informed and authoritative exposition of the sociology of religion.

I read a number of previous attempts to interpret Paul psychoanalytically. Two are worthy of note: Sidney Tarachow, "St. Paul and Early Christianity," in Warner Muensterberger and Sidney Axelrad, eds., *Psychoanalysis and the Social Sciences*, vol. 4 (New York: International Universities Press, 1955), and Oscar Pfister, *Christianity and Fear: A Study in History and in the Psychology and Hygiene of Religion* (London: George Allen & Unwin, 1948). However, my own stress on Paul's vision of Christ as the Last Adam gives my work a very different perspective than either Tarachow's or Pfister's work.

Franz Alexander, "Buddhistic Training as an Artificial Catatonia: The Biological Meaning of Psychic Occurrences," in Alexander, *The Scope of Psychoanalysis* (New York: Basic Books, 1961), was crucial to my understanding of the equivalence of Nirvana-womb-"all in all" as the culmination of the eschatological process. Thomas J. J. Altizer,

The Descent into Hell (Philadelphia: Lippincott, 1970), suggested the same insight from the perspective of contemporary theology.

Finally, I have utilized as authentic letters of Paul: I Thessalonians, Romans, Galatians, I and II Corinthians, Philippians, Philemon, and Colossians. Where, as in Philippians 2:5–11, I have discussed a fragment whose authorship is contested, I have so indicated in the notes.

INDEX

Abraham, 76, 110
Adam, first Adam, 10, 144-173
  is the first exile, 144
  original condition of, 147
  rabbinic speculation concerning, 145-149
  sin of, 148
  see also Last Adam
Altizer, Thomas J. J., 164
apocalypse, Paul's, 169
apostate, Paul as, 4
Apostolic Council, the, 123, 124, 127, 188
Arendt, Hannah, 140
Atonement, Day of, 13
Auschwitz, 115
autonomous man, modern ideal of the, 154

Baeck, Leo, 114
Bakan, David, 65-67, 75, 178
baptism, 51, 54-77
  as the circumcision of Christ, 74
  as tomb and womb, 64-65

before Paul, 57
John's, 57
new parent at, 65
Paul's doctrine of, 39-40
baptismal waters, the, 54
  as tomb and womb, 61
Barrett, C. K., 137, 145, 150, 160
Barth, Karl, 26, 34, 175-176
Baur, Ferdinand Christian, 2, 187
belief, shift of, 90
Bettelheim, Bruno, 71
birth and death, order of, 62
Bligh, John, 187-188
blood, taboo against drinking, 104
body, the
  and Christian experience, 26
  of Christ, 31, 99, 101
Bornkamm, Günther, 63, 144
Brown, Norman O., 139, 164, 177-178
Buber, Martin, 114
Bultmann, Rudolf, 2, 63, 102, 191

charismatic individuals and religious institutions, 118

Christ
    and the paschal lamb, 106-110
    as a mediating figure, 85
    as the elder brother, 33
    as the Last Adam, 169-170, 172
    as the truly righteous man, 154
    atoning death of, 82
    belief in resurrection of, 62
    dream of one humanity united
        in, 143
    his obedience, 157, 161
    his self-sacrificing, 84-85
    identification of the Church
        with, 49
    "in," 55-56
    Risen, the, 40, 89, 100
        Paul's vision of, 48-50
"Christ mysticism," 24, 52
Christian, the, enters new life at
    baptism, 55
Christian psychological revolu-
    tion, 29
Christian religious revolution, 22,
    77
Church, the, 52
    and the Synagogue, 5, 135-143
    in Paul's thought, 24-25
circumcision, 69-77
    shift from to baptism, 69
Cohn, Norman, 180
collection of money, Paul's, 131-
    143
communion, sacrificial, 93, 99
conversion, see Paul of Tarsus:
    his conversion
Corinth, 132
cosmic restoration, the drama of,
    77
Cullmann, Oscar, 88, 91, 171
Cybele, 72
Cyril of Jerusalem, 54

Davies, W. D., 103, 145, 184
death, 14, 41, 64, 154, 169
    and birth, order of, 62
    as punishment, 68
    origins of, 144
Diaspora Jews, 129-130
Didache, 91
dietary laws, 9
disobedience, 153-154, 157-158,
    160-161
Dodd, C. H., 105, 115
Don Pablo de Santa Maria, 116
drowning, dreams involving, 67

ego, the, 30, 38
election of Israel, Paul's reinter-
    pretation of doctrine of,
    136
Eliade, Mircea, 61-62, 71
Erikson, Erik, 178
Esau, 136, 138, 142
eschatological speculation, 148
eschatology, 37
eternal life, 40, 151
Eucharist, the, 87, 91-93
    backward- and forward-look-
        ing, 113
    Pauline type of, 94-95
    Paul's teaching about, 95-113
    shift in practice of, 90-91
exclusivism of biblical religion,
    138
exile and return, 171
    human existence as drama of,
    144
experience, authority of in Paul, 6

Father, right relationship with
    the, 83

feelings, 36
Ferenczi, Sandor, 57-60
Fiedler, Leslie, 163
fraternal strife, conflict between
    Church and Synagogue as,
    5, 135-143
Freud, Sigmund, 1, 18, 27, 30,
    36, 58-60, 65, 66, 73, 75,
    78-86, 87, 93, 109, 110,
    111-112, 128, 154, 161-
    162, 170, 172, 178
    as secularized mystic, 22

Galatia, 132
Galatians, 10
Gamaliel, Rabban, 38
Gentiles, mission to the, 124, 125,
    127, 139
God, 6, 8, 65, 167-168
    acceptance by, 21
    as the Divine Infanticide, 15-
    16, 65-66
    becomes "all in all," 170, 172
    hatred of, 10
    -who-acts-in-human-affairs, 20
"God-fearers," 70
guilt, 12, 134

Ha-Levi, Rabbi Solomon, 116
Hegel, Georg Wilhelm Friedrich,
    84, 172
Héring, Jean, 96, 99, 151, 156,
    169, 170
Heydrich, Reinhard, 116
Holy Communion, 81, 82, 83, 87
Houlden, J. L., 156, 177
human solidarity, 112
Hutner, Rabbi Isaac, 16

id, the, 29, 30, 38
identification, 27-29, 51-52
    acts of, 79
    model for, 29
    with the elder brother, 23, 28,
    93, 98-99
    with (the Risen) Christ, 33,
    35, 83, 92
immersion, ritual, 61
immortality, 14-15, 33, 37, 51
    Paul's yearning for, 14
incest, taboo against, 80
infanticide, 75-76, 157
    as temptation for father, 75
Infanticide, the Divine, 15-16
instinct, 58-59
interim period, the, 64
Isaac, 76, 135-136, 138, 142
    and Jesus, 109
Isaiah, 119, 127-128, 132-133
Ishmael, 136, 138, 142
Israel, conversion of, 140
Israelites, the, 97

Jacob, 135-136, 138, 142
James, William, 175
Jeremiah, 127-128
Jerusalem, 132-133
    see also New Jerusalem
Jerusalem Church, the, 117, 122,
    132
    and Paul, 122-126
Jesus of Nazareth, 52, 88, 92
    and Isaac, 109
    and Judaism, 121-122
    and the Law, 122
    his antifamilial bias, 63
    his atoning death, 109-110
    Jewish attitude toward, 114

Jesus of Nazareth (*con't*)
  Paul's first response to resurrection of, 43
Jewish Christians and Paul, 123
Jewish religious system, viability of, 19
Jews, Nazi extermination of, 8
Johanan, R., 146
Judaism
  and Jesus, 121-122
  and Paul, 127
  normative, 36
  Paul regarded as apostate in, 4
  rabbinic, 65, 75-76, 133
  repression of female deities in, 163
  teacher-pupil relationship in, 134
Judeo-Christian encounter
  is fraternal, 142
  mutual envy in, 140
justification by faith, doctrine of, 13-14, 24, 150-151

Kabbalism, Lurianic, 167-168
Käsemann, Ernst, 96, 97, 99, 169, 189
Kierkegaard, Sören, 2
Knox, W. L., 148

Last Adam, the, 10, 60, 77, 85, 144-173
  Christ as, 40, 169-170, 172
  Messiah as, 144
  see also Adam
Last Supper, the, 88
Law, the, 11, 12, 18, 40-41, 120-122, 125-126, 155
Leitzmann, Hans, 89, 90, 94, 95

life to come, the, 168
Lohmeyer, Ernst, 158
Lord's Meal, the, 85, 87-113
  improper participation in, 98
Lord's Supper, the, 28, 78, 81, 82, 87
  elements of, 102
  Paul's understanding of, 104
lustrations, purificatory, 56
Luther, Martin, 98
  and Paul, 134-135

mankind, Christ's liberation of, 156
Manson, T. W., 91
marriage, Paul's views on, 62-65
martyrdom, 45
masculine orientation of divine-human encounter, 162-163
Mass, the, 82
Melville, Herman, 153
Messiah
  as the Last Adam, 144
  crucified, a, 43
Messianic Age, the, 36, 115
messianism, 37
  Jewish, 35-38, 44
messianist(s), Jewish, 36
  Paul as, 35
Micah, 132-133
mortality
  as punishment, 68
  escape from, 16
Moses, 95, 119, 120, 128, 134
mother
  fear of, 67, 69
  reunion with the, 163
Munck, Johannes, 124-125, 129, 132, 133, 137, 187

Munck-Nickle hypothesis, the, 133, 135
mystics, Jewish, 22

narcissism, primary, 30-31, 37
Nazi extermination of the Jews, 8
New Jerusalem, 164
New Testament, the, 5
Nickle, Keith F., 132, 133
Nietzsche, Friedrich, 12
Nirvana, 164, 165, 167, 168, 171, 172, 192-193
Nock, Arthur Darby, 179

obedience, 9, 154-155
    the act of, 11
    to the Father, 28, 33
observer, importance of point of view of, 3
Oesterley, W. O. E., 107
omnipotence, 33, 50, 83-84, 105, 158, 161, 167, 173

parent, quest for a new, 68
parricide, 82
    myth of, 78-79, 85
particularism, Jewish, 129
paschal lamb, the, and Christ, 106-110
Passover, the, 106-110
Paul of Tarsus, 13, 22, 173
    after conversion, 40
    and conflict between experience and tradition, 6, 118, 119
    and mankind's fundamental problem, 23
    and Martin Luther, 134-135
    and observance of the Law, 40-41, 121
    and Peter, 122-123
    and Sigmund Freud, 85-86, 111-112, 161-162
    and the difficulty of genuine obedience, 12
    and the Jerusalem Church, 122-126
    and the Pharisees, 114-115
    and the rabbis, 4, 19
    appraisals of, 1
    as a persecutor, 38-39, 42, 46
    as a Pharisee, 38-39, 45, 46, 53
    as apostate, 4, 116, 126
    as Apostle to the Gentiles, 127, 129, 139, 141
    as a twice-born man, 6
    as Jewish messianist, 35, 115
    at crossroads of rabbinic Judaism and Christianity, 23
    expressed the redemptive yearnings of his contemporaries, 110
    his authority, 133
    his background Hellenistic or Jewish, 19
    his conversion, 34-35
        as attempts at self-liberation, 173
        loss of normal ego functions in, 46-48
        recovery of capacities in, 50-53
        vision of the Risen Christ, in, 48-50
    his desire to bring about conversion of the Jews, 127, 129, 131
    his emotional upheaval, 113
    his eschatology, 24
    his final vision, 172-173

Paul of Tarsus (*con't*)
    his religious symbols, 20
    his symbolic consciousness, 30,
        128, 138
    his teaching about the Eucha-
        rist, 95-113
    "historical," the, 2
    his universalist vision, 129
    his yearning for omnipotence,
        50, 52
    Jewish attitude toward, 114
    knew weakness and pain, 45
    not an anti-Semite, 115
    opposition to, 124-125, 130
    upbringing of in Tarsus, 129
Pedersen, Johannes, 108
Peter and Paul, 122-123
Pharisees, the, 117, 118
    and Paul, 46, 114-115, 141
    heirs of, 117
Philippians, 17
pidyon ha-ben, 76
prenatal existence, 147, 165
primary process level of mental
        functioning, 12-13
    and Paul's thought, 32
    Paul's thought dominated by
        imagery of, 29
psychoanalysis, 26-27
psychological man, 21, 86

Rab, 146-147
rage, 8
reality principle, the, 30
    conflict of with the pleasure
        principle, 37-38
rebirth, 55
redemption, 149
Reik, Theodore, 44, 178
religious symbols, Paul's, 20

resurrection, 64
    of Christ, 51
    of the body, 151
Rieff, Philip, 21
Rigaux, Béda, 175
rite(s), initiatory, 61-62, 69
Robinson, John A. T., 25-26, 29,
        49, 96
Romans, 5, 11, 14, 20, 34, 149-
        151
Rubenstein, Richard L., 5-22, 180
    and Paul, 14

sacred, the, and the taboo, 103
sacrifice, the Communion, 81-82
    see also totem sacrifice
Sadducees, the, 117, 118
Schmithals, Walther, 125
Schnackenburg, Rudolf, 29, 74
Schoeps, Hans Joachim, 40, 114,
        179, 186
Scholem, Gershom, 19, 36, 49
Schweitzer, Albert, 23-24, 25-27,
        55, 96, 156
Scripture, Paul's reinterpretation
        of, 117-118
Scroggs, Robin, 145, 151
Scrolls, Community of the, 117
self-acceptance, 21
sexuality, Paul's views on, 62-65
sin, 41, 148, 153-154
Smith, William Robertson, 81
sonship, 16
Spiegel, Shalom, 109
Spirit, the, and the letter, 119-
        120
Stendahl, Krister, 20, 41
Stephen, 46
subject-object dichotomy, 166
Suffering Servant, the, 45

Synagogue and Church, 5, 135-143

taboo, the, and the sacred, 103
theology of covenant and election, 117
Thessalonika, 130
time, Judeo-Christian experience of, 171
totem sacrifice, 80, 87
twice-born man, a, 6-7
   Paul as, 6

unconscious, the, 49
   in Christianity, 105

unity, 32
U-N'sane-Tokef, the, 15-16

Virgin, the, 67-68, 162

water, 60-61
   and womb, 60
Weber, Max, 119
womb, 58, 164
   and tomb, 57
   and water, 60
World to Come, the, 145-147
worship, sacrificial, 112

Zvi, Sabbatai, 35, 36

72 73 10 9 8 7 6 5 4 3 2 1

Identification 27
Groaning to be set free 31
Paul on Judaism's obedience to Father 33
Immortal life as omnipotence 51
"In Christ" – 56
"Ontogeny follows phylogeny" – 58
Sexuality – & the coming End – 64
Paul – no need to be circumcised 69
Baptism obliterates male – female distinction 70
Freud – Xnty illusory 86